New patterns of work reform

The case of Norway

Bjørn Gustavsen and Gerry Hunnius

New patterns of work reform

The case of Norway

UNIVERSITETSFORLAGET
Oslo – Bergen – Tromsø

© Universitetsforlaget 1981
Omslag: Rolf Michaelsen
ISBN 82-00-05525-6

Printed in Norway by
Lie & Co.s Boktrykkeri, Oslo

Contents

Acknowledgements   9
Foreword 11

Chapter I
Labour relations in Norway – an overview

Introduction 15
Historical notes 16
The Norwegian Federation of Trade Unions (LO) 20
The Norwegian Employers' Confederation (NAF) 21
The relationship between the LO and the Norwegian Labour Party . . 22
Wage solidarity and centralized decision-making 23
Conflicts and productivity 24
Conflict resolution and the role of the state in labour relations 25
Tripartite cooperation 28
Collective bargaining and conflict resolution 29
Incomes policy and tripartite bargaining 31
Concluding remarks 35

Chapter II
The industrial democracy programme

Introduction 37
The issue of industrial democracy 37
Industrial democracy and partipation 40
Organization of work, psychological requirements and productivity . 41
Participation, research and action 43
The socio-technical perspective 48
Turbulence, survival and participation 49
Field experiments 51
A case: Hotel Caledonian 51
The initiative 51

The first development: Caledonian Dancing 52
Horizontal diffusion 53
Autonomous work groups and broader organizational changes 54
The role of organizations 55
Long term perspective 56
Concluding remarks 56

Chapter III
The industrial democracy programmes: Discussion and diffusion

Introduction 57
Patterns of diffusion 58
Diffusion – some tentative conclusions 64
The relationship to the main goal of the programme 67
Work reform and productivity 69
Limitations to diffusion – an overview 72
Lack of worker interest 73
Collaboration and conflict 75
The role of research 79
Dissolution of meaning 81
Concluding summary 82

Chapter IV
Employee representation on the board of directors and the company assembly

Introduction 85
The formal system 86
The debate on employee representation 87
Some results 90
A general evaluation 94
The context of the board 96

Chapter V
The background of the work environment reform

Introduction 101
Why improvement of the work environment? 102
The environment debate 105
Patterns of industrial conflict around 1970 106
Some general political aspects 108
Some indicators on the developement of Norwegian working life ... 109
The initiative 111

Chapter VI

A critique of the conventional approach to safety and health in work

Introduction 115

The rule-based strategy for workers protection 116

Limitations of efforts 119

Proof requirements 119

The problem of interaction 121

Demands for experts and pressure on public resources 123

«Frozen standards» 124

Lack of long term development 124

Administrative practices 125

The traditional approach and the role of research 126

Concluding summary 129

Chapter VII

The merger between work environment and participatory democracy

Introduction 131

Freedom, competence and worker control: Ability to cope with work
environment loads 131

Job characteristics, work environment and safety work 133

Concluding remarks 137

Chapter VIII

The Work Environment Act of 1977 – Legislation in support of local activity

Introduction 139

Priority on the work environment consideration 141

Minimum standards and the demand for improvement 141

Emphasis on issues demanding local experience for their settlement . 143

A holistic approach 144

Improved legitimacy to the experiences and evaluations of those
who «have» the problems 144

Shifting the burden of proof 146

New concepts of casuality 147

New ways of tackling work environment problems 148

A learning process 148

Rules on the organization of work 149

The formal work environment organization on enterprise level 152

The development of a work environment improvement programme –

the case of Berger Langmoen A/S 156
The initiative 157
The chief purpose of the project 157
Organization 158
Education and training 159
Mapping of problems 159
Stucturing and priorities 160
Programme 161
Execution of the programme 161
Using the Work Environment Act Sect. 12: The letter department,
Oslo Post-Terminal 163
The initiative 163
Sect. 12 and the mapping of problems 164
Problem structure 166
The holistic perspective 167
Programme for improvement 168
Some social perspectives 170
Concluding remarks – the current status of the reform 172

Chapter IX
Concluding remarks on work reform and contemporary problems in Norwegian society

Introduction 175
Centralization, decentralization and strategy 176
Economic instability 178
A note on work organization and health 181
Concluding remarks 183

References 185

Appendix
Selected parts of the Work Environment Act 193

Acknowledgements

We wish to express our gratitude to colleagues and friends who, in various ways, have helped us. Steven Deutsch, University of Oregon, Eugene, and Eric Batstone, Warwick University have both commented extensively on an earlier manuscript; Steven Deutsch has also written a foreword to the book. Richard P. Shore, Department of Labor, Washington, and Albert Cherns, University of Loughborough, have both given encouraging comments on earlier drafts; Albert Cherns has also suggested some of the points which we draw upon in our analysis of the Norwegian work environment legislation. Ragnvald Kalleberg, University of Oslo, has participated in a number of discussions on the relationship between work reforms and participatory democracy.

Numerous contributions have been given by colleagues at the Work Research Institutes, Oslo, of which we can mention only a few: Per H. Engelstad has made suggestions concerning the presentation and analysis of The Industrial Democracy Programme. Ståle Seierstad has commented on Chapter I on general labour relations in Norway as well as provided case material, the last together with Jan Irgens Karlsen, Øyvind Ryste and Ingrid Greger Ramberg. Lars A. Ødegaard and Tor Norseth have helped control some of the information given in the book. Ellen Berglie and Line Harsheim have done the typing.

We will also take the opportunity to express our thanks to all who have taken part in the development of ideas for work environment reform, particularly Bertil Gardell, University of Stockholm; Arvid Eskild and Knut Grøholt, Ministry of Labour and Local Government, Oslo. Taking up the task of writing this book has been encouraget by the establishment of Research Committe 10 under the International Sociological Association on Participation, Self-Management and Industrial Democracy, who, under the chairmanship of Veljko Rus, University of Ljubljana, is working on the international diffusion and comparison of ideas.

We also express our thanks to the administrative staff of the Work Research Institutes, who, under Dag Mathiesen, has provided efficient assistance on administrative and economic issues pertaining to Gerry Hunnius' stay as a visiting researcher at the Work Research Institutes, and to Arbetslivscentrum in Stockholm for their collaboration in making Hunnius' visit to Scandinavia possible.

We are grateful for the financial support given to Hunnius by the Social Sciences and Humanities Research Council of Canada.

A few words about the book: To keep it relatively brief has been an overriding consideration. Consequently, we have had to make a selection among all the topics which can possibly be taken up when the working life of a society, as a whole, is to be treated. We have chosen to focus on three reform «campaigns»: an industrial democracy programme departing from the need to change organization of work; employee representation on the board of directors; and a work environment reform emerging from health and safety considerations in a narrow sense but which eventually came to include such issues as psycho-social loads, organization of work and industrial democracy. The last of these efforts is given the broadest treatment here as it is the newest and least dealt with in literature available in English. We also stress the links between these reform efforts, in locating them within an overall pattern of development. Such topics as the organization and functioning of the bargaining system is dealt with briefly and mostly as background material. The same is the case as concerns the system of joint committees dealing with issues of collaboration, the development of which started just after World War II but has now matured into a highly complet system of bodies and activities.

As concerns references we are, of course, aware that reference to texts available only in Norwegian or one of the other Scandinavian languages is of limited interest to most English language readers. We have consequently as far as possible referred to literature written in English. However, as only a limited number of the studies etc. dealing with work life issues in Norway, or in Scandinavia in general, is available in English, while we have felt it necessary to comply with the ordinary rules for the use of references, a certain degree of referring to Scandinavian texts has been unavoidable.

Oslo, June 1980

Bjørn Gustavsen   *Gerry Hunnius*
Work Research Institutes   *York University*
Oslo   *Toronto*

Foreword

Emerging out of the post World War Two era, western industrial nations have seen a major new concern with quality of life issues. Quality of urban environment issues have developed in the wake of automobile-centered cities and new industrial waste by-products affecting air and water resources. With the growth of centralized state decisionmaking there have come many grass-roots political movements concerned with neighbourhood control, local self-reliance and participatory structures to challenge the hegemonic control over citizen's lives. In many societies this mood has paralleled the push for individual rights and we have witnessed an extraordinary climate of social-political change.

At the same time there has been a quieter if less revolutionary fervor brewing in the world of work. As capitalist industrial states entered a period of economic crises they lost their ability to pay off. The traditional assumption that greater productivity and corporate profits would filter through improved wages to advance the life styles of the working class, was increasingly invalid. High inflation, growing unemployment and job insecurity, run-away shops and plant closings, and other structural features of Western economies have shaken the belief in many countries that collective bargaining and peaceful labor-management relations can work to the benefit of labor. Of course that never was an assumption accepted in all quarters, but the rising militancy in the 1960s and 1970s has accelerated and expanded. As the 1980s unfold we see ever greater signs of worker discontent and demands for worklife reform. The quiet rumblings during the period of relative economic expansion in the 1950s and 1960s have risen into a crescendo of opposition to management and state apparatuses designed to quell workers' demands and maintain workers as the victims of economic crises.

It is important to understand the changing conditions in the world after the Second World War and the reform efforts which have emerged in recent years. This book is not global in coverage, and while the situation in Norway differs in many respects from that of, for example, the USA and Canada, it offers keen insights into the dynamics and issues of all industrial nations. The experimental efforts to democratize worklife in Norway have parallels throughout the West. We see corporate board participation by labor as a newly emerging point of discussion in North America, so that it is important to assess the experience in countries which have legislated such structures. The dramatic incidence of occupational health and safety casualties has gained wide popular awareness and has challenged most societies to seek solutions. The Norwegian case is very important and offers considerable provocation in terms of theory, strategies for reform and implementation of reform at various levels.

Bjørn Gustavsen and Gerry Hunnius have written a book which is challenging and useful, both in its practical application and larger theoretical utility. They are not abstract theoreticians and «value free» academics. While this book is well grounded in a broad theoretical literature on work reform the authors come from applied involvement in worklife reform. Gustavsen, Director of the Institute for Work Psychology, at the Work Research Institutes, Oslo, lawyer and social science researcher is one of the key architects of the Norwegian work environment reform and has worked closely with public authorities as well as with the labor market parties in Norway. In a similar fashion, Hunnius, professor of social science at York University of Toronto, Canada, and recent visiting researcher at the Work Research Institutes, Oslo and the Swedish Center for Working Life, Stockholm, is a labor educator and resource person for unions, labour departments and various organizations. The authors are unusually qualified to write such a book from a vantage point of active involvement, clear advocates for democratizing work and improving the quality of work life for working men and women in all countries.

While the text outlines the important features of the Norwegian system, it is important to place this study in a broader context. Norway has a national approach to industrial relations, rather than a local collective bargaining strategy which characterises some other societies. The centralization of its tripartite industrial relations system, involving government, labor and management, is a key and important for its success. While national economic planning and national strategies of labor relations have been discussed in countries such as Britain, Canada and the United States, the local bargaining approach has tended to keep power relationships assymetrical and as a result there are wide disparities within those countries in wage packages, health and safety compliance and a wide range of quality of work life issues. While Norway is a country with a small population, innovations and reform in its working life have gained international attention. The re-

12

cent work environment reform has already come to be seen as a model by organizations and persons in many countries. My own belief is that this law is extremely useful as a challenge for legislative reform in the USA. While many practitioners will balk at the idea of using one country's experience in their own setting, I think it is ever clearer that global markets, multi-national managements, international labor federations all push in the direction of inter-relationships, if not standardization. If work reform does affect productivity, obviously the developments in other countries interests management and labor everywhere. The pressure to reform the workplace will increase in the coming years and the challenge will be to find the appropriate strategies for change.

It is my hope that forces for progressive change, in the labor movement, in governments and elsewhere, will utilize this volume as part of a strategy for social-political-economic change which will increase the dignity of working men and women on the job and the control which workers have over their jobs. The days are gone when workers should be required to give up their democratic rights as they pass through the factory gates or enter the office; workers' health and safety should not be for sale. Should this book contribute towards such changes, as well as the readers' understanding of Norway, it will surely have served the key purpose of the authors.

Steven Deutsch
Labor Education & Research Center
University of Oregon, USA.

I. Labour relations in Norway – an overview

Introduction

The purpose of this chapter is to pull together those aspects of Norway's social, political and economic life which are essential to an understanding of the innovations and reforms which constitute the main part of this book. We will pay special attention to certain features in the system of labour relations which set Norway apart from most other industrialized societies.

Norway, today, is an industrialized society with a high standard of living. In 1978, per capita gross domestic product (at market prices) in Norway stood at US$ 9778, compared to 9602 in the USA, 8766 in Canada, and 5514 in the United Kingdom. Per capita private consumption in 1977 was US$ 4940 in Norway, 5600 in the USA, 4870 in Canada and 2580 in the United Kingdom.

The distribution of the labour force is not unlike that of other Western industrialized countries. The percentage of the total civilian labour force employed in industry (including mining, manufacturing, construction and utilities) in 1978 was 31.6 percent in Norway, 31.2 percent in the USA, 28,7 percent in Canada and 39.7 percent in the United Kingdom (OECD, 1980).

But large nos of v. small organisations

The trade union movement in Norway is one of the most centralized in the Western world. The main employee organization is the Federation of Trade Unions (LO), which encompasses 37 national unions. In addition to the Federation of Trade Unions, a number of other organizations and federations exists, giving a total percentage of organized employees in Norway of around 80. In the brief description and analysis to be given in this chapter, we will focus on the Federation of Trade Unions, as this is not only the biggest but also the oldest and politically most significant employee organization in Norway.

The traditional counterpart of the Federation of Trade Unions is the Employers Confederation (NAF), which covers, however, a smaller part of working life than LO, as LO organizes people also in the public sector as well as in parts of working life where special employers organizations exist, such as in shipping and trade.

Recently, a proposal for the creation of an employer organization for companies where the state has a majority of the shares, and withdrawal of these companies from the Employers Confederation where they are presently members has been put forward. If this proposal is acted on, it will have a major impact on the organization of employer interests in Norway, as the state owns about 50 % of all shares in the bigger industrial companies (Norges Industri, 1975) and has a majority position in relation to some of the biggest companies, such as Norsk Hydro (the biggest industrial group in Norway) and Årdal & Sunndal (the biggest aluminium company). The fate of this proposal is at the moment undecided.

Historical notes

Industrialization came late to Norway, at least in comparison with Britain and such areas of Germany as the Ruhr district. In the second half of the 19th century industrial development, largely in textiles and machine shops, began to increase but it was not until the first decade of this century that cheap hydro-electric power enabled the economy to "take off".

Norway's trade union movement, like that of most other nations, is the product of the industrial revolution. Led by the formation of craft unions in the 1880's it was preceded by massive labour agitation in the 1840's, and early 1850's, this was a period of economic instability and high unemployment. Led by Marcus Thrane, nearly 300 workers' associations with a membership of 30,000 workers were formed within a few years. At a time when the entire number of industrial workers was only 13,000, this was a remarkable event which left a deep impression on the country.

Marcus Thrane's political ideas were drawn from various sources. Born in 1817, he went to France in his young days where he became acquainted with French socialist ideas. He was strongly radicalized by the 1848 revolution in France. His later work in the Norwegian labour movement was based on a class analysis of society with the owners of property on the one hand, and the majority of the property-less on the other. In 1851, Thrane was arrested and jailed and the movement he helped to create was crushed. He eventually migrated to the United States where he spent the rest of his life until his death in 1890. The impact of his revolutionary work did, however, not end in 1851 and re-emerged with the birth of industrial unionism in the last part of the century. The significance of Marcus Thrane and the ideas and struggles of the labour movement in the late 1840's can be sought along the following lines:

- The need for workers to organize on a class basis as contrasted to craft-based unionization.
- The class-based organization of workers must encompass society as a whole, local units must unite in a national organization.
- His awareness of revolutionary movements in other countries linked the Norwegian labour movement to broader socialist developments of that period.

After the authorities crushed the Thrane movement, a couple of decades passed before the labour movement started to recover. The formative years of the Norwegian labour movement, from about 1870 to 1935 when the first Basic Agreement with the employers was signed and a Labour Government came into office, can not be discussed here in detail. Since the developments of that period gave the labour movement its present shape, we will, however, briefly outline the political parameters of that period:

The first unions formed in Norway were craft-based, including masters, as employers, as well as journeymen, apprentices and other workers. These craft unions maintained a loose affiliation to the so-called Left Party, which was, however, not left in the modern political sense, but rather resembled the British liberals.

The next step saw the emergence of a social-democratic labour movement. Craft-based unions were replaced by industrial unions with unskilled workers as the backbone of the union movement. The former masters with their contacts to the liberals disappeared and the Norwegian Labour Party was founded in 1887. In spite of its name, the party was originally intended to function as a union movement. With the founding of the Norwegian Federation of Trade Unions in 1899, the labour movement was separated into a union branch and a political party. They remained, however, closely linked to each other and when we speak today about the labour movement in Norway, both parts are included by this term. The policy to emerge in the early period of the modern Norwegian labour movement, was moderate social-democratic.

The next important political development emerged during the First World War with the victory of the Bolshevik revolution in Russia, which was clearly not unrelated to the second period of strong radicalization in the history of the Norwegian labour movement. It is intimately linked to the ideas of Martin Tranmæl, who was the major theoretician and agitator e in the Norwegian labor movement in the period around 1920. He was a socialist who believed in revolution as the vehicle for bringing the working class to power. Under the revolutionary impetus of this period, the Norwegian Labour party joined the communist international (Comintern) when it was formed in 1919.

New conflicts, however, were soon to emerge. The more reformist, social-democratic ideas were still alive and started to reassert themselves. While the Norwegian Labour Party at that time took a more radical position than did labour parties in most other countries, there were few indications that the labour movement was ready to take revolutionary steps in the implementation of its aims. There was little discussion, and no agreement, on the goals of the revolution, and the entire campaign remained largely on the verbal level (Torgersen, 1974). An additional conflict, which emerged at that time, related directly to the politics of the Comintern. A core element in the communist international was the so-called Moscow theses which, among other things, underlined the supremacy of the Soviet party and the need of all other parties to subordinate themselves to Moscow. This strategy presupposed, furthermore, a very centralist organizational structure for the entire labour movement, making the movement controllable by a small elite at the top. Tranmæl, by far the most important figure in the radical wing of the labour movement, opposed the main elements of the Moscow theses. Tranmæl was strongly influenced by the syndicalism of the International Workers of the World (IWW). He had spent four years in the USA and brought these ideas back to Norway. He was in fact highly critical of the relatively centralized union structure that had already emerged in Norway. He advocated instead increased power to the grass roots, without, however, wanting to loose the unifying element of a national organization.

The struggle now turned into a struggle between three competing tendencies in the labour movement: The Tranmæl supporters, the more reformist social democrats, and the pro-Moscow section of the labour movement.

In organizational terms, these conflicts resulted in a split in the Labour Party and the creation of a Communist Party which remained loyal to Moscow. While the Communist Party has participated in parliamentary elections it has not received significant support from the electorate with the exception of the immediate post World War II period when eleven Communists were elected to the Norwegian Parliament.

The labour movement to emerge out of these conflicts, was characterised by a stepwise merger between the Tranmæl wing and the social democrats. The Comintern membership was brought to an end in 1923. The Norwegian labour movement was, however, still a highly radicalized movement. Up until 1935, when the first Basic Agreement was signed between the LO and the NAF the policy turned more and more towards a social-democratic line, with emphasis on elections as the road to political power, and on the development of an ordered structure of bargaining and agreements in working life. How can we explain this relatively sudden shift, from a revolutionary labour movent, to one ready to enter into co-operative relationships with the employers?

We have already indicated that the revolutionary nature of the Labour movement had remained largely at the verbal level. We should, perhaps, not exaggerate the importance of that point given the prevailing economic conditions of that time and the relatively weak position of the labour movement in the 1920's. The economic conditions were certainly not conducive to a strengthening of the power of the labour movement. In the twenties and early thirties Norwegian economy went through three major recessions, at one point as much as one third of the total membership of the LO was unemployed. The recessions turned the attention of unions to defensive strategies and must have had a negative effect on the further development of a revolutionary programme. Another factor of possible importance was the slow but steady increase in the parliamentary strength of the Labour Party. The possibility of gaining political power via electoral politics, may well have had a moderating impact on the labour movement. In 1918, the Labour Party had only 18 elected members in the Norwegian Parliament, its strength increased to 29 out of 150 in 1921, to 59 in 1927 and 69 in 1933. In the middle thirties the Labour Party came into government, to remain there almost continuously up until the present (1980). The breaks that have occurred in this pattern, emerged in the form of center to right coalition governments for some periods in the sixties and seventies.

The increasing strength of the Labour Party coincided with a tendency in the international socialist movement to see the seizure of state power as the number one priority in the creation of a socialist society. In the Norwegian context, with the growing influence of the parliamentary wing of the labour movement, these factors should be considered in any attempt to explain the victory of social democratic tendencies in the labour movement. State intervention as a mechanism in the achievement of economic control in society entered the picture of practical social democratic politics with the development of just such a plan by two Norwegian economists, Colbjørnsen and Sømme, who, like Wigforss in Sweden, pioneered the development of concrete economic policies along the lines generally associated with the name of Keynes.

Before we turn our attention to the contemporary system of labour relations in Norway, we must give a brief account of the organizational structures of the two dominant parties in the labour market: The Norwegian Federation of Trade Unions (LO) and the Norwegian Employers' Confederation (NAF).

The Norwegian Federation of Trade Unions (LO)

Centralization of Norway's labour movement began as soon as local unions were organized in the 1880's. Isolated small local unions soon saw the benefits of uniting in a central organization. Similar developments in the other Scandiavian countries, discussed at the first meeting of the Scandinavian Labour Congress in 1886, speeded up the unification of the labour movement. The Norwegian Federation of Trade Unions (LO) was formed in 1899 to be followed one year later by the founding of the Norwegian Employers' Confederation.

The Norwegian Federation of Trade Unions is an organization of 35 national unions with a combined membership, in 1979, of 740 000 wage and salary earners out of a total number of employees (people who work for others for pay) of somewhat in excess of 1,8 million (Central Bureau of Statistics, 1980). Each national union, in turn, is composed of branches or local unions of which there are more than 4000 (OECD, 1979). All manual workers in a given plant will normally belong to the same union, although some union locals may encompass more than one workplace. White collar emplyees in a given workplace, however, may belong to several different unions.

Concerning general policy, the LO is the governing body of the trade union movement. Through its three levels of authority – Congress, General Council and Executive Board – the federation formulates and administers policy for organized labour (LRN, 1975). A brief look at the structure and the corresponding decision-making power of each level will illustrate this high degree of centralization (figure 1).

The supreme authority is the Congress which, however, meets only once every four years. Between sessions, authority is vested in a General Council which meets at least once a year. The General Council is a large body of 120 members, elected by national unions and regional groups with the addition of the 15 members of the LO Executive Board. It is the Executive Board, which includes the LO President, Vice-President, Treasurer and Secretary, which in practice exercises the power of the federation. This Executive Board meets weekly and

20

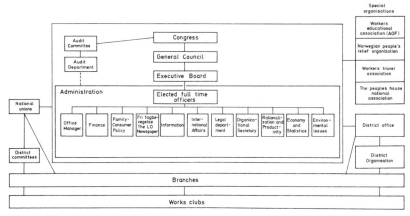

Fig. 1. The formal structure of the Norwegian Federation og Trade Unions (LO).

controls the day-to-day developments in the union movement.

A number of unions have remained outside the LO. Out of the total of 1,5 million employees, approximately 1,3 million, or 80 %, belong to an employee organization. Excepting the LO, these organizations range from small unions with a handful of members to federations with a membership around 100.000 (for a review, see Central Bureau of Statistics, 1978). They comprise mostly non-manual employees and professionals. Their significance in the over-all development of labour relations in Norway has until recently been overshadowed by the dominant position of the LO (LRN, 1975): This may possibly undergo some changes in the future, a point we can not, however, pursue here.

The Norwegian Employers' Confederation (NAF)

The early centralization of employers and the creation of the NAF in 1900 is no doubt directly related to the centralization of the labour movement which preceded that of the employers by one year. There is no counterpart to the NAF in either the United States or Canada. While the highest decisionmaking authority is the General Meeting which usually takes place once a year, for all practical purposes it is the Central Board which has effective policy-making power while day-to-day decisions are made by the Executive Committee headed by a chairman who is also the Director General and thus the highest officer in the Confederation. It is this committee which conducts contract negotiations. Administratively, the NAF is divided into six negotiating departments with responsibilities for the various industrial sectors. No individual NAF member may negotiate directly with a trade union. Such negotiations are conducted either by the NAF or in some instances by appropriate national associations. The power to

21

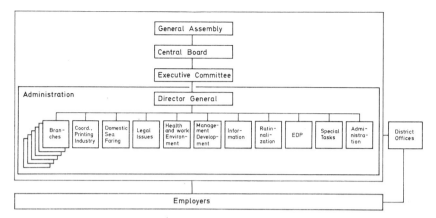

Fig. 2. The formal structure of the Norwegian Employers' Confederation (NAF).

declare a lockout is vested in the Central Board and requires a three-fourth majority before being implemented. In instances where a lockout would involve more than a quarter of workers under the NAF, the decision must be made at a special session of the General Meeting where it requires a three-fourth majority. The right of an individual employer to engage in a labour conflict is thus severely limited as is the right to engage in collective bargaining (LRN, 1975).

A number of employer associations remain outside the NAF; the most important being the Norwegian Shipowners' Association and commercial wholesale and retail outlets, but in collective bargaining in particular, these groups are strongly influenced by the prevailing policy of the NAF.

The relationship between the LO and the Norwegian Labour Party

A factor of considerable significance in the political life of Norway is the close link between the Norwegian Labour Party and the Norwegian Federation of Trade unions (LO). Prior to the creation of the LO, the Labour Party in fact performed, what one might call, trade union functions. In 1889, for example, the party came out strongly in support of a strike by 300 female match workers and organized nationwide support for the strikers (LRN, 1975).

The links between the LO and the Labour Party, which has been in power for most of the period since World War II, have remained strong. On a formal level this co-operation is anchored in a committee of co-operation where all questions of importance to the labour movement are being discussed. Additional informal contacts, dual membership and a common ideological position have helped to create a unified labour movement which is strategically separated into a political party and a trade union movement.

Wage solidarity and centralized decision-making

A feature which has achieved much prominence in Scandinavian countries is the union policy of wage equalization, or as it is sometimes called, wage solidarity. Organized labour in Norway, particularly at the level of the LO, has generally advocated a lowering of wage differentials between the white- and blue-collar sectors as well as within the sectors themselves. This policy should be seen in the context of the relatively strong egalitarian tradition in Norwegian society. The trend toward an equalization of incomes between blue- and white-collar employees since the turn of the century has been marked, as emerges from Table 1.

Table 1. Selected white collar occupations' yearly income as compared with that of industrial workers*, 1900 – 1965.

Occupation	1900	1910	1920	1925	1930	1935	1940	1950	1965
Industrial worker	100	100	100	100	100	100	100	100	100
White collar (government employed):									
Train conductor	152	142	109	–	108	–	104	101	99**
Head, government office	443	376	298	210	255	265	212	200	206
White collar (employed by Oslo Municipality):									
Office clerk	212	184	121	134	139	137	135	102	100
'Secretary' (head of office)	602	481	224	259	289	284	230	173	172
White collar (private):									
Bookkeeper	–	157	–	–	–	–	–	119	114

* The comparison is between full-time employed in all occupations.
**The figure is for the year 1963.
Sourec: Seierstad, 1974.

More recent figures pertaining to industrial wage differentials produce a rather mixed picture. Despite the egalitarian profile of recent wage settlements which resulted in above average increases to lower income groups, the wage structure has remained largely unchanged. Taking the industrial average as 100, unskilled workers, for example, have improved their position only slightly: from 92 in 1971, to 94 in 1978. The traditional low income sectors, such as textiles, wood, shoe and food and beverage industries have remained at, or below, the 90 mark in relation to the industrial average, while construction and printing have remained above the average. Female workers, however, have increased their income from 78 of the industrial average in 1971, to 84 in 1978 (OECD, 1980).

Another traditionally low income sector is presently experiencing a substantial increase. The 1976 combined settlement (see below) resulted in a larger than average increase for farmers. This increase is to be seen as the first step towards an agreed-upon equalization of farm and industrial incomes by 1982 (OECD, 1979).

The policy of wage solidarity is generally applied at the level of centralized and combined settlements. It is in fact one of the positive justifications for centralized bargaining. To the extent that wage drifts occur, they tend to have their origin in local bargaining and the application of production premium wage systems.

Even the income of management personnel shows to some extent the impact of the egalitarian tendencies in Norwegian society. Figures for 1979 show the following spread for middle to upper-middle managerial (monthly) incomes: They range from 17.634 Norwegian Kroner (US $ 3.600) for technical directors to 11.759 N.kr. (US $ 2.400) for heads of purchasing departments. (Norsk Arbeidsgiverforening, 1980). Given the high level of income tax in Norway, particularly at levels above that of the average income of industrial workers, management salaries in Norway must be considered to be modest.

Conflicts and productivity

Norway has experienced a relatively low level of labour conflicts, particularly during the last few decades.

The relatively low level of conflicts can perhaps be explained along the following lines: The highly sophisticated and centralized apparatus for conflict resolution both, within the LO and the NAF, is clearly important. An equally relevant factor is the close collaboration between the LO and the Labour Party which has been in power for most of the post-war period. It seems evident that the low level of unemployment in Norway is to some extent the outcome of government planning. Given the close collaboration between the Labour Party and the LO we can assume that full employment has emerged as a high priority in the deliberations within the labour movement. The unions in turn, have never seriously opposed the principle of increased productivity. Increased productivity, including the introduction of new technologies for that purpose, is seen by the labour movement as an essential part of a viable national policy and as a pre-condition for the achievement of a democratic socialist society. Organized labour does not, on the whole, see increased productivity as an attempt to extract additional surplus value from the workers. The acceptance of increased pro-

24

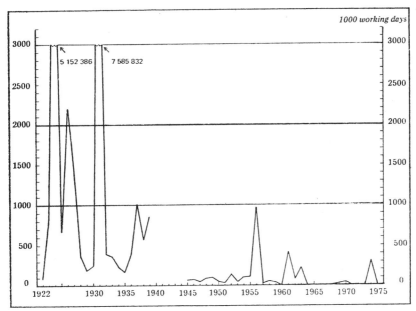

Fig. 3. Work days lost as a result og labour conflicts 1922–1975.
Source: Central Bureau of Statistics,1978

ductivity by the labour movement is certainly a key element in the generally peaceful co-operation between unions, employers and the government. Agreement on this important issue removes a potentially serious source of conflict from the bargaining process.

Conflict resolution and the role of the state in labour relations

We can perhaps best view this phenomenon along three interrelated lines. We will first deal with parliamentary acts and institutions created specifically to deal with labour disputes. This will be followed by a brief description of various tripartite bodies set up for the purpose of developing and administering policies in the area of labour relations with a strong emphasis on tripartite cooperation and the advancement of the "national interest". Finally, in the context of discussing collective bargaining, we will deal with the role of the state in the bargaining process.

The most important parliamentary act dates back to a series of massive labour conflict starting in 1907 with a lockout affecting the entire pulp and paper industry and culminating in a massive strike in 1911 when miners walked out followed by a NAF directed lockout in saw mills, the paper industry and the iron industry. The government re-

25

sponse, after mediation and arbitration had resulted in a compromise solution of the conflict, was to prepare a bill which was finally passed in 1915 as the Labour Disputes Act. The most significant aspect of this Act is that it distinguishes between disputes of right and disputes of interest. The former are disagreements over an existing contract and cannot be settled by strikes or lockouts, they must be submitted to the Labour Court. Disputes of interest are conflicts emerging in the process of negotiations for a new contract. Such conflicts must be submitted to a mediator but should mediation fail, strikes or lockouts can legally be initiated. The final step in preventing or ending a conflict is compulsory arbitration through an act of parliament. Such action is in practice not frequently taken. These principles of the Labour Disputes Act govern the entire system of labour relations.

The Labour Court dates back to the same period and should be seen as complementing the Labour Disputes Act. It is composed of three neutral members, including the chairman, and two persons each nominated by the employers and the unions respectively. The chairman and one of the neutral members must have the qualifications of a Supreme Court judge. The jurisdiction of the court extends only to disputes arising from existing collective agreements (conflicts of right). There is no appeal from a decision of the Labour Court except on questions of the Court's jurisdiction (LRN, 1975).

The present institutional mechanism for resolution of conflicts of interest will be presented in more detail below, as we need to include the role of the state to give an adequate picture. The pattern of resolution of conflicts of rights (legal disputes) emerges from Figure 4.

A number of observations are relevant here. While the parties in a «dispute of right» are unions and employer associations, complaints frequently originate with individual workers. These complaints are then raised by the union in the context of the contract. Such grievances are handled extremely rapidly. As a rule only a few weeks elapse between the filing of a grievance and the hearing before the court. While decisions of the court are made by majority vote of its seven members, in practice unanimity prevails whenever the three neutral members agree on a given issue. Decisions of the Labour Court are regarded as a precedent, a principle which possibly explains in part the surprisingly small number of cases handled by the court. During the period of 1916 – 1940 about 1600 complaints were filed but only half of them were actually dealt with by the court. The remainder were either settled by court mediation, a practice which has been encouraged from the beginning, or were withdrawn. Similar to the reality in the USA and Canada, approximately two-thirds of the grievances originate with unions.

26

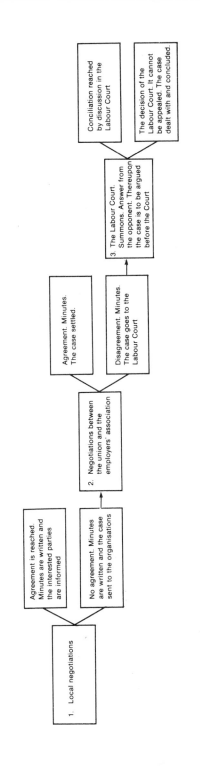

Fig. 4. The institutional mechanism of resolution of conflicts of rights.
Source: OECD, 1979

Tripartite cooperation

The various councils, committees, directorates and services mentioned in this section deal, broadly speaking, with government, labour and employer cooperation in industrial planning, employment policy and the preparation of labour legislation.

The Joint Industrial Councils, or Industrial Development Committees are tripartite industrial planning agencies. They have been in existence since 1947 and they function as advisory bodies to the ministry in question. Between 1947, when the first nine councils were established, and 1967, eight new councils were created covering a substantial part of industry in Norway. Their size varies from 8 to 12 members. The chairman as well as one or two additional members are selected by the government, three members are nominated by the employers and three by the unions, two representing industrial workers and one the white collar employees.

The supervision of employment policy is the function of another tripartite agency, the Directorate of Labour, including, in addition to the central directorate itself, a network of county employment and development committees as well as local employment committees. As outlined in the Employment Act of 1947, «The Directorate of Labour shall watch the development of employment in the country, strive to achieve a steady and adequate level of employment and advise the Ministry of Labour in matters relating to employment and unemployment» (LRN, 1975). The directorate is also responsible for vocational guidance and the administration of the unemployment incurance programme. It is governed by a board of seven members. Three are selected by the government and two each by labour and the employers.

By an act of parliament, the entire labour inspection service was centralized. The Directorate of Labour Inspection with its regional and local offices is governed by a board of seven members including two representatives each of labour and the employers.

A further institution with strong tirpartite characteristics is the Work Research Institutes, where the state as well as both parties are represented in the board. This board handles, however, issues of economy and personnell, while research policy is mostly left with the institutes. Of such institutes there are three, two in occupational medicine, one which covers organization of work and related matters, and one laboratory for muscular physiology.

The final arena of tripartite cooperation we will mention relates to the preparation of labour legislation. Most legislation presented to the Storting (Parliament) is prepared by specially appointed committees. Proposals dealing with labour relations and working conditions usually include representatives of employees and employers. Their participation almost certainly affects the content of labour legislation. In cases of strong disagreement at the committee level, both the majority as well as the minority views will be presented to the Storting which of course will make the final decision (LRN, 1975).

Collective bargaining and conflict resolution

The system of collective bargaining reflects the centralization of the main actors and exhibits a high degree of institutionalized conflict regulation. Contract preparation, particularly in the form of discussions and the articulation of demands, take place at all levels in the union structure, ranging from the local to the LO. The most important preparations, however, take place between national unions and employer associations on the one hand and the LO and the NAF on the other. While the LO council approves the general principles for each set of negotiations, the real work in formulating contract policy is done by the Executive Board. Contract demands by a local union, if considered to be unreasonable, can be vetoed at the level of the national union, while the LO can weed out demands by national unions which it considers excessive (LRN, 1975).

The Basic Agreement is a unique innovation which is used only in Scandinavia. It has existed in Norway since 1935 and forms the first part of every collective agreement. It is negotiated separately between ·the LO and the NAF and removes a considerable area of conflictual issues from the regular bargaining process. Like the Labour Disputes Act, the Basic Agreement distinguishes between disputes of right and disputes of interest. Disputes over an existing contract must be submitted to the Labour Court. Strikes and lockouts are not permitted while the collective agreement is in force. The Basic Agreement also recognizes the right of employees and employers to organize and includes provisions outlining the responsibilities and the protection given to the local shop stewards. The local stewards perform an important role. They are consulted by local employers on all issues relating to changes in the production process and the work environment. Frequently, shop stewards will enter into special written agreements with employers concerning wages or working conditions. This practice is not prohibited by the Basic Agreement as long as these agreements do not conflict with the master contract for the enterprise (LRN, 1975).

The Basic Agreement recognizes the right of unions and employers to stage work stoppages over disputes of interest. It also recognizes the right of both parties to stage sympathy strikes and lockouts. This right to stage sympathy stoppages in support of another conflict applies even during the contract period, provided that the original dispute is lawful. In practice, however, this does not lead to many sympathy actions since such action requires the prior approval of the LO or the NAF.

Collective bargaining in Norway can take various forms. The common approach has been for the LO to bargain centrally for its affiliated unions. The negotiated contract is then put before the membership for approval or rejection. If there is an overall majority of the entire membership in favour of a proposal then it is accepted even if there is a majority against it in any one or more national unions (OECD, 1979). Individual national unions, as well as locals, then bargain with their employer counterpart on issues of particular relevance to their members. This bargaining must, however, be within the framework of the overall general agreement.

Of the 17 negotiations which have taken place between 1946 and 1974, all but six have been centralized. Decentralized negotiations, which are less frequent, take place between national unions and their respective employer counterparts. Wage negotiations between all levels of government and its employees are always conducted on a centralized level (OECD, 1979).

A further aspect of the system of labour relation which reduces the area of potential conflict is the fact that many so-called «fringes» are legislated and thus removed from the bargaining process. Two further institutions in the conflict-reducing arsenal of the main parties concerned need to be mentioned briefly. Mediation, in existence since 1915, enters the process of negotiations in almost every case which threatens to erupt in open conflict. The «cooling off» period imposed by the State Mediator or the District Mediators frequently leads to a settlement. It has been reported that over any representative period as many contracts are signed through mediation as through direct bargaining (LRN, 1975).

Free collective bargaining, as we have seen, includes the creation of institutions and processes to regulate and reduce conflict. The final weapon in the hands of the state, that of compulsory arbitration has on the whole been resisted by both the LO and the NAF. The government has, however, introduced compulsory arbitration from time to time, but compulsory arbitration has never become a permanent institution within the framework of Norway's labour relations system.

30

Incomes policy and tripartite bargaining

It is not our intention to review the details of incomes policy in Norway. It has existed, in one form or another since the end of the Second World War. A new trend has emerged in the 1970's which has brought the government more directly into the negotiation process. As this is of direct relevance to the issue of conflict resolution, we will review the main parameters of this development here. We will not go into the details of the origin of this approach (Cf. OECD, 1979) but it can be said in general terms that its introduction and use was related to the deteriorating economic conditions of that time. What is of direct relevance to us here is the institutional framework which has been created. While combined, or tripartite agreements had been implemented in 1973 and again in 1975 (OECD 1979), we will illustrate this new institutional arrangement with occasional reference to the 1976 settlement since it is of a more comprehensive nature than the preceding ones.

Two new institutions, created in the 1960's, play an important role in the new system of combined bargaining and settlements which emerged in the 1970's. The Contact Committee, with the Prime Minister as chairman and including the relevant Cabinet Ministers, representatives of LO and NAF as well as the organizations of farmers and fishermen, was initially seen as a discussion forum where the various parties could exchange opinions and discuss their basic assumptions prior to finalizing their respective strategies and demands for wage negotiations. In 1965, the government appointed an expert committee of three economists (the so-called Aukrust Committee, named after the research director of the Central Bureau of Statistics) to support the work of the Contact Committee. Two years later, under the chairmanship of Aukrust, the committee, now called the Technical Expert Group, was enlarged to include representatives from LO, NAF, fishermen and farmers as well as the relevant ministries concerned. The technical expert group, which became permanent in 1969, issues regular reports of alternative estimates of income and price developments (for details of the various models used, see OECD, 1979). The work of the Contact Committee has undergone important changes. While it functioned originally as a discussion forum, since the mid-1970's decisions of central importance are hammered out in the Contact Committee. The institutional machinery for the 1976 combined settlement included, in addition to the Contact Committee and the Technical Expert Group, various other committees. Issues of a more political nature were dealt with by a committee headed by the Finance Minister while more technical issues were handled by several technical working groups. A newly created Internal Steering Group, consisting of representatives from the relevant ministries, did much of the necessary coordination. All affected parties were included in the work of the Steering Group.

The negotiations themselves proceeded on a centralized basis, partly on the traditional bilateral model and partly with the participation of the government, but the basic approach as well as the parameters of the settlement were already agreed upon by all parties at the level of the Contact Committee. The government approach, which was announced to the Contact Committee in January of 1976, was based on the following points (OECD, 1979):

  i) to moderate price and cost inflation,
 ii) to safeguard employment in the exposed industries,
iii) to secure an average increase in real disposable income for wage earners of 3 percent, a somewhat larger increase for pensioners, and a considerably larger increase for farmers,
 iv) to reduce direct taxes.

In the area of wage settlements, coupled with government initiatives in taxation, social security payments, food subsidies and other actions aimed at controlling price developments, Norway is developing a fully integrated wage policy which is probably the first of its kind in a market economy (OECD, 1979). Such a policy, to be successful, requires a high degree of centralization and integration, which can only be maintained by intensified co-operation between the government, the trade unions and the employer organizations.

We have given a very brief and simplified description of a very complex arrangement. It seems likely that combined bargaining will continue to be used in Norway, particularly in times of economic difficulties. In the 1978 settlement, the combined and coordinated approach was used again, but even though general agreement was reached in the Contact Committee, subsequent negotiations between LO and NAF broke down, mediation failed and the settlement was finally imposed by compulsory arbitration. The issues pertaining to combined negotiations and settlements are a topic of intense and lively debate and we can not be certain of the outcome (for reactions from trade unionists, see Korsnes, 1979).

At the time when the final draft for this book is concluded, the 1980 settlement draws towards an end and it can be worthwhile adding some comments on this settlement as it introduces an element of solidaristic wage policy which has to do with transfers *between employees*. The Iron- and Metalworkers Union has for some time had the

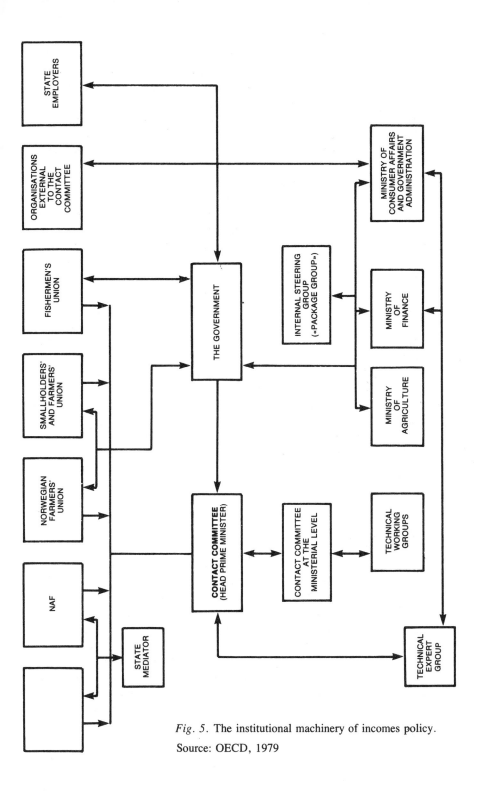

Fig. 5. The institutional machinery of incomes policy.

Source: OECD, 1979

clause in its agreements that nobody is to earn less than 87% of the avarage wage in this industry. In the last settlement this principle was introduced as a rule to apply generally within the part of working life covered by the LO – NAF agreements. The way it was actually done is so complex that it can not be spelled out in detail here. The main outline is as follows: The first step is to define a limit below which nobody is to be, in the 1980 settlement this was set at 85 per cent of the average wage in industry. To get everybody above this limit, various steps are taken, the primary one is still to distribute the total wage rise in such a way as to ensure that the low-income groups recieve the highest percentual increases. However, this mechanism may not be sufficient to raise the low income groups above the critical limit, as relatively too much of the total increase can still go to the middle and high income groups. Hence, a further support to the low income groups can be achieved through transferring money from those who earn more to those who earn less. In essence, the high income groups will pay some of the wages of the low income groups and there is some automatism built into the system to ensure that some compensation is made for income distributions that do not take sufficient care of the need to raise the low income groups. This principle of transfer was introduced in the last settlement. It was, however, not stretched very far in this settlement, as the amount to be deducted from the wages is around 20 øre pr hour (about 4 US cents). This amount is deducted from everybody and then distributed to the low income groups.

In a so-called combined ballot, where the votes from a number of unions are counted together, the settlement, largely developed by the parties together with the state mediator, went through, but with a very narrow margin. The majority was just above 50%. This probably has less to do with resistance from some unions against this expression of a solidaristic wage policy than with other aspects of the Norwegian system, which were perhaps more clearly brought to light by the 1980 settlement than what had been the case under the earlier settlements. The high degree of centralization seems, for example, to lead to a slow but steady curtailing of the local bargaining rights which in some unions, for example the Iron- and Metalworkers Union, has enabled the workers to take out productivity increases in the contract period in the form of a locally negotiated wage drift. The settlement took, furthermore, quite a long time, about half a year. This implies that price level and other relevant conditions can change while the negotiations are going on. Furthermore, union officials with whom we have been in contact argue that the complexity of the settlements has now become so high that the average member has great difficulties in understanding not only what goes on but how much money he or she will get. In centralized, tripartite settlements it is also necessary for organizations outside LO to agree to the same pattern as LO does. In the 1980 settlement compulsory arbitration has been used to bring other organizations to comply with the LO – NAF – State pattern. This in spite of the fact that compulsory arbitration is not supposed to be used to bring organizations in line with each other, but only when a conflict is a major threat against important interests of society as a whole. Some further remarks on possible instabilities in the Norwegian economic system are made in Chapter IX.

Concluding remarks

We have now presented, however briefly, the individual parts which shape, direct and influence Norway's labour relations system. One aspect above all stands out: The high degree of institutionalization of labour relations in general and conflict resolution in particular.

The high degree of state intervention, both direct and indirect, the participation of employers and unions in policy formation as well as in the administration of labour related legislation is strengthened by the existence of the highly centralized organizations of employers and employees. A great deal of potential conflict is absorbed, resolved or suppressed before it reaches the top level of LO and NAF.

But there are other factors which help to explain the high level of cooperation between the state, the employers and the unions. The late arrival of industrialization in Norway meant that democratic institutions and processes were relatively developed with the result that many of the bitter industrial struggles we have witnessed elsewhere in Europe and North America have no parallel in Norway. A case in point is the right to organize which was never seriously challenged in Norway.

The German occupation during the Second World War and the need to unite efforts in a major reconstruction when the war ended, has probably contributed to the relatively peaceful picture which Norwegian labour relations present. The relatively peaceful picture presented by Norwegian society in general, and working life in particular, sometimes brings observers from other countries to presume that Norway is an almost conflict-free society. This, however, is not the case. There is a strong consensus concerning methods of conflict resolution, but there is no similar consensus on what policies to pursue. In fact, the existence of a strong labour movement with a recent history of radicalism, combined with a system of free enterprise makes for a number of debates and conflicts over such issues as socialization, public control and so on, whose parallels are not found in, for ex-

35

ample, the United States or Canada, at least not as broad debates engaging the political «mainstreams». The conflict between various socialist positions and between the socialists on the one hand and the proponents of a liberal-capitalist society on the other is a marked feature of everyday Norwegian politics, and will continue to be so in the future.

II. The industrial democracy programme

Introduction

The first effort at reform in working life on which we will focus in greater detail, is the so-called Industrial Democracy Programme (ID-programme, for short) which was launched in the early sixties. Based on collaboration between the main parties in working life and researchers, the idea was partly to analyse some of the conventional approaches to industrial democracy, such as employee representation on the board of directors, partly to study the importance of the way work is organized for the problem of democratization, and to perform experiments with alternative forms of work organization. The programme is described and documented in various English language publications, such as Emery & Thorsrud (1969; 1976), Thorsrud (1970; 1976), Herbst (1974), Qvale (1976), Engelstad (1980).

There are some difficulties attached to giving a description of the ID programme that will satisfy everyone. It has given rise to a number of debates and discussions, both in Norway and elsewhere. The programme is part of a broader international development of what many call «job re-design programmes», or «socio-technical changes», which have brought forth a number of issues and debates in addition to those emerging in Norway. Hence, as this presentation has to be relatively brief, and we had to make a selection of what topics to treat, we have chosen to concentrate on those aspects of the programme that pertain to *participative democracy*. As will be seen later the programme can be said to have been based on three major arguments: a psychological argument, a productivity argument and a democratization argument. A few comments will be made on the psychological argument and the productivity argument, but emphasis will be on the democracy argument and on the role of work in a democratization process.

The issue of industrial democracy

«Industial democracy» is one of a number of concepts which cover a particular area of problems and efforts. Other concepts are participation, co-determination, self-management, to mention a few. Thorough analyses and definitions of these concepts are not necessary in this connection. They belong, generally, to those concepts which are relatively well covered in social analysis and social research. (General treatments are found in e.g. Clegg (1960); Emery & Thorsrud (1969); Walker and Bellecombe (1974); Batstone and Davies, (1976); Bernstein (1976); of governmentally initiated reports the "Bullock committee" (1977) can be mentioned). How the issue of industrial democracy was defined in this particular Norwegian programme will be described below.

Industrial democracy has emerged as an issue of relatively great political importance a number of times in Norway. If we limit the review to this century, a debate including some issues pertinent to industrial democracy emerged just after its beginning. The background was the emerging technological possibilities for the utilization of waterfalls to generate electricity and the resulting possibilities for the development of industry, particularly electrochemical industry. Such industry was costly to develop, and Norway did not have a capital market able to carry these investments. Hence, the entrepreneurs of the period went abroad, particularly to Britain, France and Germany to raise the necessary capital. This brought foreign investors into an ownership position in relation to Norwegian industry, and a debate emerged about the wisdom of this development. The relationship between workers and owners was no major part of this debate, but it played some role. The outcome of this round of discussions was a series of concession laws which made it necessary for foreigners to get government concession to acquire waterfalls rights.

The next time industrial democracy became an issue of importance in Norwegian politics was after the Russian revolution and the resulting upsurge in socialist movements. This was a period of rapid economic expansion, accompanied by a steady growth in union membership. Growth was particularly impressive in the General Workers' Union, the backbone of the radical wing in the Federation of Trade Unions (Cf. Chapter I). It was in this context of rapid growth and radicalization of the trade union movement that the government brought in a law introducing works councils. The law achieved, however, very little as a relationship of competition seems to have emerged between the councils and the trade union movement. The issues raised in the works councils tended to relate directly to time/wage questions, issues which are of course traditionally dealt with by unions (Dorfman, 1957). Unions had in fact not supported the introduction of works councils: they quickly lost their importance and the law was eventually abolished.

38

Industrial democracy surfaced for the third time in connection with the post-war settlements in 1945. The war period and the German occupation of Norway brought forth a new level of cohesion and solidarity across the ranks of the population and this new solidarity was to be given expression in the new order to be introduced when the war ended. The specific outcome was in fact not a politically defined and legally sanctioned effort at all, but an agreement between the main organizations in working life – the Employers Confederation (NAF) and the Federation of Trade Unions (LO) – about production committees. This idea was taken from war-time Britain. The committees were to function primarily in relation to shop floor issues. They were created on a parity basis (equal number of representatives from management and the workers) and their role was consultative unless management entrusted them with powers to make legally binding decisions. In a revision of the basic agreement in 1966 these committees were further developed. For an early analysis of this system, see Gullvåg (1953); in the seventies an analysis was made by the LO – NAF joint council for cooperative issues (Samarbeidsrådet, 1975).

In 1947 the employees in state owned companies over a certain size were given two representatives on the board of directors to be appointed by the general assembly members but upon suggestions from the employees. This system came to encompass a handful of companies; an analysis can be found in Emery & Thorsrud (1969), see also chapter IV.

Excepting a certain degree of discussion about socialism and ownership issues, the fifties were a quiet period from an industrial democracy point of view. Economic life went through a rapid development. Part of this development was a rather intensive use of scientific management and related techniques and ideas. This portfolio of ideas, by the way, did not reach Norway in any great measure until after 1945.

Together with economic progress, the Scandinavian type of welfare society was developed. Emphasis was put on equal distribution of income and wealth, but mainly through efforts which function after the wealth is generated (equalization through the tax system, the social security system and so forth). There was less public interference in the production and marketing processes. There were some exceptions to this pattern: a relatively broad law on public control of prices and agreements in restraint of competition, was passed in the early fifties, after a very heated public debate. A new work environment act was passed in 1956, but this act did not constitute a major break with the patterns of health and safety work already established (cf. Chapters V and VI).

Towards the end of the fifties, however, the issue of industrial democracy again started knocking on the door. The spirit of the reconstruction period started to fade away, and a more future-directed outlook emerged.

The discussion was opened by an analysis of industrial democracy centering heavily on certain aspects of the formal enterprise organization (Anker Ording, 1965). The framework was as follows:

- The enterprise must be seen as a system for distribution and excercise of power.
- As such it is organized in a hierarchical pattern.
- Industrial democracy efforts, to have any real impact, must consequently aim at the top of this system.

At this point the debate was entered by Emery & Thorsrud who pointed out another aspect of the issue.

Industrial democracy and participation

Emery & Thorsrud (1969) argued that the hierarchical power model overlooks a highly critical aspect of democracy: *the possibilities for participation by the individual:*

Democracy can not be fully specified in terms of a particular social structure, it is also a question of *how the structure has been generated:* i.e., who has influenced the generation process. If a structure is developed without any contributions or any sanctioning from the great majority of those concerned – the workers in the case of industrial democracy – it can not be called democratic. Democracy has, in other words, a *process perspective.*

Given this, the *problem of participation* becomes crucial: what possibilities does each worker in an industrial organization have for taking part in the development of a new enterprise organization?

To answer this question, it is necessary to consider the enterprise as a *place of work* and not only as a system for the exercise of power. Emery & Thorsrud pointed out that democratic participation by the individual was largely blocked by the prevailing ideas about organization of work. Scientific management, which in the early sixties had achieved a solid grip on working life in Norway, implies as specialized and heavily controlled work roles as possible, and as direct and comprehensive supervision of the individual as could be defended from an economic point of view. Hence, the individual – and this pertained with particular strength to people on the shop floor, – was left with a work role that allowed for very little in terms of development and maintainance of skills, very little freedom to take initiatives, perform judgments and make decisions, and very limited possibilities for developing contacts with fellow workers. Such patterns of organiza-

40

tion are an obstacle for the development of participation and democracy in working life. Hence, to further industrial democracy it would be necessary to solve the problem of *participation:* to change work roles in a direction more consistent with such basic prerequisites for participation as a reasonable degree of freedom and competence in work. This implied, at the same time, the definition of democratization of working life as a multi-step *process* where efforts had to follow upon each other in sequence and where a variety of means and methods would need to be employed. The need to focus on the work situation was supported by a survey of workers in the Oslo area where 56 % of the blue collar workers and 67 % of the white collar said that they would like to participate more in decisions concerning their work and work conditions (Holter, 1965).

Organization of work, psychological job requirements and productivity

We have so far located freedom and competence in work within the framework of a democratization process. In Emery & Thorsrud (1976) one finds, however, that job reform, or the introduction of a new paradigm of work (Emery, 1978) is argued for also from two other points of view:

Firstly, a productivity argument is given. It is mentioned that around 1960, Norway had reached a stage where continued increases in productivity could no longer be achieved through conventional efforts such as scientific management or an exclusive reliance on techonogical development. It would instead be necessary to seek new ways of utilizing the human resources in working life. Better utilization of human resources would demand changes in the organization of work.

Secondly, one finds a psychological argument, or what can possibly be called a «theory of man». It was argued that people are the bearers of certain requirements pertaining to work:

1. The need for the content of the job to be reasonably demanding (challenging) in terms other than sheer endurance, and yet providing some variety (not necessarily novelty).
2. The need for being able to learn on the job, and go on learning (which imply known and appropriate standards, and knowledge of results). Again it is a question of neither too much nor too little.
3. The need for some area of decision-making that the individual can call his own.
4. The need for some minimal degree of helpfulness and recognition in the workplace.

5. The need to be able to relate what he does and what he produces to his social life.
6. The need to feel that the job leads to some sort of desirable future.

These are commonly referred to as psychological job requirements.

Looking at the relationship between these three arguments, which can be called the democratization argument, the productivity argument and the psychological argument respectively, it seems reasonable to believe that Emery & Thorsrud consider them to overlap to a large extent. Bringing the three arguments together will give the following picture:

Industrial democracy is founded on a theory of man, and this theory can be expressed as psychological job requirements. If these requirements are met, people can have an active, creative relationship to their work. This active, creative relationship to work is expressed in high productivity. At the same time it constitutes the basis for participation necessary to a democratization process. In a real democracy, human and technological resources will interact in an optimal way, and one expression of this is a high level of productivity.

As concerns the validity of this «merging» of the arguments, opinions may differ. We will not perform a thorough analysis in this book, but mention a few points only.

Concerning the productivity argument, we will return to it, albeit briefly, in the next chapter. However, when evaluating this argument in the context of the Norwegian ID programme, it is necessary to be aware of the point that the labour movement in Norway in the post-war period generally has expressed itself in favour of productivity. Why productivity is such a positive goal, not only for the Labour Party which, after all, has generally had the responsibility for the nation's economy, but also for the union movement, has something to do with characteristics of society and such power relationships in working life as mentioned in Chapter I. Productivity is not considered primarily in the light of something which the employer «extracts» from the workers, but rather as something pertaining to national welfare. This view is of course not universally shared, but is much more prominent in Norway than in societies like the United States or Canada. Furthermore, the productivity argument put forth by Emery & Thorsrud is a broad argument pertaining to society as a whole and very different from seeing productivity as a question of squeezing as much as possible out of the workers in terms of units produced per hour or similar dimensions. Given the Norwegian setting as it was in the early sixties, the linking of the democracy argument to the productivity argument was well founded.

More criticism can, in fact be raised against the psychological job requirements, at least insofar as such requirements are thought to follow from inherent tendencies in man, rather than from values and processes in society (Gustavsen, 1980 c). On the other hand, the psychological job requirements are redundant in the sense that they are not needed as basis for the ID programme. The democratization argument alone is more than enough to justify the programme and the steps taken to implement it.

The democratization argument does not have to depart from any thesis about inherent needs in people, be it for certain types of jobs nor, for that matter, for democracy as such; what it says is that *if democracy is to be striven for, then it is necessary for people to have a work situation which makes participation possible. Why* democracy should be an overall aim in the development of society can be seen to follow from certain critical historical choices already made in the earlier development of society (cf. Gustavsen, 1980 e).

Participation, research and action

The contribution of research to development of possibilities for participation can take on various forms. Traditionally, the contributions of research are thought to be theoretical or descriptive, such as finding out what factors become of critical importance to the development of freedom and competence in work. This aspect was included in the research strategy developed by Emery & Thorsrud. However, a major dimension was added when it was argued that research should also go *into action*. Research should not only sit on the sideline and give more or less well founded analyses and advice, it should also share the responsibility for the development of concrete solutions to the problems emerging in the workplaces.

To go into action, it is necessary to have ideas about social change. The ideas to guide the development of the ID programme were initially drawn from a programme of development in Australian agriculture (Emery & Oeser, 1958) according to which change can be seen as a process evolving around the following main steps:
- Conceptualization
- Information
- Commitment
- Action
- Diffusion

Conceptualization will usually imply a description of how the world «is» and how it «ought to be». For a social science conceptualization to catch sufficient interest from other people to be able to link into broader events, certain conditions must generally be present. Such conditions demand a broad analysis, which can not be done here. It is clear that the conceptualization of the issue of industrial democracy which was introduced by Thorsrud & Emery caught on and was perceived as fruitful and relevant to a degree sufficient to start the process of implementation.

By saying this, a comment has already been made on the next issue – information. For conceptualization to lead to socially relevant changes, it needs to be made known to those concerned.

Knowledge itself is, however, not enough. People generally become acquainted with a broad spectrum of ideas without necessarily acting upon them. In fact, in a modern «communication» or «media» society, people can incorporate only a very small share of what they are exposed to; hence, the crucial role of the process of commitment. The Norwegian Industrial Democracy Programme was based on the idea of defining the leadership of Norwegian working life, as found at the top of the LO and the NAF and in various more informal circles relatively closely affiliated to it, as the critical element. Commitment from the leadership was thought to lead eventually to a broader commitment including the membership of both labour market parties. This was in line with the diffusion experiences from Australian agriculture on which the initial part of the programme was built.

Involving the leadership on the employer as well as on the employee side implied making the ID programme a joint one and to base it on the collaboration of both parties in working life with an equal or balanced influence over the programme.

When a certain conceptualization of the problem is done, and a network of people with ability to influence real events is established, the issue of *action* can be considered. The ID programme was based on the idea of going into a number of worksites to initiate experimental changes. These changes would fulfill various functions, ranging from demonstrating the feasibility of certain ideas about alternative forms of work organization, via testing the ability of researchers to share responsibility for field efforts, to the provision of inputs into a broader diffusion and learning process encompassing successively broadening circles of workplaces.

Given the aims and the basis of the ID programme, specific organizational changes had to start on the shop floor. It is on the shop floor that the possibilities for participation are generally most limited and it is consequently here that changes are most urgently needed. The chief reason for starting higher up, with management, is that management can be in charge of diffusion of the changes downwards in the organization. Hill (1971) describes such an example from a British setting, and even though the example does not constitute an unconditional failure, its positive results were not prominent enough to warrant a major re-evaluation of the shop floor approach. Earlier projects, particularly the one in Glacier Metals (Brown & Jaques 1965; Jacques 1951) indicated the major difficulties in getting changes originating on higher levels of the organization to overcome «the split at the bottom», cfr. Lysgaard (1960).

The selection of sites for the first series of local actions is of critical importance, and this selection raises a number of issues. The work-sites must, for example, be reasonably representative of important branches of working life, if results are to have a broader impact. It is, however, necessary to consider further points: it is mentioned above that a network of people committed to the ideas of the project must be developed before the field work can start. One function of this network is to help the researchers find relevant worksites as well as to endorse the researchers in relation to local management and workers. This makes it necessary to seek field sites within those parts of working life to which members of the network have access, not only in formal terms but also in terms of personal contacts. One must, of course, also to some extent consider the possibilities of success. However impressive it may be to change the most difficult workplaces, the problem is that the chances of failure will be high if such places are chosen. Failure means initial defeat and often the halting of the whole programme. On the other hand, sites must not be chosen from which experience can be rejected on the grounds that they are «too special». Between this version of Scylla and Charybdis the choices must be made. The considerations taken when the first sites of the ID programme were elected, are described in Emery & Thorsrud (1976).

When the first series of local actions are carried through, experience will be fed back into the conceptualization, the information process, and so on, and lead to improvements in all links of the total chain of steps in the action programme. When such considerations are done, the broader diffusion emerges as the main next step.

Briefly, these were the basic points of departure for the programme. The programme is often associated with such concepts as «autonomous work groups», «socio-technical design» and such like, and these elements were of importance, but the unique contributions of the ID programme are to be sought in ideas about *social change*. We believe, it is possible to argue that even though ideas about change and the use of research in action were not new, the Industrial Democracy Programme represented an important new effort for the purpose of achieving changes in society.

45

The programme was, more specifically, divided into the folowing steps or phases:
- Firstly, an analysis of various formal approaches to industrial democracy (an aspect not to be treated here but to which we will return in chapter IV).
- Secondly, a series of field experiments with alternative forms of work organization in selected field sites.
- Thirdly, diffusion of ideas and results from the experimental phase.

The socio-technical perspective

The socio-technical approach is a particular frame of reference for analysis of man-work relationships. It can, like all other frameworks, be used as a basis for development of efforts and action, but is in itself «a theory», in connection with a system of insights. Concepts like «socio-technics» might of course be used, as everybody has the right to his or her concepts, but has no anchoring in the way this framework was used in the ID programme. Nor does the use of a socio-technical frameworks necessarily imply neglect of other frameworks (as suggested by e.g. Pugh, 1966 or Silverman, 1970). The point is that in an action situation a *selection* must be made as there is no possibility of bringing «all knowledge» to bear on the situation (Gustavsen, 1980 e).

Given the need for reorganization to achieve increased freedom and competence in work, the set of ideas developed through the Tavistock coal-mining studies and experiments in the forties and fifties seemed relevant and potent and were brought in when the chief action parameters of the first series of field experiments were to be decided on.

The socio-technical framework is so well known and described in English language literature that no presentation will be attempted here (see for example Trist & Bamforth, 1951; Emery, 1959; Herbst, 1974; Emery, 1978). Briefly, the core element is to view work roles and work organization in the light of technology and the tasks and task interdependencies which technology generates. Neither technology nor tasks are, however, taken as given. The socio-technical approach has demonstrated that a given technology often lends itself to different definitions of tasks and task relationships and hence to possibilities for organizational *choice* (Trist et al., 1963). The framework has, furthermore, provided important contributions to the understanding of how systems need to be changed if the changes are to be socially relevant in facilitating a process towards improved freedom and competence in work.

46

The most widespread relevance of the socio-technical framework is perhaps to be found in suggestions concerning the restructuring of tasks to achieve broader work roles with improved possibilities for learning, for making judgments, taking initiatives and establishing social contacts. Generally, this has meant that the tendency to fragment larger jobs into smaller task pieces and the allocation of the smallest possible number of task pieces to each work role (Gustavsen & Ryste, 1978; Herbst, 1975) had to be opposed in favour of bringing task pieces together to form larger wholes, to stop the fragmentation process in the first place if possible, and to redesign work roles and work relationship structures to correspond to the demands created by broader tasks and the need for stronger collaboration between the workers.

In the ID programme, the following principles of job design were applied:
1. The need to bring together such tasks within the job as makes for optimal variety for the operator.
2. The need to bring tasks together in jobs in such a way that they form a meaningful pattern with as much resemblance to an overall task as is possible.
3. The need to develop an optimal length for each work cycle. While the need to provide for longer work cycles is evident, these must not be so long as to make it impossible for the operator to develop a reasonable work rhythm.
4. Some scope for the operator for setting standards of quantity and quality of production and suitable feedback of knowledge of results.
5. The inclusion in the job of some of the auxiliary and preparatory tasks.
6. The tasks included in the job should include some degree of care, skill, knowledge or effort that is worthy of respect in the community.
7. The job should make a perceivable contribution to the utility of the product in the wider society.

At group level:
8. Provision should be made for interlocking tasks, job rotation or physical proximity where there is a necessary interdependence of jobs.
9. Provision should be made for interlocking tasks, job rotation or physical proximity where the individual job entails a high degree of stress.
10. Provision should be made for interlocking tasks, job rotation or physical proximity where the individual job does not make an obviously perceivable contribution to the utility of the end product.

11. Where a number of jobs are linked together by interlocking tasks or job rotation they should as a group:
  - have some resemblance to an overall task which makes a contribution to the social utility of the product,
  - have some scope for setting standards and receiving knowledge of results, and
  - have some control over the boundary tasks.

The importance of «autonomous work groups» (Herbst, 1962; Gulowsen, 1971) is partly to be sought in the point that re-grouping of tasks and redefinition of work roles must generally be done on the level of the group, as most interdependent sets of tasks in modern service or production systems go beyond what can be handled by an individual. A group context makes it, furthermore, possible for the individual to become part of a social system which can take care of those social and psychological functions which can only be performed in the near and close environment, such as social support (Herbst, 1974; Emery & Thorsrud, 1976).

Autonomous work groups are not *ultimate* solutions in the development of industrial democracy. They are a core element in a system of ideas about forms of work organization that give the operators more in terms of freedom and possibilities for the development of competence than what conventional patterns of work organization generally do. So far, autonomous work groups belong to the level of *prerequisites* for a democratization process rather than to the level of the aims of such a process. On the other hand, as *some* of the problems of democracy belong to the level of the near environment of the individual, autonomous work groups also emerge as part of the larger network of solutions to organizational issues which need to be developed as part of an overall democratization process. It can be said that *autonomous work groups bridge the gap between participation and enterprise organization.*

The systems perspective

The introduction of a systems perspective was particularly helpful in understanding the complexity of organizations as a whole. It was introduced, to some extent, as an integrated part of the socio-technical framework and to some extent as an independent factor (Emery 1959; 1969). The importance of the systems framework for the actual steps taken in the participating organizations can be found within such areas as analysis of input and output on group, department or higher levels and in the understanding and analysis of variations, and of how

48

to adapt to, or control them. Suggestions for redefinition of managerial roles emerged from this framework in that it pointed out «boundary functions» as a set of tasks that need to be taken care of in an organization, and opened up the possibility of redefining inward-directed management roles in the direction of handling transactions across the boundary: between enterprise and environment for top management, between different departments for departmental heads, and so on. Such definitions of managerial roles opened up possibilities for shifting the right to make decisions pertaining to day-to-day work downwards in the organization.

The socio-technical frame of reference, together with the systems approach, were the theoretical pillars on the enterprise level. The framework did, however, not stop here. Less well known in the Scandinavian countries, but nevertheless of crucial importance, was a broader theory of society giving, among other things, some of the chief arguments for democratization (Emery, 1967).

Turbulence, survival and participation

Industrial democracy can be argued for as having value in itself. It is, however, possible to move beyond this level of argument and pose the problem of the «utility value» of democracy with respect to *other goals*. Democracy does, in other words, not only have to be valuable in itself, it can have value beyond this:

In Emery's line of reasoning on this, an analysis of environments, or situations, is the point of departure. Using degree of organization and complexity as the chief dimension, Emery & Trist (1969) distinguish between four ideal types of environments: the placid, random environment; the clustered environment; the disturbed-reactive environment, and environments were turbulence can occur. English language presentations of the environments and the underlying theory are available, and no further analysis will be given here (cf. Emery, 1967; 1969).

Turning to the problem of industrial democracy, environments with possibilities for turbulence can be taken as the point of departure. In such environments, acts, campaigns, disturbances can have far-reaching and unpredictable consequences. The underlying reason is the existence of links and ties which encompass the whole environment and make it possible for acts taking place in one location to achieve effects in other, and quite unpredictable, locations. When the environmental categories were originally introduced, the point of departure was the enterprise environment. Later the analysis was broadened, and the categories were used to describe characteristics of society. When possibilities for turbulence exist on the level of society, it becomes a task on this level to avoid the negative consequences such turbulence can have, such as events going out of control, major crises, etc. How, then, is sufficient control over the environment to be achieved?

The next step in the line of reasoning is that «rational instruments» like decision theory, planning techniques and such like do *not* reflect the real complexity of the situation and are consequently unable to produce relevant guidelines for policies and action. When rational instruments can no longer do the job, there is only one option left: the development of *values* which can function as «field forces» (Lewin, 1951) and give direction and stability to people's behavior.

How, then, are values created? Values of relevance to coping with complex environments cannot be decided on and installed by an elite in society. For the necessary commitment to be achieved, people must have the possibility for influencing the values – for taking part in their creation. Consequently, conditions must be created for this influence to be effective. Through this line of reasoning we are back to the problem of participatory democracy. Social organization must be developed so that this influence, and hence the necessary commitments, become possible. This line of reasoning puts democratization into a position where it has instrumental value in relation to such problems as the stabilization of society.

This brief presentation does not do justice to this complex but elegant reasoning. These arguments were never broadly diffused in Norway as part of the ID programme, and views on their validity did consequently not play any role of importance for the fate of the programme. When we come to the work environment reform (Chapters V – VIII) it will be seen that the instrumental value of democratization emerges again. The context is somewhat different from the one drawn up by Emery but there are also clear parallells. A core element in the work environment reform is to give those concerned, those who experience a work environment from the «inside», improved rights to define the issues and problems as well as to develop the solutions. Among the reasons for this we find not only the point that «democracy is good in itself» but also that the task of performing a national environment reform is so great and complex that «rational bureaucratic approaches» have no chance of coping with the problems.

Field experiments

From the middle sixties a series of field experiments were launched as part of the ID programme. The purposes of these experiments were primarily the following:
- Firstly, to demonstrate the viability of alternative forms of work organization, based on more freedom and competence for the workers, under «real conditions» in working life.
- Secondly, to demonstrate that researchers could share responsibility for generating practical solutions to workplace problems.
- Thirdly, to generate experience from which others could learn and that could function as a nucleus from which a diffusion process could begin.

The first four of these experiments – a wire drawing mill, a mechanical assembly plant, a pulp department and a fertilizer plant – are described in Emery & Thorsrud (1976), a broad description of the pulp department project is found in Engelstad (1970). As these experiments are already reported in English, another one is chosen as an illustration here: a project in a hotel and restaurant company: Hotel Caledonien. This project started in 1970, some years after the first efforts were launched. Substantial developments concerning both, the organization and the generation of changes at the enterprise level took place in the period between the first project in the wire drawing mill and such projects as Hotel Caledonien. These are described in Emery & Thorsrud (1976) and will not be treated here.

A case-study: Hotel Caledonien

Hotel Caledonien is a hotel & restaurant company located in Kristiansand, one of the southernmost towns in Norway. The hotel was built in the sixties, and opened in 1969. Originally, it could accommodate 250 guests in 130 rooms. Its capacity has now been doubled through the construction of a new wing. The hotel has a number of restaurants, including a large banquet hall seating 350 people. The hotel is also involved in the conference and convention market. In 1970, a project within the Industrial Democracy programme was started in this company.

The initiative

The specific initiative for the project came from the chairman of the board who was also managing director of the pulp and paper factory where one of the first field experiments of the ID programme took place.

When the board and management was interested in testing out new ideas for organization of work, the motives were probably mixed. Hotel Caledonien was a new venture at the time and had as yet not found a stable and rewarding location in the market. It can hence be said to have confronted problems of economy. These problems were, however, defined more as a question of «image» or «institutional characteristics» (Selznick, 1957) than as a question of increased effort from the workers. The problem of Caledonien was not too low productivity, but too few customers on which to apply its productivity. Something had to be done, and the board and top management invited the workers in to make this a *joint effort* rather than an effort defined by top management alone, to be installed from the top.

The initiative for a project was initially discussed internally between top management and the local union representatives. They agreed to launch a project, and put the issue before a meeting of all the employees. After approval on this level, the project was launched. (Cf. Karlsen, 1976 for a report in Norwegian).

The first development – Caledonien Dancing

It was decided to start the project in the main restaurant: Caledonien Dancing. With its old-fashioned formal style, high prices and few guests, it was an obvious point of departure. Initial discussion led to the emergence of various points which needed to be considered. These included lighting and decoration, the type of image the restaurant presented towards the guests, the organization of work, the addition of a bar within, or linked to the restaurant and the physical access to Caledonien Dancing, as its location in the building made it difficult to reach.

The organization of work was of the conventional type. The waiters had specialized work roles in the sense that each was assigned a set of tables (a station) for which he or she alone was responsible. Above the waiters was a headwaiter, who distributed guests on the various stations and in general acted as first line supervisor and manager. This system was supported by an individual accounting and control system: each waiter had his/her own file on the cash register, to which only he/she had the key. Hence, the economic performance of the waiters could be controlled individually. The waiters had, furthermore, an individual incentive wage system in that their wage was determined by the economic turnover on the station.

The weakness of such a system is that an imbalance can easily occur between the workload on each station and the people available to meet that workload. If a group of guests arrive in the restaurant in an otherwise slack period, the waiter on the station to which they are showed by the headwaiter gets his hands more than full, while the waiters at the other stations can be standing around with little to do.

The economic controls and the wage system reinforced this link between the waiter and «his/her tables». The system can, furthermore, foster competition between the waiters to attract guests to their stations, and gives the headwaiter who distributes the guests a very strong position of power over the waiters. When the individual waiter has to meet all types of workloads on his/her station without any help, the work gets heavier and the possibilities for giving good service are reduced. The image presented to the guests, with a few waiters being very busy while others stand around is, of course, not the best.

It was decided to try an autonomous work group solution in the restaurant. This process implied that the waiters had to take joint responsibility for the work in the whole restaurant. The stations were abolished in favour of waiters working together if the situation called for such collaboration.

Together with this, a change was made in the accounting and control system, doing away with separate files and having only one file where all transactions from the entire restaurant were registered. Instead of wage levels being decided on the basis of economic turnover on the individual station, wage levels now became dependent upon the total sales of the restaurant. This implied absolutely equal pay for all the waiters. Money coming in from tipping was pooled and shared equally.

The traditional headwaiter's role was eliminated. The waiters took over the headwaiter's function in the restaurant, such as allocation of guests to tables. This change was faciliated by two of the headwaiters going on to other jobs, while those remaining were given new tasks.

Together with the changes in the organization of work, a major rebuilding of the restaurant and the access to it took place and a bar was build adjacent to the restaurant. These changes, together with the changes in organization and patterns of work and service, changed the image of the restaurant thus attracting a broader clientele.

Horizontal diffusion

After the changes in Caledonien Dancing, the programme was broadened to include other departments of the enterprise, among these, the other restaurants. Like in most larger hotel and restaurant companies, the restaurants and cafeterias are designed to cater to different types of clientele, making it possible to have something to offer to everyone.

This, however, makes for rather substantial differences in the kind of jobs the various establishments have to offer. Such differences made it necessary to develop new solutions when ideas were to be diffused from the first restaurant to the others.

In attempting to develop patterns of work organization where the employees share responsibility for more than one restaurant, efforts were made to cut across restaurant boundaries. This has met with only limited success. Generally, however, it is quite clear that a new type of restaurant organization has been developed, built much more around multiplex horizontal links between people than the old one, and where the amount of management and supervision «from above» is very limited.

The enterprise does, however, not only consist of restaurants but also of the kitchen, and of various administrative units in the hotel. Restaurant kitchens are traditionally organized according to a strongly hierarchical pattern, with the chef at the top, followed by a descending order of cooks, down to the unqualified hands. Certain changes were made in this hierarchical pattern mainly by bringing employees in unqualified work roles, like scrubbing, into more qualified kitchen work for part of their working hours. Changes have also taken place on the boundary between kitchen and restaurant, a boundary which is often the source of tensions and conflicts. In a grill restaurant, where the kitchen function is closely related to the serving of the food, an agreement was made, bringing the waiters and the cooks together into one work group. Together they share the responsibility for preparing as well as for serving the food. One of the obstacles to be overcome in this context, was the wage system. While the waiters are generally payed according to an incentive scheme, the cooks are generally on fixed salaries. For this group, it was agreed to create a wage system based on a general, fixed basic wage with a bonus on top, the bonus to be determined by the sales of the restaurant.

Autonomous work groups and broader organizational changes

In the Caledonien project, efforts have been made to expand the democratic solutions, partly by shifting as many decisions as possible from higher level management to the work groups and partly by reorganizing higher organizational levels into patterns which can support the new type of work organization.

Looking at decisions allocated to the groups, the following pattern emerges:

It has already been mentioned that the waiters take care of organization and distribution of work in the restaurants. In addition to this, they also handle, as a group, recruitment, the question of leaves, settlement of rosters and shiftplans, issues of organization to meet the holiday seasons, and day-to-day eonomic control. Efforts at moving beyond this, and entrusting the waiters with the total economic planning and budgeting on the level of the restaurant have, however, not met with the same success. The problem here seems to be primarily caused by the working hours of the waiters who generally work in the evenings while the administrative staff is present in the daytime. A certain degree of collaboration between the administrative staff and the waiters would be necessary if the waiters were to be in charge of budgeting. This collaboration on the practical level is not easily achieved between people who are generally not present at the same time.

The development of multiple links between the people on the «shop floor» has greatly reduced the need for middle level management and coordination. The contacts between the different departments are largely handled directly between those concerned and without involving higher level management. The managerial and administrative staff is for this reason smaller than what is ordinarily the case for hotels of this type and size. In addition to budgeting, management and administrative staff mainly handle the outward directed activities, like marketing. The chief task of the head of the restaurant department as well as of the previous headwaiters is to develop and maintain contacts to clients and users, and to help them plan special events such as banquets, conventions or social occasions.

A more collaborative form of planning and information sharing has also developed at company level in the form of weekly «mail meetings». Here top management meet toghether with representatives from all departments, including department heads and workers, and the shop stewards and discuss incoming mail, all arrangements for the coming week, last figures on sales, complaints or any other type of issue relevant for that particular time. The meeting is quite informal in style, and anyone can bring up an issue. The chairmanship is rotated between those usually meeting, management and workers alike. There is no formal election of representatives to this meeting, the workers in any particular department decide from time to time who is going to represent them.

The role of the organizations

Both the Hotel and Restaurant employers organization, and the Hotel and Restaurant Workers Union have been involved in various ways.

Agreements on new wage systems, for example, had to be dealt with on this level to establish the necessary exemptions from existing rules.

Generally, the hotel and restaurant sector is a part of working life where the degree of organization is not as high as traditionally found in industry. When the project started, only about 25 percent of the people working in Hotel Caledonien were members of the Hotel- and Restaurant Workers Union. This percentage went up as the project developed, until about 80 percent were organized. At a particular point in time a conflict emerged between the Caledonien workers and the union, resulting in the Caledonien members resigning from the union. This conflict had, however, little to do with the project, and pertained mostly to other issues, particularly to general wage issues. After a while, the conflict was settled, and the Caledonien workers again joined the union.

Long term perspective

There is no doubt that Hotel Caledonien has achieved what one set out to do when the project was launched in the early seventies. From a difficult start, the economy has improved steadily until this company today emerges as one of the most successful hotel and restaurant firms in Norway. The profits have been solid since 1973 – 74 and the physical facilities have been expanded to include more rooms and restaurants. No major setbacks have occurred. No interest has ever been expressed by management nor workers for a return to the conventional patterns of organization.

Concluding remarks

We have so far traced the Industrial Democracy Programme up until the end of the first experimental phase. The programme does not stop here, but from here and onwards changes started to emerge. In various ways these changes are linked to discussions and evaluations emerging on the basis of the first series of field experiments. Hence, the programme and the evaluations of it can not be kept apart. In the next chapter diffusion and evaluation will be discussed as interdependent developments.

III. The industrial democracy pro- gramme: Discussion and diffusion

Introduction

Before proceeding with a description of the Norwegian development, we will take a brief look at two critical views on the Industrial Democracy Programme:

One view, which has been expressed by many (e.g. Bull, 1979) is that the field experiments of the sixties and early seventies did not lead to any diffusion at all. Another view, which has emerged primarily among radical social scientists within the Anglo-American tradition, and which pertains to job redesign programmes in general, is that they are above all a new management technique (e.g. Braverman, 1974; Nichols 1976; Edwards, 1979). This last argument amounts to saying that such changes are a new version of «human relations man-agement». Despite what is said about psychological needs and demo-cratization, the point is really to give management new methods for control over the workers, methods that have their main appeal in be-ing less obtrusive and more refined than scientific management or the «older» human relations approaches whose limitations have become fairly obvious. It is also quite clear that a case like Hotel Caledonien can be taken to support such a view: management had, among other things, economic motives for advocating this project. These motives were, at the same time, not of the simple productivity kind that can be satisfied through increased output per time unit or similar crude effici-ency improvements. The problem was more subtle: the development of a market image that could attract sufficient customers to bring the company into a better economic position. A managerial strategy for such «institution building» (Selznick, 1957) needs to rely on the cons-cious use of psychological and social mechanisms to create solidarity among all employees around common goals.

When these two views are put forward it is because they are per-haps the most widespread critical positions of such innovations as the Industrial Democracy Programme. They are also, to some extent, op-posing views. If it is true that the main function of the innovations is as a management technique, one would expect relatively broad diffusion. It is, of course, possible that management does not know what is in its own best interest and that this is the reason why these ideas are not put to use. However, if one looks at the extremely broad diffusion of the original human relations approach, as emerging from the Hawthorne (Roethlisberger and Dickson, 1950; Mayo, 1945) the explanation is somewhat difficult to accept. Management may be critisized on various grounds, but lack of ability to see what is in its own best interest has rarely been a justified element in such criticisms. Hence, both these views can hardly represent a reasonable overall characterisation of one and the same programme. As concerns the Norwegian development, there is a need for the application of a more differentiated outlook. It is clear that there have been diffusion *problems*. To say that there has been no diffusion is, however, a far too negative view. It is, furthermore, quite clear that there have been instances where management's participation in the programme has been strongly influenced by a need to acquire new techniques to control and mobilize the workforce. This does not mean, however, that all actors shared the same motives nor that a reasonable overall sociological interpretation of the programme must naturally focus on this as the main perspective.

Despite the fact that productivity and control considerations have played a role in some instances, productivity perhaps in most instances, in retrospect we view the radical critique as inadequate in the Norwegian setting. As we will return to more in detail below, and in later parts of this book, we do this for the following main reasons: The ID programme should not be evaluated in isolation from later change efforts, particularly the changes associated with the Work Environment Act of 1977. The programme was the result of struggles and demands by the labour movement, and should not be evaluated in the same manner as similar changes in other countries which have been implemented more exclusively through employer initiatives. Given the powerful position of the Norwegian labour movement (Chapter I), motives and reasons of individual employers in Norway do not have the same significance as they would, for example, in the USA or Canada. Equally important is the related fact that the trade union movement in Norway has not, on the whole, resisted increased productivity – on the contrary, it has supported it (Chapter I).

Patterns of diffusion

Passing any judgment on diffusion of ideas in a society as a whole, even if it is a small one like Norway, must rely upon judgments and impressions. We have as yet no possibilities for applying an unequi- vocal «scientific approach» to this issue, and we probably never will. Even if we had the theory and methods necessary for an exact de- scription of complex social developments, we would nevertheless confront a number of issues where we would have to rely on judg- ments. One example is the issue of diffusion as such: what is to be understood by diffusion? What characteristics must y have for us to say that it has something to do with x via a mechanism for diffusion? It is easily seen that a whole host of problems, relating to causality and a number of other highly problematic issues, emerge. We will not pursue these issues here: the points are mentioned to underline the need for judgment (for some further comments, see Gustavsen (1980e).

As emerges from Chapter II, the ID programme was based on the idea of a multi-step development: changes were to start in selected field sites on the shop floor and move from there to encompass larger areas of the shop floor organization of the participating enterprises. When sufficiently broad changes in the organization of work were achieved, a basis for participation in relation to broader enterprise is- sues would be established and changes in overall patterns of organiza- tion and decision-making on the level of the enterprise as a whole would emerge. When discussing diffusion and changes it is in prin- ciple necessary to distinguish between these three steps, even though it is not always easily done in practice. The reason why it is necessary to make this distinction is that a change programme can be halted on any of these levels.

As diffusion was thought to take place in expandling circles from a number of experimental sites, it is also relevant to distinguish between diffusion within particular organizations, e.g., from an experimental site to the rest of the organization, on the one hand, and diffusion to other organizations, or external diffusion, on the other.

When these perspectives are pointed out, it is to underline some of the dimensions that need to be considered. In our relatively brief pre- sentation we can not pursue these aspects separately, but must limit ourselves to relatively broad overall views.

In discussing diffusion from the ID propgramme, the following main types of developments need to be considered:

- Direct replication. By this is meant enterprise projects conducted along the same lines as in the first generation of experiments. ⌐
- Change projects that are linked to the orginal projects but which also imply important changes.
- The ID programme implied the use of a number of means, such as

59

job rotation, new training methods, etc., within an overall framework. Such means can, however, be used as more isolated efforts, without the overall framework of the projects within the ID programme. Hence, diffusion of means is a third possibility.
– We also need to consider developments that have some of their roots in the ID programme, but where ideas form this programme have merged with other ideas to from partly new structures and developments.

A relatively thorough effort at estimating the impact of the ID programme was done by Bolweg (1976). On the basis of information up to late 1974, he develops the following picture:

In addition to the enterprises where the first four demonstration projects took place, Christiania Spigerverk, NOBØ, Hunsfos Fabrikker and Norsk Hydro (See Emery and Thorsrud, 1976) he finds that there are five further enterprises where substantial changes have been accomplished: those five are Hotel Caledonien (Chapter II; Karlsen, 1976), Norsk Medisinaldepot (The Norwegian State Medical Supply Depot: a state owned monopoly for pharmaceuticals on the wholesale level), Norsk Shell (Shell Norway) (Gustavsen og Skaarud, 1971; Gustavsen, 1972b; Gustavsen and Ryste, 1978), Siemens (subsidiary of Siemens, Germany) and Block Watne (a producer of prefabricated houses and building elements). He lists 14 additional enterprises that «are in the planning or early implementation phase» and a further 13 where projects have been planned «but never started, or failed in the early implementation phase.» It is possible to argue the allocation of the headings for some of the enterprises Bolweg mentions, and to some extent also his categories, however, as a rough picture of the situation in Norway in the middle seventies his summary seems correct enough. The number of relatively direct replications of the first field experiments was low, while a number of enterprises tried to relate to the programme, more or less successfully.

The situation at this time can be characterised as unstable. The possibilities for a major setback and almost complete failure were clearly present. Setbacks did, for example, occur not only in enterprises trying to relate to the ID programme, but also in two of the first demonstration enterprises (Christiania Spigerverk and NOBØ) and to some extent also in some participants in the «second wave» of experiments. As concerns one of the two remaining enterprises from the first generation of experiments, Gulowsen (1974) paints a picture of the development in Norsk Hydro which is perhaps somewhat darker than the one given in Emery & Thorsrud (1976). In spite of this, a total reversal, however, did not occur. Instead, the overall development continued in a positive direction. It was still slow, but the danger of going back to «square one» did not materialize. In retrospect, five years later (1980), we can put the number of enterprises that have in some way or other related to the programme, and with some positive results to show for the effort, around fifty. In this we include enterprises taking part in a programme in the commercial navy that has been going on since the latter sixties (Roggema and Thorsrud, 1974; Johansen, 1979). A number of these positive developments are limited to moderate changes on the shop floor. The number of organizations where broader changes have occurred and stabilized has, however, also grown, in that such companies as Øglænd (bicycles and textiles) and Mjellem og Karlsen (shipbuilding) can be added to the list.

When giving this estimate around fifty enterprises we do, however, move from the first to the second pattern of diffusion: from relatively direct replications of the first experiments into changes that are linked to the first ones, but where more substantial changes in strategy have occurred. Comments will be made below on some of these changes. They primarily imply a changed balance between the researchers on the one hand and the people in the enterprises on the other, in the definition and implementation of changes. The researchers show a «lower profile» and generally leave more of the development to local definition, which allows for a broader range of solutions and approaches.

A substantial number of the enterprises that can show positive results have participated in a job design workshop described in Engelstad and Ødegaard (1979) This workshop, which is a continuous service to organizations who want to start development programmes, is based on the participation of a limited number of organizations each time, each organization being represented by management as well as workers. To participate, the enterprise has to commit itself to actual change and development and to the use of the workshop in support of this. The individal enterprise participate more than once to make it possible to utilise the workshop as support to a developmental process over time.

A third pattern of diffusion was loosely called diffusion of means, relating to the more «tactical» steps taken, particularly to achieve increased freedom and competence in work on a group basis. A number of such means were brought to bear on the problems in the experimental sites under the first part of the ID programme, pertaining to recruitment, training, job allocation, participation in planning, and so forth (see Emery and Thorsrud, 1976). One of the most marked features of the development is a fairly wide diffusion of these means, such as changes in wage systems, introduction of job rotation, but outside

61

the overall context provided for by the ID programme. This implies that this type of diffusion has its questionable aspects. At this point we may be close to the «new management technique» perspective mentioned above. When a particular method is introduced outside the context of a broader programme for democratization, it does not necessarily function in a way which is positive for the workers. The clearest example may be job rotation: a number of examples are know where job rotation has been introduced on management initiative with the intention of increasing the flexibility of the workforce, making people more multi skilled and more used to being shifted around. Increasing the skill level and the flexibility of the workers is a positive factor if the resulting rotation is controlled by the workers. It is rarely positive if the system is imposed from above without worker participation in design and implementation. In the last case the situation is characterised by improved competence of the operators but without a parallel increase in the right to decide when the various skills are to be used. Hence, it is highly important to consider the issue of competence *as well as* the issue of freedom.

When particular and isolated means are used outside the context of the ID programme the effect does, however, not have to be negative. There are examples of more positive developments as well, for example as concerns the abolishment of the piece rate wage system. In the seventies the use of piece rates was drastically reduced in Norway. The number of workers on piece rates in the mechanical industry seems, for example, to have declined over a decade from about 80 percent to about 20 percent. The type of wage system which replaces individual piece rates is generally a fixed salary with a bonus on top. The bonus is determined by quality and quantity of production (Engelstad, 1973) and is generally settled on group or higher level, not on an individual basis. Such bonus should, furthermore, not constitute too large a share of the total income and should consequently not exceed 20 percent of the income. The drift away from piece rates was motivated by more factors than the ID programme, but it is quite clear that this programme was one of the reasons that brought this development about. In the later seventies it seems, by the way, as if this development away from piece rates has slowed down. The introduction of a price-wage freeze in 1978 (Chapter V), and the increased problems pertaining to wage settlements (Chapters I and IX) seem to have functioned in favour of forcing the workers to maintain piece rates as this is the wage system which seems to lend itself most easily to wage drifts, at least in a society where the central control over wages is relatively high.

When looking at the issue of diffusion, it may also be useful to

62

quote from the current Basic Agreement between LO and the NAF, a section which was developed in the 1970's in collaboration with the Work Research Institutes:

"In the efforts to give those working within the individual departments or working groups more opportunity to make decisions on their own during their daily work, it is, among other things, important to promote understanding for and insight into the financial position of the undertaking. Learning, development, information and consulation will increase the possibilities of the individual employee for a meaningful work situation. The organizations therefore presume that the works and working environment council – or the works council and the working environment committee – of the individual undertaking will see it as an essential task to promote proposals about what can be done within the various fields of the undertaking to adapt conditions for such a development.

Experience shows that it is of little use to change jobs or positions in isolated cases, or to try to change the forms of organization and management within an individual group or department without any connection with the rest of the undertaking. Such changes need the support and active cooperation of the rest of the organization and may lead to smaller or larger changes also in other parts of the organization. Therefore, representatives of the various parts of the undertaking must be included in such developmental work.

The organizations emphasize that it is the duty of the top management and of the employees and their shop stewards to take the initiative and actively support and take part in such developmental work. For their part the organizations will, jointly and separately, support this work through various actions".(From Part B, the Basic Agreement).

This belongs, in itself, to the level of general declarations, which do not necessarily lead to specific positive developments. In fact, the «various actions» mentioned at the end of the quotation, can probably be counted on the fingers of one hand. Nevertheless, it is worth noting that the ideas introduced in the ID programme have received this type of institutional sanction.

The last pattern of diffusion occurs when a set of ideas become linked to other ideas and issues to produce new combinations. Such links have, for example, been forged between the ID programme and education (Blichfeldt, 1974; 1975). Another example, which we will treat in depth later in this book is the work environment reform to emerge in Norway on the latter seventies (Chapters V – VIII): Bolweg (1976) notes, in his evaluation of the ID programme, that the union movement by the middle seventies showed a limited interest in pursuing the ideas of the ID programme and that it was much more preoccupied with health and safety issues in the workplace. This is true enough, but Bolweg has for some reason left out mentioning that already in the middle seventies the elements of a *merger* between ideas from the ID programme on the one hand, and ideas pertaining to a workplace reform in health and safety on the other, had already started to emerge. In a programme for work environment reform developed jointly by the Federation of Trade Unions and the Labour Party in connection with the parliamentary elections of 1973 (LO-DNA, 1973, see Chapter V), the need to consider organization of work as part of a work environment reform was taken up. The Work Research Institutes had already embarked on a study of the organization of health and safety work on enterprise level, the result of which meant a further step in the bringing together of these two sets of ideas; the report from this study was published in 1975 (Karlsen et al, 1975). This merger between ideas about work and participatory democracy as found in the ID programme, and ideas about how to further health and safety work in the workplace has of course meant that both systems of ideas have undergone changes. The work environment reform to emerge in the later seventies deviates to some extent from the ID programme, but there are also clear links between them and they both form part of a total process of development.

Before leaving the issue of diffusion from the ID programme it can also be mentioned that the Norwegian programme triggered off parallel developments in Sweden and Denmark. These developments will not be treated here. As concerns Sweden, see, for example, Bjørk et al (1972), SAF (1975), Agurén et at (1976), Agurén and Edgren (1979), for critical comments see, e.g., Gunzburg (1976) and Dahlstrøm (1978). A brief overall comparison between Sweden and Norway can be found in Gardell and Gustavsen (1980). The main series of sociotechnical projects in Denmark is described in Agernsap (1973); critical comments can be found in, for example, Jensen (1977).

Diffusion – some tentative conclusions

In drawing some tentative conclusions on the basis of the picture sketched above, one may start by saying that the point of view that little or nothing came out of the programme is clearly not valid. There has in fact been a relatively broad diffusion. The problem is rather what yardsticks are used: negative evaluations of such efforts as the ID programme are often linked to the use of unrealistic criteria. Instead it is necessary to ask what expectations one can legitimately entertain in an analysis of such a programme. What developments are to be included when diffusion is discussed, and what criteria are to be used when a given process is evaluated?

As concerns expectations, it seems quite clear that a rather long time span must be expected for changes to encompass a broader part of working life of a society. It is not realistic to assume that major changes can be achieved in a few years or even a decade. Instead, time horizons of twenty to forty years seem more realistic.

When relatively long time spans must be accepted, a new problem emerges: what is to be understood by diffusion? An event taking place in society, such as a series of field experiments with alternative forms of work organization, does not occur in isolation, but in a context made up of numerous other events and developments. If the experiments have any significance at all, they will enter into relationships with some of these other ongoing streams of events, eventually to produce new outcomes which may resemble, but also in important respects may differ, from the original input. Hence, what can be called «linear diffusion», where ideas are spread in the form of «more of the same», will rarely occur in the social field. When ideas are diffused, they will also to a greater or lesser extent change. These changes can, of course, be so major that the original ideas are turned into something quite different and one then confronts the question of having to draw an ultimate line between what is considered diffusion and what is something almost wholly new.

A third aspect relates to what yardstick is to be used when the significance of a particular development is to be evaluated. As concerns the ID programme, a number of dimensions can possibly be introduced. Let us here mention only two: the programme can be evaluated as a social science research effort or as a political development.

In the first instance we will have to compare the ID programme to other social science-based efforts at changing organizations and society. Insofar as this is the frame of reference it is beyond doubt that the programme has been succesful. There may be comparable and equally successful programme in other societies, but the Norwegian ID programme was clearly the first of its kind and opened up a new way of using social science resources.

By political significance is meant the extent to which the ID programme really came to function as a major factor when various questions pertaining to working life came up on the political agenda in the period from the late sixties and into the seventies. To what extent did, for example, the basic strategy of the programme, the step by step development towards improved industrial democracy emerging from changes in organization of work become acceptet as *the* valid approach to industrial democracy? To what extent did the Norwegian union movement come to accept the notion that the changes emerging from the ID programme were to be the main thrust at the grass roots in Norwegian working life? It is quite clear that in relation to such criteria the impact of the programme was limited. As will be seen from the next chapter, employee representation on the level of the board was introduced in the early seventies with no consideration for the chief argument behind the ID programme. As Bolweg (1976) rightly notes, in the middle seventies the union movement discussed health and safety and not democracy and organization of work. The elements of a merger between ideas about participatory democracy on the one hand, and problems of health and safety on the other, were as yet only present in an embroyonic form among a few trade unionists and researchers. Most initiatives for specific projects within the ID programme emerged with managment, indicating that a broad grass roots movement in favour of new patterns of work organization was not present at that time. This lack of a clear political significance for the ID programme by the middle seventies does, of course, not necessarily reflect on the quality of the programme. Lack of political significance may occur for various reasons, for example that ideas are put forward before the time is ripe for them. To some extent this may in fact have been the case for the ID programme.

It is mentioned above that approximately fifty enterprises, or rather organizations, as some are found in the public sector, have been involved in developments radiating from the ID programme. In a number of these the changes are relatively modest. Even where the changes are most broad, in the sense that they encompass most or all of the shop floor, what has emerged in terms of *further* organizational changes, such as delegation of management decisions to the work groups as demonstrated in the Caledonien case is still limited. In organizations that the Work Research Institutes has had occasion to follow, various changes pertaining to «higher levels» in the formal organization have emerged, particularly within the following areas:

In the roles of foremen and other first line supervisors: from their traditional control function towards a coordinative function, frequently across departemental boundaries.

In the use of experts: from their previously dominant role as change agents towards a function as resource persons on the shop floor.

Within the field of planning and budgeting: from the traditional model and towards increased delegation to, or participation from, the workers.

66

In the broad use of project groups and similar units of organization where the workers are given broad representation on an equal footing with management and experts on the basis of the assumption that work experience is a valid input in the design of, for example, new production systems.

Within the field of managerial structure, towards more integrated managerial functions which make the lower levels less exposed to the previously detailed and often controversial requirements emerging out of a highly specialized and consequently fragmented managerial structure (Gustavsen and Ryste, 1978).

In a few organizations developments can be seen within all these and perhaps other areas (e.g. in Mjellem & Karlsen, a middle sized ship-building company, and in Øglænd, a bicycle and textile company, see also the Swedish Almex case as reported by Gardell and Svensson (1980). In other organizations we find developments within some of these areas . Even if such trends and developments can be seen, however, they are still too scarce, and with a few exceptions too limited, to make it possible to say that we are on the road towards broad and major changes in the overall pattern of enterprise organization. Hence, a further tentative conclusion is that diffusion has so far been more successful «along the shop floor» than «higher up» in the organization. This, of course, also means thant there are limitations on what changes can emerge on the shop floor, as there are limits to how far these can go before they confront limitations following from the patterns of organization on higher levels in the formal structure.

As an overall conclusion, it is clear that the problem of diffusion is the one that must be given most consideration in the context of the ID programme and related efforts. In the last part of this chapter, where some further points of analysis and evaluation will be raised, this will be the point of departure. Before proceeding to this, however, a few comments will be made on the relationship between enterprise development and the goals of the ID programme.

The relationship to the main goals of the programme

As emerges from Chapter II, there were three main arguments behind the ID programme: a psychological argument, a productivity argument and a democratization argument. To what extent were these aims fulfilled in the various enterprise developments that occurred as part of, or in the wake of, this programme?

As pointed out by Srivastva et al (1975) in relation to the productivity argument, it is not always easy to assess an outcome with an absolute certainty. This is linked to the reporting from the various projects, which often deviates from «ideal scientific norms», particularly if these norms are interpreted in a naturalistic direction. Field projects in social research tend to be reported in ways which are strongly influenced by local characteristics and developments and hence they vary from case to case. «Naturalistic» ideals of science can rarely be met in social research (Gustavsen, 1980a; 1980e; 1980f). Consequently, it is necessary to rely on overall judgments when main results are to be assessed.

Starting with the psychological argument, Blumberg's well known point that there is hardly an investigation which does not show that work satisfaction increases after an increase in the decision-making rights of the workers (Blumberg, 1968) generally applies to the Norwegian developments. Measurements were not always made, nor are those made always comparable, but as an overall impression this clearly holds. On the other hand, these authors are generally skeptical towards the use of this dimension. In line with, for example, Thurman (1977), Taylor (1977) and Roustang (1977) we generally do not believe job satisfaction to give a reasonable intake to important issues in working life. We believe, furthermore, that this reflects underlying difficulties in using «psychological needs» as key to social development (Gustavsen, 1980c). These issues will, however, not be pursued here.

Of greater importance is the issue of productivity. Again, there is no unequivocal picture to emerge from the Norwegian projects in terms of reporting, but it seems fairly clear that improvements in productivity occurred in most cases, provided that productivity is given a broad definition. This is in line with conclusions drawn by, e.g., Srivastva et al (1975) and Cummings and Molloy (1977) with reference to job redesign programmes in general.

As far as the democratization argument is concerned, it may be more of an open issue what dimensions to use in the evalution of results. However, changes in patterning of organization and decision-making as such, seem to be the most relevant aspects. Hence, there is no need to add dimensions to those already present when project developments and results are described as changes in organization and decision-making. There is, for example, no need to evaluate a democratization process in terms of degree of satisfaction expressed by those involved in it. In fact, such an evaluation can be misleading, as democracy does not always function best when people are most satisfied (Gustavsen, 1980c). In an enterprise experiment described by Karlsson (1971) no correlation was found between job satisfaction among the workers and demand for influence. So far the evaluation done within the ID programme is good enough, as all cases are described in terms of changes in organization and decision-making (such as the Caledonien example given in Chapter II. The majority of case reports are available in Norwegian only) One weakness, however, is pointed out by Gardell (1976) and Bolweg (1976) when they make the point that it is of major importance to see to what extent improved freedom and competence in work, through the development of, e.g., autonomous work groups, actually lay the foundation for a broader democratization process, or at least, produce a pressure from the workers in this direction. The empirical demonstration of this link will validate the chief dynamic assumption of the programme, at least insofar as one focusses on the democratization perspective: that autonomous work groups mediate between work and a broader process of democratization. On this point the various reports from the ID programme are relatively weak and unsystematic. They do not give a clear and unequivocal support for the thesis that increased freedom and competence in work leads to an increased pressure for broader organizational changes. There are, however, other studies pointing in this direction, see for example Gardell (1976) and Elden (1977); in fact, the evidence in support of this link has been piling up throughout the seventies.

Work reform and productivity

Critics of job redesign programmes have argued that the productivity aim can function contrary to the interests of the workers. Kelly (1978) argues, for example, that it leads to «intensification of work», which implies that the employers and managers extract more from the workers. The relevance of the productivity argument becomes even more pronounced if we apply a broad view to the issue of productivity: the Caledonien case demonstrates, for example, that economic survival and growth can be dependent upon market image, and that the basic productivity problem is the development of such an image rather than squeezing more output out of the employees. The productivity argument can also be said to cover such issues as are raised by, for example, Burns and Stalker (1962), Lawrence and Lorsch (1967) and others, when they argue that survival and growth can depend upon such dimensions as flexibility in adaptation to changing external conditions and ability to create new products and services. Given such broad definitions of productivity, it is quite clear that the relevance of job redesign programmes is great. Scientific management will rarely provide for greater flexibility or more creativity − rather the opposite. And as Emery and Thorsrud (1976) clearly depart from such a broad concept of productivity, the relationship between this aim and the interests of the workers is worth commenting on.

There is no doubt that the productivity argument accounts for much of the management interest that emerged in relation to the ID programme. It is reasonable to say that in Norway in the sixties and early seventies, there was a widespread, but not exclusive, management view that productivity gains were essential for them to be willing to invest in changes. The question is to what extent this constituted a goal in conflict with worker interests.

Even though there are differences of opinion within the union movement, and perhaps now and then a gap between the leadership and the grass roots, it is beyond doubt that the Norwegian union movement has been in favour of increased productivity in the post World War II period. There may be a slight change at this moment, due particularly to increased uncertainty about future employment in the light of technological development (Grøholt et al, 1979), but the support for productivity was quite clear in the late fifties and sixties, the period which constituted the context of the ID programme. As we have indicated elsewhere, the union movement had come to accept productivity as a goal of overall national importance, and not as something «extracted» from the workers (Chapter I). A number of unions, such as for example The Chemical Workers Union, had a vision of their membership as being in transition from a mass of relatively lowly skilled people and towards becoming qualified experts operating advanced technology. (cfr. Blauner, 1964). The realization of such a vision can not take place unless patterns of work organization are changed towards a group pattern where highly trained operators make joint decisions about complex technology. That such qualified people operating advanced technology will in most respects show a higher productivity per person than the less qualified operators, is beyond doubt. They will also be much more higly paid. The relatively strong position of the trade unions, their link to the governing Labour Party and a strong faith in state socialism probably explains why the union movement found it possible to back productivity in the belief that this would be for the best of society as a whole. It is, of course, possible to question the realism of this position of the unions: should they have done something different? Have they fallen victims to a subtle employer strategy? To the extent that such points are raised with people with responsibility for labour policies in the post World War II period, they will point out that Norway has one of the highest standards of living in the world, a higher degree of income equalization than practically any other society and one of the highest degrees of political participation from the grass roots. The policy has, they argue, given practical results.

Even though the productivity aim behind the ID programme was anchored in a broad national consensus on the legitimacy of increased productivity, this does not mean that the productivity goal did not give rise to problems.

One of these problems had to do with the relationship between management and the workers on a more day-to-day level in experimental enterprises. Even though there may have been an overall consensus on productivity on the national level, the pursuance of productivity aims in specific settings can nevertheless influence worker-management relationships in a problematic direction. If psychological aims or democratization aims are pursued, the workers automatically acquire a broad right to define what should be done and to evaluate the results: one's psychology is after all one's own and management can hardly claim advances in job satisfaction if the workers feel more dissatified. Similarly, democracy has to do with the influence of the majority, and the majority in the workplace is the workers. However, when the focus is on productivity, «management ownership» becomes a much more prominent feature. Productivity is the core of management responsibility and the bulk of their legal and organizational rights are designed to make it possible to pursue productivity aims. Hence, the relative position of the workers, in defining action and evaluting results is adversely affected. The problematic aspects of this situation are strenghtened by the fact that even when the question of productivity is raised in a specific setting, there are still possibilities for different definitions of productivity. One experience that emerged in some of the projects was that management changed its definition of productivity as the project developed, so as to be able to continuously put forth the argument that «we expected productivity improvments but have not seen any». What can be gained from such tactics is to maintain focus on productivity and keep the psychological and democratization aims in the background. It must, however, be added that this was not a major problem, but rather one of the many problems that invariably emerge when one tries to take action in «real life».

Another version of the productivity problem is mentioned by Gulowsen (1975). On the basis of an analysis of 13 projects within the ID programme, he draws the conclusion that labour market relations were one of the chief management reasons for engaging in projects: Management interest emerged primarily in situations where the enterprise had difficulties in recruiting and maintaining a workforce which fulfilled certain characteristics in terms of stability and competence.

This is another version of a broadly interpreted productivity argument. To the extent that it is valid, it implies that if the labour market problems disappear because of changes in the labour market, e.g., increased unemployment, then management interest in a work redesign project will also disappear and projects can be halted. Furthermore, enterprises without labour market problems will not engage in work redesign projects. On the other hand, Gulowsen does not explain why the many enterprises that obviously had such problems in Norway in the sixties did *not* engage in projects under the ID programme. As a positive motivator for management, this aspect of labour market relations can obviously be only one of many. Enterprise projects which began later than those included in Gulowsen's analysis to some extent support the labour market argument. In the period when the off-shore development started there was, for example, an over representation of enterprises, from this western Norwegian region in the previously mentioned job design workshop. These enterprises clearly had problems in maintaining their workforce when faced with the personnel demands and higher wages of the oil industry. However, it can also be said that a number of the arguments for job reform (cf. Emery and Thorsrud, 1969; 1976) are such that they predict just such labour market problems for an increasing number of enterprises and hence lead to the point of view that it is just those enterprises that experience labour market problems that are in greatest need of changes.

As concerns productivity it can be mentioned that this will often be a result of more rational patterns of organization, whatever the reasons may be for the introduction of these patterns. An example: Within the framework of the work environment reform (Chapters V – VIII) a series of new enterprise developments have emerged. One of these, in which the Work Research Institutes is involved, is in a mechanical assembly plant which produces stoves and fireplaces (Kråkerøy Verk). Most of the production is for export. On the basis of work environment considerations a production line structure was changed into a group pattern. One of the results of this was a productivity increase of about 40 %. The wholesale value of this 40 % increase is, for the production of one day, equal to the total cost of the change programme. It is hard to find a more dramatic example of a productivity increase.

Limitations to diffusion – an overview

The last part of this analysis will depart from the point of view that there have been difficulties in achieving the diffusion sought for. Choosing this point of departure is primarily a way of ordering points and arguments and not a subscription to the belief that diffusion would have been very different if other approaches or strategies had been chosen when the ID programme was launched.

This point of departure gives rise to a number of discussions and arguments. We will touch upon the following issues:

- A possible lack of worker interest in such changes as were advocated in the programme.
- The issue of worker-management collaboration versus the application of a conflict model. Together with this we will touch upon the enterprise as a system for the exercise of power and the issue of functional necessities behind hierarchical structures.
- A further point is the role of research
- A last point to be included here can be called dissolution of meaning.

Lack of worker interest

The *embourgoisement* of the workers is a point of view which has played a major role in post World War II analyses of the workers (e.g. Goldthorpe et al, 1969). Such a view can imply various things, particularly a shift in focus away from the traditional goals of the working class, such as power over the enterprises and the process of production, in favour of goals pertaining to material standard of living, passive comsumption of the products of the entertainment industry, self-actualisation in free-time, and so on. If such a development actually takes place, democratization arguments will lose much of their ·force, as the workers are no longer interested in industrial democracy and self-management, but are quite willing to let management decide as long as their material goals are satisfied. Efforts to improve industrial democracy will meet with limited success. The same happens to improvements emerging from the psychological arguments, as the workers will have long ago given up any interest in the satisfaction of «intrinsic» needs, in favour of stressing the «extrinsic» ones, particularly those relating to pay and free time. Generally, the workers become passive and disinterested in workplace reforms.

An evaluation of this argument, with respect to the Norwegian situation is not easily made. As mentioned above, by the middle seventies the workers showed limited interest in developing the ID programme. This may, on the other hand, have been a time-bound reaction. Furthermore, there has quite clearly been a very broad mobilization of worker interest and worker activity around the work environment reform (Chapters V – VIII). There was also, in the early seventies, a fairly broad workplace mobilization against Norwegian Common Market membership. *General* passivity does, in other words, not seem to dominate the Norwegian workers. That the workers have become more preoccupied with material issues along with the possibilities of acquiring more material goods is true enough. It is also quite clear that there is a marked reduction in open labour-employer conflicts, compared to the pre World War II period (Chapter I). This reduction can be interpreted as resulting from decreased support for traditional working class goals and strategies. On the other hand, the surrounding society has also changed, and changes in patterns of activity by the workers do not necessarily reflect a shift away from the classical goals but can instead imply that the struggles for these goals are finding new expressions. The reduced rate of conflict in Norwegian working life can, for example, be argued to have paralleled a continuous development of political influence for the workers via the Labour Party and state socialism. We do not argue that this is surely the case, but it is a possibility which needs to be looked into to make an assessment of the *embourgeoisement* hypothesis with reference to Norway. A further problem pertains to what can possibly be uncovered through social science investigations that do not include any action and hence to not generate *changes* in worker conditions. It may, for example, be that workers are manipulated into a situation which changes their focus of interest towards bourgeois goals, but that specific changes in conditions can create a new situation and a re-awakening of such goals as democratization. To the extent that this is true, it constitutes an argument for researchers to go beyond a purely descriptive and interpretative role and participate in action. In fact, this is what was done in the ID programme. There are, furthermore, a number of studies which show that increasing freedom and competence in work results in worker demands for increased influence over the organization of the enterprise and related issues (Chapters VII and IX). It is also worth noting that the embourgeoisement argument has not emerged on the Scandinavian scene with any great strength. In the Scandinavian countries it has, by the way, been much more common to point at *lack of resources for participation* as the chief reason why democratization efforts bear limited fruit; many people lack the possibilities for utilizing democratic structures. The concept of «poverty of resources» *(ressursfattigdom)* is one of the most widely used concepts in Scandinavian social research as well as in public debates and policies. Recently, however, there is a growing tendency to question the relevance of the traditional content of this concept and to depart from the point of view that all people have resources but that the utilisation of these resources are blocked by the dominant social structures, alternatively that it is these structures which *define* people as poor in resources and through this act of definition, prevent them from participation. This emerging tendency is in fact in line with the orginal democratization argument of the ID programme.

This resource perspective opens up a further · issue: in various spheres of the modern welfare state it has turned out that programmes in support of those «poor in resources» do in fact not reach those who are poorest, but rather those who alrady have at least some resources. To phrase it like this, it takes resources to utilize offers of more resources. Gulowsen (1975) makes, on the basis of the 13 cases covered by his analysis, this point as concerns the ID programme: if we look at who have benefited most from the programme, it is workers who had a reasonable position from before as freedom and competence in work is concerned, while those in the weakest position – e.g. unskilled assembly line workers – generally were less able to draw upon the programme to improve on their position. Unlike the labour market argument which Gulowsen makes (above), this point has, however, not been borne out by experiences later than those he analyses. The enterprises whose development is linked to the job design workshop described by Engelstad and Ødegaard (1979) do not support this point.

Collaboration and conflict

The aspect of the ID programme which has attracted most criticism from other Scandinavian social scientists is clearly that it was based on collaboration between the workers and management, centrally as well as locally – a strategy, is argued, that will have to be at the expense of the workers. Again, we touch upon a broad issue where a number of points can be raised, for as well as against the approach used in the ID programme.

Here we will depart from one of the arguments *for* the ID programme – the idea that it is only through trying to come to grips with issues in real life that various critical problems can be settled, such as for example what is possible and what is not under given forms of ownership and control in working life. Such a point of view rests on rather strong metascientific considerations (Gustavsen, 1976b, 1979b, 1980e, 1980f). To the extent that there are limitations on what can possibly be uncovered through theoretical-descriptive and non-involved research, the problem of what should be done is transformed from a problem of «what theory is right» to *what action is possible*. The most valid criticism of the ID programme will hence be the development of alternative action programmes.

75

Alternatives to the ID programme have clearly emerged in the Scandinavian countries. Examples are the Norwegian Iron- and Metalworkers project (Nygaard and Bergo, 1974), the Demos-project in Sweden (Sandberg, 1979) and a number of projects developed in the seventies at the Work Research Institutes (see for example Chapter VIII) to mention some of the developments implying research-union collaboration instead of the tripartite model of the ID programme where the employers also took part. However, the relationship between such projects and the ID programme is complex. There are clearly elements of disagreements and differences as to what constitutes the most adequate approach but in Norway there are also elements of continuity and development. At the time when the ID programme was launched, the unions had no experience in direct collaboration with social researchers on development projects pertaining to issues of organization. In the early sixties it would at best have been very difficult to develop an action programme based on collaboration with the workers only. The unions at that point in time were in all probability not ready to struggle unilaterally, or for that matter with researchers, for industrial democracy. Throughout the sixties and early seventies the unions continuously developed their ability to use research as a resource to further their interests, and the possibilities for new types of collaborative relationships were developed. This happened, however, to a large extent as a result of experience gained through the ID programme.

Turning from these general points to specifics, there is a more concrete issue pertaining to the conflict problem which is important and this is the issue of *legal domain*. When the ID programme started, organization of work was an area which legally belonged to management alone. According to law as well as agreements, the right to define, distribute and organize work was one of management's prerogatives. This prerogative was subject to various constraints, but it was nevertheless clear enough. This legal situation made it possible for management to change, and to reverse, structures developed through such efforts as the ID programme. It was not even necessary for management in general to want such a reversal, one single plant manager could sometimes reverse changes brought about through heavy investments not only from external resources like researchers, but also from the workers and management as well. This gave new forms of work organization a precarious legal position, a point which in all probability had an inhibiting effect on the willingness of the unions and workers to engage themselves in this type of development. The Work Environment Act of 1977 has as one of its legislative backgrounds the need to level out some of these legal differences between

76

management and the workers within the area of organization of work. Similarly, the Swedish Co-determination Act is a response to the same problem, albeit based on a somewhat different strategy (Gardell & Gustavsen, 1980).

The discussion on the relationship between collaboration and conflict can give rise to a number of more specific points and debates. It will be remembered that Emery and Thorsrud launched their arguments to some extent in opposition to the point of view that the enterprise must be understood primarily as a system for the distribution and exercise of power (Chapter II). It can be argued that Emery and Thorsrud went too far in their attempt to de-emphasize the issue of power and conflict (Kronlund, 1975; Karlsson, 1975). As legal changes have been a main feature of the development of Scandinavian labour relations in the later seventies, this gives some degree of support for the view that power issues need to be considered to a greater extent than what was the case in the ID programme. On the other hand, this programme was necessary to clarify some of the issues that, at least in Norway, came up for legislation in the later seventies.

When the issue of power is raised, the total enterprise organization is automatically placed in focus. We have previously touched upon the point that changes in overall enterprise organization have to some extent emerged as part of the ID programme or of diffusion in the wake of this programme. The cases of major changes, such as in Mjellem & Karlsen or in Almex in Sweden (Gardell & Svensson, 1980) are, however, still too isolated to unequivocally document that major changes away from the conventional patterns of hierarchical organization can be achieved on a broad front under contemporary conditions in society. A chief problem for the future is obviously to test further what possibilities and constraints one confronts in this area.

A very important point to emerge from Gulowsen's analysis (Gulowsen, 1975) was that there did not seem to be any link between shop floor experimental development and top management support for changes. Positive developments on the shop floor did not result in increased top management support for changes, nor did negative results, for that matter, automatically reduce top management support. In other words: the enterprise organization did not function as a mechanism for diffusion from the shop floor to top management but rather as a buffer mechanism preventing changes from influencing top management. Given the diffusion theory of Emery and Thorsrud, according to which positive developments in experimental sites were to give rise to further changes via the commitment of expanding circles of people, and where elites were to play a crucial role, this limitation is obviously of critical importance. Later projects have as yet not been analysed with a view to seeing to what extent this obeservation stands up. It is an obvious task for future research to do this.

A point which needs to be considered is that the lack of major changes on a broad front may, at least partly, be owing to lack of ability of the researchers to develop alternative solutions. The ID programme was based on the idea of a step-by-step development where the broader organizational changes would not be developed until the issue of participation was solved. The reason for this relates to the obvious point that a democratization process requires the participation of everyone concerned. It is not only a question of implementing certain organizational changes, it is above all a question of *who* has participated in the development of new organizational patterns. Hence, the researchers can not specify certain organizational characteristics and say that «this is democracy and this is what you should strive for». It is in this transition from participation to broader changes that experience is still too limited and fragmentary for us to be able to draw firm conclusions. It may be that the researchers have actually contributed too little to these further steps. Even though people themslves must participate in the development of new patterns of enterprise organization, this does not mean that researchers should not be active in this part'of the process, for example in providing ideas and help. In fact, efforts have also been made in this field. Members of the Work Research Institutes have attempted, for example, to generate a broad and systematic programme within this area in the early seventies (Herbst, 1975; Gustavsen & Ryste, 1978) but it had to be given reduced priority when the work environment reform emerged. These threads are being taken up again in the eighties. In spite of the fact that «theories of organization» have been a major topic in social research from its infancy until the present day, there is still a shortage of ideas as concerns «organization and change»: for example, what particular aspects to focus on when the aim is to achieve certain types of changes and what issues to use as levers in the change process. Most ideas about organization and change which are anchored in action efforts on the part of the researcher have emerged as human relations-inspired efforts at «organization development», and even though these ideas are to some extent useful, there is clearly a need for ideas more specifically related to issues like democratization and work environment.

A further problem to emerge here is to what extent hierarchical and «un-democratic» organizations are functionally necessary. Abell (1980) has, for example, advanced some rather strong arguments in favour of the necessity of a certain degree of hierarchization. To the extent that hierarchization is necessary to maintain rational problem solution and coordination in organizations, and not because it ex-

78

presses power interests and ownership preferences, there will of course be limitations to the development of participatory democracy. Eckstein (1966) seems to go as far as to say that enterprises can not be democratized at all. Again, only further experimental efforts can tell what is possible and what is not.

The role of research

Emery and Thorsrud (1976) have argued that the researchers showed too high a profile in the initial experiments, and took too much responsibility for initiating and defining events. This had a negative effect on the willingness and ability of other people to take over and carry the process further. This is one version of a problem basic to all efforts of democratization, and which in logical terms constitutes a dilemma. A democratic organization is not only a question of organizational characteristics, it is also a question of who has defined and implemented these characteristics. Hence, the problem of participation becomes crucial, and the first step of a democratization process is to generate the conditions conducive to participation.

But then the question emerges as to what these conditions are, and who is to decide on this issue. As long as conditions for participation are not established, and this will in principle be the case in the initial part of a democratization programme, the workers cannot participate in deciding what conditions are relevant. Hence, the only way to the introduction of new conditions is in principle the authoritarian one. A point parallel to this is made by Kelly (1978) when he argues that autonomous work groups are in fact a structured and standardized type of solution to certain organizational problems and not a form consistent with the possibilities for «organization choice» on the part of the workers.

When the problem is posed in the form of a logical dilemma it is unsolvable. In practical situations, however, dilemmas are rarely as absolute and as logical as they appear on paper, and what Emery and Thorsrud argue is that there are options and that a less directive role than the one actually chosen by the researchers can in principle be better suited to the furtherance of a broader diffusion process. One reason why the researchers have options, is that even though lack of possibilities for participation may be a broad overall problem in industrial society, the degree of actual participation will nevertheless vary in different parts of working life. By linking to those parts of working life where participation is (relatively) high, it is possible to validate to some extent certain types of solutions before they are used as model in planned change efforts.

As concerns autonomous work groups, it has, for example been argued that this is actually an old form of work organization developed within the workers' own culture, which has largely become lost under modern industrialization (Trist et al.; 1963; Gulowsen, 1971). Kelly's specific point that autonomous work group is a model decided on by researchers rather than developed by workers under conditions of possibilities for choice, must be evaluated against the fact that after about thirty years of rather intensive theoretical as well as practical work with «alternative patterns of work organization» there are still only two main patterns of solutions that have emerged: one is the «job enrichment» approach largely based on finding individual solutions; the other is the autonomous work group pattern. As concerns autonomous work groups as a model for organization it is necessary to be aware of the point that even though some rather specific definitions have been made (such as Herbst, 1962; Gulowsen , 1971) these definitions and descriptions are nevertheless conducted with the help of variables that are highly abstract. Hence, in terms of the specific social meaning it has for the workers, the concept of autonomous work group can cover a broad range of alternative patterns.

In terms of research role, at least three main types can be said to have emerged as part of the development of the ID programme (Elden, 1975; 1979).

In the initial part of the programme, the researchers showed a «high profile». This implied taking a broad responsibility for defining solutions and actions. Such a role is consistent with a traditional «action research» approach, where the researcher has done the research before the action starts, and hence knows what is to be done.

The second step is the development of a role based on a more balanced relationship between the researchers and other people; goals and steps are developed in participation where the parties have an equal position.

A third pattern emerges when the researcher acts as a resource to other people, to *their* development of ideas and solutions. The emergence of this last type of role is linked to the realisation that there is a fluid and gradual boundary between research and other activities (Gustavsen, 1980 e) and that one can well imagine that people do research themselves (Lindqvist, 1978) but can gain from being supported by researchers.

Within the framework of the ID programme the development has been from the first and towards the last of these roles. This does, however, not mean that the last one is more «valid» than the first. In actual practice there is a need for all three roles; what approach is most fruitful can vary from situation to situation. In the initial part of a change programme the researchers will sometimes have to take a broad responsibility, the point is rather to change the role when moving from demonstration and into diffusion.

Dissolution of meaning

We have already touched upon the point that specific efforts at change take place in a society, where the efforts become linked to other events. Such emerging links can affect the original ideas in various ways, and what can be called dissolution of meaning is one possibility.

The various ideas upon which the ID programme was built are presented in Chapter II. One of the points necessary to recall is the «utility» argument for democracy: that democratic forms of work and enterprise organization are necessary to allow for the value-generating process needed to stabilize an over-complex world. It cannot be said that this idea disappeared as the ID programme went into the diffusion phase, as this whole line of reasoning was not known in Norway beyond a limited circle mostly made up of the participating researchers. There was consequently nothing to be dissolved. That this line of reasoning was not grasped and understood is, however, of importance to the understanding of the fate of the programme. When the «necessity of democracy» is not part of the argument, democratization is often pushed into the realm of «luxury problems», problems which may be important, but which will have to wait «until the economic problems are solved» or until some other important issue has been settled. As these issues that need to be settled «first» are, of course, never settled, democracy has a tendency to be postponed. One of the major functions of the work environment reform (Chapters V – VIII) has in fact been to reintroduce the point that participation in working life is *not* only a question of ideals, it is also a necessity if society is to solve increasingly complex and pressing problems.

The second point that can be brought forth when we talk about dissolution of meaning, is the multi-step character of the strategy. When specific efforts like job rotation, new traning methods. etc. were introduced in particular settings, it was not because such means are inherently good in themselves, but because they could contribute to the aim of increasing the level of autonomy of the operators. In relation to the issue of freedom and competence in work, such efforts as job rotation can be characterised as «tactics». When it is used out of context, such as provided for by the ID programme, the effect can very well be negative. When diffusion of such means took place to a relatively large extent, dissolution of the original meaning of the programme is one part of the explanation.

The strategic concept above the level of such means as job rotation, was autonomous work group. This is the next level where the chain of arguments can be broken, and to a large extent also was broken. Such a break implies that the perspectives *beyond* autonomous groups are lost. The establishment of such groups come to be seen as the ultimate goal of a democratization process, rather than as a stepping stone to further changes.

Concluding summary

The Industrial Democracy programme was the first of a series of job- or work redesign programmes to emerge in various countries in the sixties and seventies. These programmes have grown out of various contexts, showing different patterns of development and impact on the surrounding society. Each such development must hence be understood on the basis of the particular society in which it emerged.

As concerns the Norwegian programme, a series of initial field experiments led to diffusion along the following lines:
- Some instances, but relatively few, of direct replications.
- A broader set of changes were spurred off by the original experiments, but also implying changes, particularly in strategy.
- A number of the specific means used within the overall framework of the programme, such as job rotation, have been taken into use as isolated efforts. This pattern of diffusion has been very broad.
- The development initiated in the ID programme has eventually come to link up with other developments in society to form new structures and patterns of change.

As time goes by, the last pattern becomes perhaps the more prominent one, as society continually develops and changes. The programme had no particular «end». Instead, it has branched off into various developments, which each have formed the basis for ongoing processes.

While the planned effort at change implicit in the Industrial Democracy Programme led to a not insubstantial diffusion to various parts of Norwegian working life, this diffusion was more limited than originally expected. The actual developments brought to light various possible constraints on diffusion, such as:
- a possible lack of real worker interest in workplace reform;
- emphasis on worker-management collaboration in a situation where a conflict approach would have been more appropriate;

- lack of new solutions to overall patterns of enterprise organization as a follow-up on shop floor changes;
- a too highly profiled research role, creating a too strong element of «research ownership» of changes achieved;
- dissolution of the socio-political meaning of changes in work organization.

These points all indicate areas to which consideration must be given and where development needs to take place without any specific area in itself being the ultimate key to the overall success or failure of such efforts as the Norwegian Industrial Democracy Programme.

IV. Employee representation on the board of directors and the company assembly

Introduction

Among the various approaches to industrial democracy, employee representation on the board of directors is perhaps the one most widely discussed in Western countries. Introduced in certain parts of German industry in the immediate postwar period, this approach has certain advantages as a political parameter: it demands no complex, long term developmental strategy but lends itself to relatively simple legislation, in actual practice in the form of amendments to the company act. It is, in other words, a parameter which is eminently suitable to high level political discussion and decision. The seeming reluctance, in many countries, to apply this approach more forcefully, is not only due to a certain resistance by management and employers but also because the outcome, in terms of democratization effect, is under some doubt. Many proponents of industrial democracy have been negative to the use of this approach (e.g. Emery & Thorsrud 1969, see Chapter II).

As mentioned in Chapter II, the industrial democracy debate in Norway around 1960 focussed to some extent on the issue of employee representation on higher organizational levels. However, when the problem of democratization and individual participation emerged, this issue receded somewhat into the background. It was, however, not dead and the leadership of the Federation of Trade Unions pushed it throughout the sixties. (Aspengrenkomitéen, 1965). A public committee headed by a supreme court justice was set up in the latter sixties, and published a white book on the issue (Eckhoff-komitéen, 1971). The committee had representatives from both sides in working life, as well as «neutral» members. The representatives from the Federation of Trade Unions argued for a system of representation which will be described below as the proposals of the Federation were eventually to become law. The committee members from the Employers' Confederation argued against the introduction of a company assembly, but accepted, with reservations, the principle of board representation. What they really objected to most was the use of legislation for that purpose. The Employers' Confederation would have preferred a more gradual approach, using the collective bargaining mechanism to bring about board representation by workers.

The formal system

In the early seventies a proposal for amendments in the Company Act was developed, to become law in 1973. This amendment gave the employees a right to elect one third of the board members with a minimum of two, in industrial companies employing more than 50 people. The system has now been expanded to cover also other sectors of working life in Norway. In addition to board representation, however, another change was made, a change which is peculiar to Norway: In companies employing more than 200, a company assembly was to be established, with a minimum of twelve members, of which one third were to be elected by the employees. In these companies board representation was not explicitly stated in the act, but it was presumed that the employees would be given such a representation if they requested it. This is what has happened in practice with the result that in companies employing more than 200 persons, employees now have double representation.

The legal status of the company assembly does not lend itself to description in a few words, as it has a peculiar place in the history and development of Norwegian company law and lacks a clear parallel in any other country (Eckhoff, 1964; Gustavsen, 1972a). The Norwegian system is not a two-tier system of the German type. The board is more of a supervisory board than a managerial board and the company assembly resembles, in its function, the general assembly (shareholders meeting) of other countries. The company assembly has taken over some of the main functions of the general assembly. It is, for example, the highest authority on investment issues. Decisions of the company assembly can not be changed by the general assembly. Its introduction has been expanded, along with the expansion of the representative system on boards, to cover most parts of Norwegian working life.

The reason why the company assembly was introduced is not quite clear, but it is reasonable to belive that the «hostage argument», often emerging in connection with the representative system, played a role. The proponents of the representative system believed that the members of the company assembly would be less closely tied to the managerial structure and decisions of the company and could therefore maintain a higher degree of independence. Another consideration of some importance was that the company assembly increased the total of seats available to employee representatives, and hence made it easier to reach agreements in cases where the employees belonged to more than one union.

While proportional voting is possible, elections, as a rule, take place on the basis of simple majority voting. Contrary to the Swedish system, participation in elections as well as board and assembly membership is open to all employees, including those not belonging to a union. A more thorough treatment of these, and other rules concerning this system, can be found in Berg et. al. (1975).

We have already mentioned that the system has eventually been expanded to cover most sectors of working life. Its introduction in shipping and in the public sector is presently under discussion. In the following we will focus on the board, and largely omit the company assembly due to the peculiarity of this last body.

The debate on employee representation

As we have seen in Chapter II, the industrial democracy programme was based on the idea that the problems related to participation need to be solved, at least to some extent, before such a «top level» system as board representation can be expected to function.

Without any worker participation at lower levels of the enterprise, board representation may not only fail to achieve positive results, but may even function contrary to the democratization of the decision-making process (Emery and Thorsrud, 1969). Even though the industrial democracy programme was criticized by the left for its emphasis on worker-management collaboration, it was nevertheless in line with a prevailing orientation of the left which insists that the power of labour must be based on work and that organizational changes must radiate from the workplace. The labour movement must create its own institutions and not attempt to take over those of the capitalist. Minority representation on board and assemblies, in this view, must be firmly rejected.

Without lower level participation and grass root support, the likely effects of board representation will be the following:

- The worker representatives become passive. They are unable to compete with owners/managers in one of the most capitalist of all institutions and they will not be able to change this particular institution as long as society in general maintains its capitalist character.

- Alternatively, the representatives become hostages of the employer.
- In either case, a gap will be created between the elected representatives and their constituency.
- At the same time, the dividing line between the workers on the one hand and the owners/managers on the other, will be blurred, thus threatening the ordinary functions of the unions.

The view that work must be the basis of worker influence and power has in fact been an important part of the general philosophy of the Norwegian Federation of Trade Unions. When this Federation has been less interested than its Swedish and Danish counterparts in pursuing wage earners funds and similar reorganizations of capital the main argument has been just this. Nevertheless, employee representation on company boards and assemblies was supported by the unions. What were the reasons for this?

One possible answer could be based on the assumption that the industrial democracy programme had achieved its aims of introducing worker participation on a broad front throughout Norwegian working life, thus preparing the ground for the introduction of a representative system on company boards and assemblies. Such an interpretation, however, would not have been consistent with the facts. As we have seen in Chapter III there has been a slow and steady diffusion radiating from the industrial democracy innovations, but no one, least of all the unions, was arguing that the diffusion was broad enough to constitute an adequate base for the introduction of a representative system. Hence, the answer must be found elsewhere.

Looking at the white book of the Eckhoff Committee (1971) it is difficult to locate the nature of the important arguments for board representation. This is all the more surprising as most of the committee members were well acquainted with the critical views of Emery and Thorsrud. One possible explanation can be found in the fact that the chief proponent of board representation, Tor Aspengren, had also been a strong supporter of the Industrial Democracy Programme. Tor Aspengren was vice-chairman of the LO from 1961 to 1969 and chairman from 1969 to 1977. It is clear that Aspengren, one of the most influential union leaders in the postwar period and a member of the Eckhoff Committee, saw the industrial democracy programme and board representation as mutually supportive efforts which could be developed side by side. The criticism by Emery and Thorsrud, as well as that of the left, was ignored − it was simply not discussed in the committee. Instead, the committee used as its general frame of reference the «balance of interest model», a model introduced and supported on the Scandinavian scene by the Swedish organization theorist Eric Rhenman (1964). According to this model, the enterprise is seen as a unit around which different interest groups cluster, the enterprise being the organization for handling the tasks which the various interest groups agree to perform jointly. The enterprise also functions to resolve conflicts which may emerge between the various interest groups. Given such clues, it seems likely that the strategic reasoning behind the decision to introduce board representation was the following:

The enterprise is admittedly the scene of disagreements and conflicts, but these conflicts involve more interests than labour and capital. The primary task of the groverning bodies of the enterprise is not to pursue the interests of one particular such group, but to settle all the interest relationships in a way which secure the necessary support and collaboration needed, for the survival and growth of the enterprise. Such interest groups as customers, suppliers and public authorities are generally not directly represented on the board. There are, however, some interest groups that can be said to have more of a stake in the individual enterprise than what is the case for the rest, because they can not as easily go elsewhere if their interests are not satisfied. This holds for those who have invested the capital, as well as for management. They can both withdraw, but generally at larger costs and more trouble than what would be the case for a customer who «withdraws» through the simple act of buying from another producer. Hence, capital and management have a privileged position in the groverning bodies of the enterprise. The workers, however, share the situation of capital and management, in as much as their fate is strongly linked to a specific enterprise. The workers should consequently be treated on the same level with capital and management and given a place on the board as well. This argument brings workers into a situation where they in a sense confront capital and management. The underlying reasoning differs, however, from the classical labour management conflict. Instead, it is presumed that social democratic institutions in a society like Norway have advanced to a point where exclusive emphasis on the labour capital relationship is no longer necessary and where a broader view of interests, conflicts and settlements can be applied while the relative importance of the «classical» model is reduced. The balance-of-interest model is part of the broader tradition of democratic theory often referred to as «elite democracy» (Dahl, 1961; 1963; Lipset, 1963; Schumpeter, 1947; see the discussion in Pateman, 1970). In this theory society is made up of interest groups and not of participants, and it belongs to smaller groups of representatives from each interest group to settle the various issues between them.

Some results

In the middle seventies, the Work Research Institutes did a study of this new system (Engelstad & Qvale, 1977). About 200 members of boards and company assemblies were interviewed. They do not constitute a representative sample of all such members. However, the results from these investigations are roughly the same as those emerging from studies in Denmark and Sweden (Westenholz, 1976; SIND, 1975) where approximately the same kind of system, without the company assembly, was introduced at the same time. They are also borne out by later experience.

A first result worth noting is that about eighty percent of all respondents declared themselves satisfied with this reform. The percentage is a little higher for employee elected representatives, and a little lower for shareholder elected representatives, but the differences are not great. There are, however, some differences in *why* the system is given a positive evaluation.

Shareholder elected members of boards and company assemblies give as main reason that they have better possibilities for communicating the goals and other considerations of the company to the workers. They see, in other words the benefits as following from a new channel of communication, *from* the board/top management, *to* the workers. The employee elected representatives argue, naturally enough, that they gain better insight into company issues and matters and improved possibilities for exerting influence over these issues.

The major question is of course to what extent the new system has led to any changes in patterns of decisions on board level. Are new issues taken up, new considerations discussed, new decisions emerging?

These questions dissolve into a number of issues, and we can here touch upon some aspects only:

There is an overall tendency in the direction of employee representatives emphasizing personnel matters, work environment issues and welfare issues as matters to be brought before the board, less in the form of new issues than in the form of considerations to be taken up in relation to cases which would also otherwise have been brought before the board (e.g. because they imply new investments of some magnitude). Such changes are in line with what was predicted by Emery & Thorsrud (1969) when they said that the workers will try to use the representative system to further concrete workplace interests (see also Gustavsen, 1972a). We can not give the exact strength of this tendency in terms of any specific figure, but on the whole one can say that it is noticeable in most boards, without, as far as we know, having led to dramatic changes in any board.

There is, however, another tendency to be seen, which partly overlaps with the one already mentioned, but which contains other elements as well. To describe this tendency, attention must be drawn to the point that all company boards are not alike in terms of the decisions they make and the degree of influence they exert over company matters. In a general study of that subject done at the Work Research Institutes (Gustavsen, 1972a; 1975; 1976c) a typology of boards was constructed:

- *The minimum board* is a board which does little more than the legal minimum and even this in a ritualistic and superficial fashion.
- *The board of consultants* gives advice and support to the managing director but makes no effort at exerting a self-determined influence over the development of the company.
- *The supervisory board* performs more of an ordinary board role in that it supervises the general development of the company and particuarly its investment decisions.
- *The limited policy making board* fulfills the same functions as the supervisory board but also takes charge of policy within certain areas, such as financing and investments.
- *The policy making board* is even more «highly profiled» in that it really performs a broad and active policy making function.
- *The administrative board* does not only take it upon itself to perform policy functions, it also more or less administers the affairs of the company.

In terms of frequencies, the first four types clearly dominated in Norwegian economic life in the latter sixties, and still do so today. The last two types are rather rare. The minimum board, and to some extent also the advisory or consultancy board, even though they are frequent, can be considered to be too passive to really fill the legal obligations of a board (Gustavsen, 1972a). This is particularly true of the minimum board.

Returning to the impact of employee representatives entering the boards, it seems as if this has led to changes in the composition of the shareholder elected members, with increased activity at the board level as the result, particularly as concerns boards that used to lean towards the passive end of the scale. Of particular importance is that the «minimum board» is now less frequently encountered than before the reform. The data in support of this point are not quite conclusive, but the indicators are fairly strong. It is known that a relatively large number of shareholder elected board members were exchanged for new

91

ones when the employees entered the boards. The average age of board members has been rather strongly reduced (Engelstad & Qvale, 1977). The study of the Work Research Institutes showed that the employee representatives on the boards of small companies believe they exert more influence than their colleagues in the boards of the bigger companies (Engelstad & Qvale, 1977). This is consistent with the view that their impact has been most noticeable on the boards where activity was lowest before the reform; «minimum boards» and related types were much more frequent in smaller companies (Gustavsen, 1972a). On the other hand, such differences in influence on the part of the employee representatives might, of course, also be partly explainable by such factors as the greater complexity of issues to be confronted in bigger companies

The study also analysed the problems experienced by the employee elected representatives in connection with their roles in the boards

Table 2. Problems as experienced by employee representatives in boards and company assemblies.

Type of problem	Percentage who states having the problem
Communications with the constituency	53
Lack of competence and insight in relation to issues one has to deal with	34
Unfamiliar ways of working	29
The need to maintain secrecy in relation to certain issues	21
Decisions are made in advance	18
Difficulties in making adequate preparations	16
Difficulties emerging in the election process	14
Unequal treatment from management (compared to shareholder-elected members)	14
The issue of economic compensation	11
Relationships to other employee groups	10
Lack of adequate activity in the board or company assembly	8
Problems in the contacts with management	6
Problems in the contacts with own union	5
Problems in relationships to colleagues	5

Source: Engelstad & Qvale (1977)

and in the company assemblies. At this point we will give the results in a table (Table 2).

It is seen that the most frequent problem confronting the employee representatives emerges from their relationship to the people they represent. There is a gap between this problem and the next one, indicating that the relationship to the «grass roots» is the most important problem.

The second most important problem has to do with the competence or insights of the representative, in relation to the issues he or she is confronting as a board member. Rather close to this issue in terms of frequency are problems related to the mode of work in such bodies as boards and company assemblies as these are unfamiliar to the employee members.

The need to maintain secrecy about some issues, and hence the lack of possibilities for taking such issues up with the constituency, emerges as a problem of some importance, but it does not seem to be as widespread as was feared by some before the system was put into operation.

The danger that the employee representatives will «leak» information to their fellow workers, with a resulting spread from them to competitors, has been one of the chief objections against giving the employees access to the board. It is argued that companies need to maintain secrecy in relation to many issues, and for various quite legitimate reasons such as competition. In Norway, this argument emerged with some strength before the reform. What can be said about it?

Table 2 shows that about twenty percent of the representatives experienced problems because of the need for confidential treatment of certain issues. To this can be added that about twenty percent of the companies studied by the Work Research Institutes had formal rules placing restraints on the board members' right to inform outsiders. Such formal rules are more widespread in the larger than in the smaller companies, twentytwo percent as against twelve percent (Norsk Arbeidsgiverforening, 1975). At the same time, complaints about the need for secrecy as a *problem* are more widespread among the representatives on the boards of the small companies than among those on the boards of the larger ones. This difference can have something to do with the higher activity level among the representatives on the boards of the smaller companies (cf. above). However, there are other possible explanations, and we are not in a position to pass any ultimate judgment on the reasons for this difference.

The overall impression is that «leakages» from employee representatives do not constitute a major problem. Few cases of such leakages with negative effects are known in Norway, and they certainly do not constitute more of a problem than leakages from other board members to *their* interest groups (e.g. in connection with the buying and selling of shares). Hence, there seems to be a tendency to reduce restraints placed on the board members' need for secrecy. The number of companies having formal rules within this area seems to have gone down. Seen from the point of view of the representative, the need for confidential treatment of certain issues constitutes a problem, but not one of overriding importance. It seems reasonable to believe that this issue is part of the background for the most frequent problem – communication with the constituency – but this problem also has a number of other components, such as the lack of any real participation from the «grass roots».

In interpreting this list of problems, consideration must be given to the fact that the study was made at a time when the system was relatively new. It is possible that the picture has changed in some respects as more time has passed and the system has become more mature. On the basis of our general knowledge about conditions in Norwegian working life we can be quite certain, however, that no major changes have taken place from the middle seventies to the early eighties.

A general evaluation

How the system of employee representation introduced in Norway in 1973 is to be evaluated, depends upon goals and expectations. One may have different expectations towards such a system. However, as efforts must at a minimum be judged against the goals of those who have brought it about, we must hold the results up against the framework mentioned earlier in this chapter – a framework made up of the idea that a representative system can be introduced, before the problem of participation at the «grass-roots» is solved. In this view, the representative system can be developed parallel to other democratization efforts on the assumption that «elites» can take care of the interests of broader groups of non-participating people. A further assumption is that social-democratic society in Norway has developed to a point where the enterprise can be considered to be a meeting place of a number of interest groups instead of being a battle ground between labour and capital; if the board is such a battle ground, minority representation is of course without value. Even when such a framework is given, it is, however, necessary to make some distinctions, as the framework can give rise to different levels of aims (Gustavsen, 1973):

94

- Firstly, one can have declarative aims. Employee representation is introduced not because it is believed that any specific and «measurable» effects will actually emerge, but simply to state that the employees are an interest group on the same level with capital and management.
- Secondly, as employee representation is thought to lend itself to parallel development with other efforts of democratization, it can be argued that a specific impact is dependent upon a combination of different threads of development. Representation as such will be part of a larger network of efforts and changes and can best be seen as the introdution of a new position, or a new resource, for the employees.
- Only on the third level do we arrive at aims related to specific changes in board, and eventually also in enterprise decisions.

Results on the first level are achieved immediately upon the passing of legislation, giving the employees access to the top level governing bodies of companies. Looking at the Norwegian reform in the light of the two other levels of aims, it seems beyond doubt that the main impact is on the second level. The employees have achieved a new position, receive more information, and gain more insight, while the actual changes in patterns of decisions and organisation must be characterized as moderate. SIND (1975) draw the same conclusion for Sweden.

Who has been proven right by the development? Does it, for example, support the left wing view; the view of Emery & Thorsrud, or does it support the line of reasoning which seems to lie behind the position of Aspengren?

The question does not lend itself to a simple answer. The main argument of Emery & Thorsrud (1969), that representation without support from a functioning participatory structure at the «grass-roots» will have limited positive effects, seems to stand unshaken. On the other hand, the possibilities for negative developments, to some extent pointed out by Emery & Thorsrud, but perhaps more central in the left wing argument, do not seem to have materialized to any important extent. No major «hostage» problem has emerged, the unions have not been weakened, and the general pattern of collaboration and conflict in Norwegian working life seems unaffected by the reform. Some instances are known where management and employees have joined forces to get external support for companies in difficulties, but such developments also took place before the representative system was introduced, and would probably have gone further without this system.

It seems, in other words, that the general development of society has in fact reached a stage where the major *negative* effects of a minority representation on the groverning bodies of companies do not emerge. To that extent, the implicit argument of Aspengren seems to be supported. To what extent employee representation will become a major *positive* contribution to a broad development towards increased democracy, the other part of the Aspengren argument, still remains to be seen. The problem here is perhaps first and foremost related to the type of development most likely to be influenced by employee representation on the boards of companies. To this issue we will turn in the last part of this chapter.

The context of the board

When employee representation on company boards is introduced as a possible approach to industrial democracy, the frame of reference is often a model of the enterprise such as the one sketched in chapter II where a few remarks were made on the Norwegian industrial democracy debate which emerged around 1960. The enterprise is seen mainly as an apparatus for the exercise of power, hierarchically organized and hence with most power at the top. Such a model is, however, somewhat too simplistic. It is clear that the board is generally «above» management, but not in every respect. It is necessary to be aware of the point that there is a certain degree of differentiation and complementarity between board and management, rather than a simple hierarchical relationship based on inclusivity. According to most legal frameworks for enterprise activity, including the Norwegian one (Gustavsen, 1972a), the board has a special responsibility for the enterprise as capital *in its abstract form* (Emery & Thorsrud, 1969; Gustavsen, 1972a; 1975; 1976a; 1976c). The special responsibility for the enterprise as «value measured in money» as something different from responsibility for the enterprise as a concrete reality of men, machines and materials, emerged historically in the earlier parts of the industrialization process. Before this process began, capital had generally two characteristics (Gustavsen, 1977b):
- It was concrete in the sense that it was identical to e.g. a real estate or a workshop.
- It was bound to, or was an extension of, specific persons or families.

The industrialization process saw the large scale emergence of organizations characterized by:
- A maintainance of a legal identity in spite of changing concrete re-

sources: a company can easily survive as an economic and legal entity while at the same time changing all its concrete resources.

- Dissolution of the link between resources and specific persons: the joint stock company made it possible for the owners to change while the company maintained its identity.

The emergence of capital which is depersonalized as well as independent of specific physical resources, brought forth a whole new set of problems pertaining to trade and credit, to the protection of investors and so forth. These problems brought about company law in its present form. (Gustavsen, 1972a; 1975; 1976c). Company legislation is rarely legislation about enterprise organization in general, it is mostly about the enterprise as capital in its abstract form. The core of the responsibility of an ordinary company board is to be found within this particular network of rules. Hence, employee representation on the board of directors must relate to this point, it is not possible to treat the board simply as the top of a hierarchy which can freely decide what it wants to do.

Whatever conditions the enterprise is confronting, the board needs to develop a strategy, in terms of investment policy, which can secure the capital against losses and preferably make it grow (Emery & Thorsrud, 1969; Gustavsen, 1972a; 1975; 1976c). Generally, the board needs to be active in relation to the broad investment policies of the company, while keeping a distant relationship to issues pertaining to the day-to-day management of resources. Hence, a dilemma easily emerges between the role of the board on the one hand and the needs the representative has to bring before the board issues emerging from the daily work of the employees on the other. It is of course possible that certain boards will allow such issues to be brought up for discussion, but where this is not the case, employee elected board members have few options. They may become passive spectators or they can attempt to become *traditional* board members. They can not, however, easily escape the basic dilemma.

The dilemma is sharpened by the fact that a number of the important premises for investment decisions are brought in from *outside* the enterprise. The board plays, to use a term from the theory of organizations, a «boundary role». The individual board will often be located within more comprehensive networks encompassing other boards and finance institutions, which provide a context for investment decisions (Gustavsen, 1976 a). The employee representative will have to compete with such a network if he wants to produce alternatives to a given investment policy. If he is not able to specify such alternatives, he will easily be forced on the defensive also in relation to other matters, as these are often determined by the basic selection of, for example, technology which is in turn dependent on investment decisions.

Such considerations lead to the argument that the issue of board representation has less to do with the internal management of the enterprise than it has to do with allocation and use of the resources of society in general (Gustavsen, 1976a). National investment policy ought to be the framework for discussing board composition. Hence, the problem of democratization through board representation becomes a problem of developing an alternative investment policy and base this on the development of alternative networks for the generation and transmission of information and for the handling of problems pertaining to protection of investments.

We arrive at the following important point: For employee board representation to become a meaningful part of a further democratization process, the general organization of capital in society becomes the critical area of further development. Here we confront an interesting situation in Norway.

The remark has already been made that the interest among the unions in a general reorganization of capital is less in Norway than it is in Sweden and Denmark. In Sweden we have, for example, the Meidner proposal for wage earners funds (Meidner, 1978; Meidner et al, 1977). No similar proposals or suggestions have as yet emerged from the Norwegian union movement. If one looks at the actual possibilities for reorganizing capital, they are, however, clearly better in Norway today than in almost any other Western, industrialized country. About fifty percent of the shares in the bigger industrial campanies are already state owned or controlled, a much higher percentage than is the case in Sweden and Denmark. The organization of the existing capital system is clearly weaker in Norway than in, for example, Sweden (Gustavsen, 1976a). The credit market is already to a large extent under direct public control. The banks have been «deprivatized» − as it is called − which means that the larger commercial banks have a so-called board of representatives which can have fifteen, thirty or forty five members, of which the Norwegian parliament elects eight fifteenth, the right to elect the residual seven fifteenth is divided between the shareholders and the employees. The influence of the state over the credit market will, furthermore, increase in the future, because of the relative importance of the oil revenues it will receive. The state is therefore well equipped to support a reorganization of capital.

While these conditions are clearly conducive to a publicly initiated reorganization of capital, whatever direction such a reorganization would take, no proposals have as yet emerged. As wage earners funds and similar solutions are relatively broadly discussed in Sweden as well as in Denmark, this is worth noting. The reasons why proposals have not been put forth are not obvious and there are various possibilities. One explanation is that just because the element of public ownership and control is relatively high already, the need for changes might be considered less. An implicit conflict between different strategies for the movement towards a socialist society may also make itself felt. If it was opened up for a broad debate on reorganization of capital, some of the suggestions put forth would be sure to imply increased local control, that is: control over the investments by the workers locally. The present structure implies control via the state apparatus. The proponents of «state socialism», and they are strong in Norway, may for reasons like this have found that one may as well let the issue rest.

V. The background of the work environment reform

Introduction

The next reform in working life to be dealt with is the work environment reform, with the Work Environment Act of 1977 as the core element, but encompassing other means and efforts as well. This reform will be treated in this, and the next three chapters. In this chapter we will review some of the events and discussions that led up to the reform and the next chapter is dedicated to a critical analysis of the conventional approach to work environment reform; chapter VII contains a brief review of some of the reasoning that brought about the merger of the concepts of work environment and of industrial democracy as mutually interdependent parts of a total reform strategy; in chapter VIII some of the main elements of the Work Environment Act will be presented, to be followed by two case studies. Before proceeding, however, a few remarks on the concept of work environment need to be made:

Work environment is a concept which has come into general use in the Scandinavian countries in the latter sixties. Like e.g. «the quality of working life» it belongs to the general terms that can be used in different ways. However, in its particular Scandinavian usage, it is necessary to be aware of this term's historical link to those issues generally called safety- and health in the workplace. As we will illustrate later (chapter VII) a chief characteristic of the work environment reform is the merger between ideas about work environment and ideas about industrial democracy. Hence, work environment has already lost it exclusive link to issues of safety and health. This notwithstanding, the historical origin of the concept needs to be kept in mind, as the following presentation will depart from the safety and health problems and then demonstrate how this particular point of departure gave rise to a line of reasoning which led to a broad reform in working life where a number of methods and organisational tools were brought together in a multi-level strategy for reform (Gardell & Gustavsen, 1980).

Why improvement of the work environment?

Walker and Bellecombe (1974) have discovered a number of aims or considerations behind the efforts to introduce industrial democracy. Similarly, we can locate a number of ideas and considerations behind the efforts to improve the work environment. It will be seen that even in the earlier phase when issues were seen in a more traditional health and safety context, the aims and considerations went beyond safety and health as interpreted in a narrow «medical» sense. Among the most important arguments were the following:

1. Improving the health of the working population.
2. Protection of the weaker part in a contract relationship.
3. Preventing exploitation of the workers.
4. Preventing conflicts.
5. Reduction of public expenditure.
6. Redistribution of wealth.

Taking care of the health of the population has been one of the most important goals of the modern welfare state. It is a goal in its own right, which does not need to be derived from any higher-level consideration. For such a goal to lead to the introduction of work environment legislation it must, however, also be accepted that public health considerations warrant *preventive* measures, not only treatment after damages or illnesses have emerged. In Norway, this shift in policy took place in the latter part of the last century, leading to the first Factory Inspection Act of 1892.

The relationship between man and work in the western world has under the influence of liberal philosophy, primarily been perceived as a *contractual* relationship. And as contracts can not be made between a person and a situation, the relationship exists between employer and employee. Initially, under the influence of a relatively «pure» liberal philosophy, such contracts were thought to be regulated in an optimal way by the market of free competition. If contract conditions were bad when seen from the point of view of one of the parties, this would be because this party had a weak position in the market. As the market mechanism was thought to lead to optimal patterns of resource allocation from society's point of view, contracts should not be interfered with. The conditions in the early phase of industrialization, such as child labour, starvation wages, excessive working hours and slum living conditions, brought about a public consciousness leading to modifications and interventions in the original (pure) liberal point of departure. Revisions in contractual law emerged, to some extent, as a result of changes within the «bourgeois» establishment, and hence took the form of «second thoughts» among those who were the primary bearers of liberalism.

The main political counterforce to liberalism is, however, socialism. Like most social democratic societies, Norwegian politics and development are strongly influenced by the tension between these two ideologies and value systems. We have indicated in chapter I that there is a high degree of consensus in Norway relating to the methods of conflict resolution. This consensus, however, must not be taken to imply a similar consensus on overall, long-term political goals. The parallel existence of capitalist market relations in combination with a strong social democratic labour movement, with historical roots in radical socialist ideas, has resulted in sharp conflicts over values and long-term goals. Thus, issues such as health and safety in working life, and improvements in the work environment in general are continually influenced by this conflict. The prevention of the exploitation of workers as a reason for work environment reform should be seen in this context.

Reduction of conflicts is one of the points which links the protection of the health and safety of workers with the issue of industrial democracy. In the same way as industrial democracy is thought by many to lead to a reduction in the conflict level in working life, so can improved health and safety conditions. The importance of work environment issues in relation to conflict was underlined in a series of labour conflicts involving work environment issues which erupted around 1970 (below).

Point five dealt with reduction of public expenditure. As long as people's health has been a public issue, it has, of course. also been a public expenditure. As public considerations have broadened from health issues in a narrow sense to the complex network of social security systems, pensions etc. characterising the modern welfare state, the relationship between health and public costs has grown in importance. People who lose their ability to work due to negative conditions in working life will end up as public costs. To save such expenditure, then, is a further argument for having as qualitatively good work environments as possible so as to be able to keep as many people as possible actively at work.

«Redistribution of wealth», the sixth and last point, should be understood in the light of the special characteristics of Norwegian society as it moved into the early seventies. At this time the economic results of the oil findings on the Norwegian continental shelf started to make themselves felt. The rapid increase in oil prices after 1973 led to an enormous increase in the value of Norwegian oil reserves. An element of «oil fever» emerged and visions of unlimited wealth were waved before the eyes of the population, a population which, naturally enough, responded by making the highest wage claims in the post-war period. These visions were eventually modified, and by 1977 one was back to more realistic assessments, followed by a complete price-wage freeze to last from the autumn of 1978 until the end of 1979. In spite of the fact that oil incomes are not an unconditional blessing, the fact that Norway will, according to current estimates, produce somewhere between five and ten times her own consumption of gas and oil every year until somewhere around the middle of the next century, obviously means that there is a need to consider the distribution of this newly earned income. Work environment demands is one factor affecting this distribution. Partly, such demands mean improvements in the quality of working life, a goal which in itself constitutes a legitimate claim on resources. More ambitious work environment demands will, furthermore, reduce the wage- and dividend paying ability of companies, and hence make some contribution to the struggle against inflation. When this argument is mentioned it must, however, also be added that it played no major role in the work environment debate in the seventies. The oil incomes have up to now not had any dramatic impact on Norwegian society. Above all, it must be underlined that the work environment reform is not dependent upon the wealth generated by the oil resources. The need to save money, particularly on the public budgets through reducing illnesses and infirmities was of much greater importance, and one can, of course, not plead the need to save on the one hand and excess wealth on the other as arguments for one and the same reform.

Such arguments as these are general ones which serve as a background for work environment reforms in many countries, albeit with some variations in emphasis. They say, however, little about the specific situation prevailing in Norway at the time when the work environment reform started to gain momentum, and the next step is to take a brief look at some of these conditions.

The factors we will look at are the following:
– The environmental debate.
– Patterns of industrial conflict around 1970.
– Some aspects of the political process in Norway in the early seventies.
– Indicators of the development of the national situation as concerns conditions in working life.

The environmental debate

One of the most important events of the sixties, was the emergence of the environmental debate. The debate started with the issue of pesticides and animal life. (Carson 1962; about the resulting debate in the USA, see Graham, 1970). Successively, the debate was broadened to cover other issues. If, for example, such industrial products as pesticides are harmful to animal life, might they not be harmful also to those who work in the factories making these products? Many workers have complained, with justification, that in the general environmental discussions and improvement programmes more interest has been dedicated to the health of animals than to the health of workers. Nevertheless, the debate eventually got around also to the workplace and the workers.

The first problem to be raised in the workplace-centered part of the debate was toxic substances. To what extent are such substances present in the work environment? What damage do they do to the health of people? Questions like these were now taken more seriously.

Whatever point of view one might have on the real dangers of chemical substances, it is beyond any doubt whatsoever that what can loosely be called the chemical complexity of the environment of man, be it on or off the job, has increased, with a resulting increase in fear, doubts and insecurity. This in itself is an important factor, and sufficient to warrant rules that can improve peoples' possibilities for coping with the situation.

Starting with chemical substances, the debate about work environment was successively broadened to cover topics that traditionally have not been raised within a work environment context. One example of such a new issue was the problem of stress, or psycho-social loads if one prefers that term. Conventional workers' protection legislation has done little to protect people against this type of hazard.

Another perspective to emerge in a successively clearer form was a need to apply a total perspective, on the environment as well as on its effects on man. Such a total perspective, inspired by ecological thinking, brought forth various important points, such as the fact that work environment loads can interact with each other and thereby strengthen each other far beyond simple addition. To deal with interaction between loads, new strategies might be called for. Looking at the effects of environmental loads, it also becomes increasingly clear that mixed or composite effects are of rising importance. By this is meant effects not easily classifiable in one or other of the special categories of a reductionistic and technologically oriented concept of health (Berg, 1975), but effects with psycho-social as well as physical

105

components in complex patterns of interaction. That some of the major illnesses have their roots in syndromes of this kind is of course not new, but the debate of the late sixties and early seventies brought this point into a sharper focus and stressed the need to develop strategies for health maintainance that could cope also with such conceptually and diagnostically difficult problems.

Patterns of industrial conflict around 1970

Statistics on number of days lost in conflict − relative to the size of the working population − shows that Norway has relatively few strikes, and that there has been a downward trend during the postwar period (chapter I). Wildcat strikes account for very little of the total figures, nevertheless, at some points in history they have played an important role.

In the late sixties an illegal strike took place in the Swedish state owned mining company, the LKAB, located in the northern mining town of Kiruna (Dahlstrøm et. al., 1971). This strike received wide publicity even outside Sweden, and came to trigger off similar strikes in other places in Sweden as well as in Norway (Karlsen et. al., 1971). Common to these strikes was that work environment arguments were raised by the striking workers as important reasons for the strikes. The work environment was, furthermore, given a fairly broad definition, covering a wide range of issues from toxic substances to the way the companies were managed.

The strikes made it clear that there was a tension between the traditional patterns of negotiations and agreements on the one hand and problems as experienced and defined by groups of workers on the other. Even though the main agreement, as well as numerous industry- or branch agreements, cover various issues besides wages and working hours, these last issues clearly dominate in the organised negotiations between the employers and employees. The emphasis on time/wage issues is strengthened by the relatively high degree of centralization in the Norwegian bargaining system. Centralization means that issues must be settled at a distance from where they actually occur. This means a preference for relatively general, quantifiable issues to the neglect of issues that need concrete insight into the situation from which they emerge and that must be settled at least partly on the basis of local conditions.

Even in a centralized system one can counteract some of the negative effects by having a differentiation of functions, with work environment issues under local jurisdiction while time/wage issues remain under central control. Such a distribution of functions has, however, only to a limited extent emerged in the Norwegian union movement. Instead, the various levels deal roughly with the same issues, and the emphasis is on wages and working time on all levels. There is, however, a possibility that this will to some extent change in the future, see Chapter IX.

The peace obligation attached to Norwegian agreements not only extends to issues explicitly written into the agreement but also to issues not covered in the contract. New issues can be introduced only when the agreement expires and ceases to be legally binding. There are, furthermore, relatively limited informal channels available to take care of problems and tensions building up in a workplace. The relatively low level of strikes in Norway do not conceal a series of informal protests such as sit-downs, work-to-rule campaigns and sabotage of production. Such non-institutionalised protests could, if they had been present, perhaps prevented, or at least reduced, the illegal strikes which emerged around 1970.

These illegal conflicts clearly put the national unions affected in a difficult situation, particularly the Chemical Workers Union, within whose domain the most widely publicized conflicts took place. The unions have to back the peace obligation, or have at least chosen to do so up to now, and this created a serious dilemma for them. They were legally obliged to control their members who had broken the peace obligation, even though the reasons for these strikes related to health and safety considerations as well as to broader issues of the work environment. Even though the unions centrally and locally stayed loyal to the peace obligation, it was of course realised by the unions that they could not indefinitely play such a role. This produced additional pressure for work environment reforms.

Criticism in this period was often voiced of the Labour Inspection for being too lenient, for not discovering problems, and for not issuing demands to enterprises for the correction of problems. These criticisms may well have been unfair or at least exaggerated given the complexity of working life problems and the limited resources available to the Labour Inspection.

Criticism was also voiced against the occupational health service on company level, its lack of presence, as well as its attachment to the employer, where it did exist. Criticism was directed against the medical profession for not being sufficiently interested in workplace problems and for not being willing to take stands in favour of the workers. A few radical doctors were among those who laid the foundations for this criticism against some of their own colleagues (e.g. Hanoa, 1971). These people also contributed to the reform, by legitimising an «illness causing» interpretation of conditions that had previously been more or less accepted in working life.

The period around 1970 also saw the emergence of a number of research projects, reports and analyses, pertaining to work environment conditions. Some examples, drawn from all three Scandinavian countries, are: Bronner och Levi (1969), Bolinder och Ohlstrøm (1971), Glud et al (1971), Attføringsutvalget ved Norsk Jernverk (1972) Studenterrapporten (1973), Ager et al (1975), Karlsen (1978).

Some general political aspects

The most important political event in Norway in the early seventies was created by the Common Market issue. The government wanted Norway to join the Common Market and so did a majority of the members of parliament. However, the forces which wanted to bring Norway into the Common Market lost in a referendum on the issue held in the autumn of 1972. The point in this particular connection, is that this issue created a split within the labour movement − to be felt particularly in the Labour Party but also to some extent in the trade union movement. It was particularly the more radical groups who assumed leadership in the campaign against common market membership and this led to a re-awakening of the left-centre conflicts within the labour movement. One would have to go back to the twenties to find a similar split in the Norwegian labour movement over as complex and many sided a problem on the level of the future of the nation. The split made itself felt in the next parliamentary elections of 1973, when the Labour Party had the lowest support of any election in the postwar period. It remained in government, however, because the Socialist Peoples' Party to the left of the Labour Party made its best election in the history of the party and secured a socialist parliamentary majority. The leadership of the labour movement in Norway has always been careful, and on the whole successful, in avoiding issues and conflicts which could divide the labour movement. It has instead focussed on class-based issues, such as for example an incomes policy based on wage solidarity, which would unite the labour movement. The common market issue was forced upon the labour movement by external forces beyond its control. Clearly, after these events, there was a need to heal the wounds and to bring the labour movement together again around common causes. The work environment reform came to be defined as such a unifying issue. A reform of this type would be of relevance not only to the Labour Party but also to the trade union movement, and could therefore repair some of the cracks

108

that had emerged in this relationship due to the government's support of Common Market membership.

A political foundation for a work environment reform was laid in connection with the parliamentary elections of 1973, in the form of a joint programme for work environment reform drawn up jointly by the Labour Party and the Federation of Trade Unions.

Some indicators on the development of Norwegian working life

General arguments and political aspects like those touched upon above are one thing, but what was the actual situation in working life? Was there a strong need for a reform? Were there any changes in work conditions, and what was the direction of these changes? This raises the question of social indicators on the national level which is a difficult and complex topic (cf. Biderman & Drury, 1976).

The Labour Inspection compiled such statistics on the basis of data on occupational infirmities and diseases. In 1966 a total of 3217 incidences of occupational diseases were registered. This figure reached a low of 1938 cases in 1970 and then started to climb until it reached 2229 cases in 1975. Considering the total size of the working population, these figures must be characterised as low. In 1975, for example, there were 2229 reported instances of occupational infirmities and diseases. With a working population of approximately 1.5 million, the figure amounts to less than 0.2 percent of the working population. These statistics gave no ground for believing that a general deterioration in conditions was under way, as was claimed by a number of critics during the debate on work environment reform. However, closer scrutiny and supplementary studies have cast grave doubts on the reliability of these statistics. Three factors in particular are responsible for this, and they may be worth mentioning as similar points can pertain to this type of statistics in other countries as well:

Firstly, we have cases that are not registered, as they do not come into contact with any part of the registration system. In a study of damages to hearing among workers in the building industry in the Oslo-area, it was found that of the first fifty cases who fullfilled the criteria for being registered (permanent damage to hearing of some magnitude) forty eight had never seen a doctor and had consequently never been in contact with any element in the registration system (Hellstrøm, 1977).

Secondly, we have cases where incidents are registered, but where information is not passed along to central bodies such as the Labour Inspection. Exact figures can not be given, but it is beyond doubt that the occupational health services on the enterprise level have generally reported only a limited number of the cases that they have come across. This may be changing now, but in the middle seventies deficiencies in the reporting system were clearly an important factor.

Thirdly, we have the question of criteria: What illnesses and infirmities are to be defined as «occupational». As there are few illnesses that are by nature specifically «occupational» this classification must relate to causes or conditioning factors. It is, however, often difficult to decide on this issue of causes, either because of lack of relevant information, or because illnesses are often of a so-called multi-factorial character. Heart diseases, for example, are generally brought about by a number of factors in interaction, few cases of heart diseases are consequently classified as occupational, even if the work situation can be an important contributing factor. The legal system in Norway generally functions in such a way that in case of doubt the classification is as «non occupational». The burden of doubt has, in other words, been *against* classifying illness as occupational. This has been facilitated by the fact that within the Norwegian social security and welfare system it is often of limited economic consequence to the ill or disabled how the cause is classified. All hospital treatment is paid for out of public budgets, and disability pensions are not greatly influenced by the cause of the disability. In societies where the economic consequences of the distinction between «occupational» and «non-occupational» causes are greater, accurate classification will be more important.

A picture somewhat different from the one pressented by the Labour Inspection emerged from a study conducted on a representative sample of members of the Federation of Trade Unions (Karlsen, 1978). Of the more than 4000 respondents, 85 percent believed themselves to be exposed to one or more work environment load or problem. The most frequently mentioned problem was noise, followed by problems pertaining to physiology or ergonomics. About one quarter of the total sample believed that these loads had negative health consequences.

A further indicator often emerging in discussions about work environment conditions is absenteeism. Registered absences due to illness in 1965 were about 6 percent for men and 9 percent for women (measured in work days lost in relation to total number of workdays per year), in 1970, 9 percent and 11 percent respectively, and in 1975, the absenteeism for men showed a slight decline to 8.3 percent while it stayed at 11 percent for women. There is a long term tendency towards increased absenteeism, reflected in data for the period after 1975. These data are, however, fairly difficult to interpret, as absenteeism can go up and down for various reasons other than the loads or stress factors in the work environment and thus this increase in absenteeism does not allow us to draw any firm conclusions. Generally, however, absenteeism is considered costly, as it takes people out of work and consequently either reduces production or creates a need for replacement.

Another set of figures that came to play a major role was the number of people receiving public pensions due to disabilities prohibiting them from taking part in working life. While this figure was around 50.000 in 1961, it had reached 150.000 by 1975. Even these figures are, however, hard to interpret. All functional disabilities are included, also those incurred outside working life, such as in traffic accidents. Secondly, it is shown by sociological studies (Kollberg, 1974) that disability pensions are used to some extent where there is no work available, as a substitute, in actual fact, for a successful employment policy (cf. also Berglind, 1978). The unemployment rate in Norway has generally been very.low – in 1978 it was, for example, 1.5 percent, or 0.9 percent if only those who registered at the employment offices are counted.

However, the changed use of disability pensions that took place in the period from 1960 to 1975 has probably contributed to this low level of unemployment. Among the 150.000 recipients of disability pensions there is clearly a number who would otherwise have been registered as unemployed. Even considering factors like these, the work environment issues clearly play a role in relation to these figures: an increasing number of people are not able to fill a role in working life, be it because of characteristics of working life or of the people – whatever it is, it is a problem, and the issue of work environment has to do with what types of abilities can be used in working life and what people can find a role there. In a public report on means to improve the conditions for the functionally disabled (NOU, 1976) it was estimated that 12.000 people are expelled from working life in Norway each year. Among the arguments drawn from official statistics, the need to do something about this «mismatch» was probably the most powerful.

The initiative

The political initiative emerged as a joint programme drafted by the Labour Party and the Federation of Trade Unions in connection with the elections of 1973 (LO – DNA, 1973). This programme for work environment reform contained a number of points and demands, of which the following were of particular importance.

- Improved protection against toxic substances.

- The need to develop a broad definition of work environment hazards or stressors.
- The need to apply a broad definition of what effects are to be considered relevant. In this connection the conventional definition of health and safety was broadened to include such issues as stress and psycho-social problems.
- In the light of the second and third consideration, the programme underlined the need to issue rules about the way work was to be organised.
- In the light of the the same considerations the programme stressed the need to put more emphasis on problems in the non-industrial sectors of working life, such as trade and service, where some of the major problems can not be attacked unless one is willing to put heavy emphasis on organisation of work and psycho-social consequences.
- The need to consider the work environment as a whole or a totality.
- The need to give more influence over the definition of problems as well as over the development of improvement efforts to the employees.

The election of 1973 produced a socialist majority in the parliament, made up of the Labour Party and the Socialist People's Party. The work with the development of the new act started in 1974.

Contrary to what is common in the preparation of legislation in Norway, a general committee, with representatives from all interested parties and organisations, was not established in this case. Instead, the Ministry of Labour developed more of a network type organisation, with four working groups as the core elements. Each group developed a part of the proposals for the act, to some extent in collaboration with people outside the group's membership. This way of working proved open and flexible and generally efficient from the point of view of bringing innovations into the process.

The Work Research Institutes was one of the organisations which took part in this process and hence came to exert influence over the development of the reform. The contributions of the WRI are to be found particularly in the development of a strategy for reform based on the bringing together of the concept of work environment and the concept of industrial democracy. This strategy will be the main object of the following presentation.

This contribution to strategy has not been limited to the development of the act itself, but has been going on afterwards as well, in various ways and on various levels. Such an act as the Work Environment Act is not a finished product when it passes through parliament; it is rather a new element in a series of continuous processes which need constant interpretation, development and support.

A draft for the new act was finished in 1976. Practically all employer- and employee organizations commented on the proposal. After some changes it was presented to parliament where it was passed (Ot. prp. nr. 3 1975/76). It went into force on July lst, 1977. Selected parts of the Act are given in Appendix.

The reactions and comments which the law attracted were manifold and cover a large number of issues. Here, we will only touch upon the main reactions of the major organisations: the Federation of Trade Unions and the Employers' Confederation.

For the Federation of Trade Unions, it was easy to react to the proposal, as it was largely based on the joint Trade Union-Labour Party programme from 1973. The proposal was, however, treated rather thoroughly within the Federation and its affiliated unions. More than 3000 study groups of workers went through the proposal on a voluntary basis and commented upon it.

Of greater interest in this particular connection are the reactions of . the employers. As we will see in succeeding chapters, the act can be said to put new and fairly broad demands upon the employers. One would, not unreasonably, expect negative reactions of some magnitude to this act. Negative reactions did in fact emerge. It is, however, beyond doubt that these reactions must be characterised as limited. There was in actual fact no broad criticism of the main thrust of the reform as such, criticism was directed at the use of legislation, instead of reliance on the willingness of management to pursue these goals voluntarily or through the collective bargaining process. The more detailed criticism which emerged pertained to specific sections of the act.

One issue to attract attention related to criminal sanctions against managers who break the law. The Federation of Trade Unions had demanded that criminal sanctions against managers/employers should be allowed on an objective basis, that is, without any demand for subjective guilt. This demand did, however, not go through. The Act as it was eventually passed allows for criminal sanctions to be initiated but without dropping the traditional requirement in Norwegian criminal law for subjective guilt.

Another issue to give rise to some discussion related to the training of employees on work environment issues. A section of the act (section 29, Appendix) expresses the principle that this training is to be done at the expense of the employer and during regular working hours.

A further part of the act to meet with criticism by the employers is the chapter on work time and shift work. This part of the act will not be treated in this book. It is a lengthy chapter, containing a number of fairly detailed rules.

To return to the main issue, one can ask why the employers did not raise a major storm against the act. The full answer to this question is not known but the following are some possible points of relevance:

It became clear immediately upon the publication of the proposal, that parliament would pass most of the act not only with a clear majority, but unanimously. The act was, in other words, supported not only by the Labour Party and the Scoialist Peoples' Party, but also by the centre to right parties in Norwegian politics. In the center we find a party with historical links to the agrarian community; a christian peoples' party; and some remnants of a liberal party that was the main opponent of the conservatives until the Labour Party took over this role (Chapter I). In addition there is the Conservative Party, the main political force in the centre to right part of the spectrum. An all-out attack on the proposal for the new Work Environment Act would most likely have come from the conservatives. The Conservative Party, however, relies on the support of the centre parties for their struggle against the socialists on a whole range of issues. Since these other parties supported the new legislation, the conservatives would have been isolated in their opposition.

Secondly, it is not correct to presume that all employers/managers are against such legislation as the Work Environment Act. The general direction of the reform was to a large extent based on past experience in working life, such as the Industrial Democracy Programme (Cf. Chapter II and III), which had been supported by a number of managers and employers as well as by the Employers' Confederation. One way of looking at the Work Environment Act is to see it as an attempt to make specific pioneering innovations generally applicable throughout the entire working environment in Norway.

There were also other factors which may have contributed to the relatively low level of opposition to the Work Environment Act. New legislation in Norway is generally prepared in committees which include representatives of the interested parties. Such a procedure gives the parties a great deal of time to discuss the proposed legislation in all its details and to bargain for changes and alternatives. The flexible work group system used in the preparation of the Work Environment Act reduced the possibilities for detailed and lengthy discussions.

Whatever the reasons may be, the Work Environment Act was passed in an air of agreement and consensus on the national level.

VI. A critique of the conventional approach to safety and health in work

Introduction

In the last chapter we presented some of the more important steps and discussions which led to the introduction of the Work Environment Act of 1977. In this chapter we will reproduce, in some detail, the more important aspects of the discussion which has taken place together with the development of an overall strategy of work environment reform. The search for an overall strategy was preceded by a critical analysis of the conventional approach to legislation and reform relating to the work environment.

One possible approach to work environment reform is to strengthen or sharpen environmental demands such as issuing lower threshold limit values for noise, toxic substances etc.. Relying exclusively on such an approach would, however, also imply problems. Firstly, some of the demands stated in the Trade Union-Labour Party programme could not easily be met through such an approach alone. Secondly, one would still be left with the problem of implementing the stricter requirements. It would, of course, be possible to expand the Labour Inspection and work research capabilities in the hope that more studies and inspections would lead to the discovery of more hazards and increased remedial action. It seems reasonable to assume, however, that in order to come to terms with an acceptable proportion of the various problems emerging in working life, this approach would require a continuous expansion of inspection and research capabilities which would exceed the limits of available public resources.

Such considerations as local initiative and worker participation in work environment issues also enter the picture when the relative importance of a rule based public approach is to be decided on (cf. Pateman, 1970, and the general debate on «elite-» versus participatory democracy).

Thus there is a need to consider *basic strategy* in a work environment reform. One part of this was to undertake a critical evaluation of the approach to legislation and reform in the field of work environment traditionally applied in Norway; an approach which is parallel to the approach used in most, not to say all, countries. To the extent that this approach has basic weaknesses the next step is to seek ways of remedying these weaknesses.

For anyone who tries to give a presentation of the Norwegian work environment reform, it would have been a great advantage if these strategic discussions had been performed at one, easily identifyable, stage in the process of developing the reform, such as in the motives for the act. This, however, was not the case. The question of basic strategy has more come to take on the characteristics of a «running debate». It emerged already in the Federation of Trade Unions-Labour Party Programme from 1973, it continued under the preparations of the act, it is part of the background of various supplementary rules and guidelines issued after the act, and it is still on the agenda as one moves into the eighties. In the spring of 1980 the work on a parliamentary report about the implementation of the act was started, and the question of basic strategy is part also of this report. In a book like this we can, however, not deal with all the steps of this debate and present it as it has evolved over time. Instead, the analysis must be concentrated, even though this gives an impression of a debate far more structured and ordered than what acutally was − and is − the case.

A further point is that one of the authors of this book has been a participant in these discussions as participant in the development of the act, as advisor to the Ministry of Labour as well as in various written studies, reports, papers and other documents (Gustavsen, 1977a; 1979a; 1980a; 1980b; Gardell and Gustavsen, 1980; Gustavsen & Seierstad, 1977; Gustavsen, Seierstad & Ebeltoft, 1978). Hence, the views to be presented and argued here to some extent reflect a «partisan position» in the debates.

The rule-based strategy for workers protection

Workers protection legislation has existed in the industrialized world for quite a period of time. In Norway the first act of this type saw daylight around the turn of the last century. This legislation has been revised at regular intervals up through the years. Generally, however, it has always been based on a particular type of strategy.

This strategy is derived from the idea of the «rule of law», as this idea has commonly been interpreted in the western, industrialized world. The point of departure is the thesis that legislation in favour of the workers is an encroachment upon the freedom of the enterprise.

116

Such encroachments, according to this ideology, must be subject to certain restrictions:

- Such legislation must be expressed thorugh general norms, that is: norms that are to hold in an equal way for everybody; otherwise competition will be influenced.
- The norms must state clearly what is allowed and what is not; a threshold limit value will be a typical example of an «acceptable» norm.
- The norms must have reasons or grounds; if it is not proven that a norm is necessary, it should not be issued.

If public efforts at reform of working life are based on norms fulfilling these criteria, the administrative practices also take on a certain character. These practices can involve various bodies, such as the Labour Inspection whose task it is to see that workers protection legislation is enforced.

The administrative practices become oriented towards the general rules. These practices will not be based on open means-end decisions, but rather on subsumption decisions (Eckhoff & Dahl-Jacobsen, 1960). A means-end decision is a fairly open selection of means guided by the ends one wants to achieve. A subsumption decision does not imply definition of ends and selection of means, but rather the «matching» of facts to rules. The solution to a problem is defined by finding the right rule or rules to fit a set of given facts. This is the type of decision made by courts.

There is in actual practice some degree of overlap between the two types of decisions, even the courts often perform more open-ended evaluations of means and ends, as for instance when they try to find the right sentence for a convicted offender. Nevertheless, the subsumption type of decision is the point of departure.

In public administration both subsumption decisions as well as means-end decisions can be found and in many varities and combinations. If we look at the bodies that have the enforcement of workers protection legislation as their main task, it seems that they have ended up relatively close to the subsumption model in its pure form.

The reasons for this are the following: The legislation and corresponding bye-laws have been more strongly oriented towards unequivocal general rules than what has generally been common in legislation in later years. In many other areas public authorities have a broader scope for discretion and means- end decisions are more frequently applied.

The relatively strong orientation towards unequivocal general rules is probably linked to an interest on the part of management of most organizations in maintaining stable and reasonably well defined conditions. Unstable and changing work environment requirements make planning difficult. Management has probably found implicit support for this point of view in the forces of society backing interests in productivity and economic goals.

This pressure towards clarity and stability has carried over from the legislative level to the level of bye-laws. Even the older work environment legislation had a number of authority norms, norms giving public authorities the right to use discretion, but these norms were often converted into bye-rules fulfilling the criteria of generality and unequivocality.

A further part of the reinforcement mechanism is probably to be found in the relationship between resources and problems. The problems generated by modern working life are extremely manyfold and complex. To penetrate them, large resources are needed. These have generally not been present in the public sector, and desicions had to be made on the basis of incomplete insights and knowledge. Under such circumstances any decision can easily be criticised on various grounds, a risk continuously run by the labour inspectors. Under this risk of criticism, for instance from lawyers and engineers working for the enterprises, the inspectors need something to hide behind, and the rules can fulfill this function. (The mechanism is the same as the one described by e.g. Merton (1940) or Gouldner (1954)). If they stick to the rules they avoid criticism, if they try to move beyond the issues where they can point at reasonably clear rules and solutions, they run the risk of criticism, appeals to higher authorities, and other sanctions.

The use of general, unequivocal and positively founded rules as the main parameter within the field of work environment has certain consequences.

Some of these consequences are clearly positive. If, for example, employers put up a fierce struggle against work environment improvements, while the alternative local forces such as unions are in a weak position, or non-existent, an approach based on rules and public inspection is probably the only solution. In, for example, North America, this type of situation seems to prevail in certain parts of working life. Employers are going against work environment standards also where this implies confrontation with unions. The contests over the promulgation of health and safety standards, citations and penalties are marked. Not only have challenges been offered in hearings designed to adopt new standards, but then afterwards there have been heated court cases involved in attempting to stay the implementation of progressive new standards, such as that for lead and cotton dust as in the US in recent years. Ten years after the passage of the Occupational Safety and Health Act of 1970 in the USA, there are major efforts by employer associations to cripple the agency and the US Congress has critical proposals before it to do just that. In Canada the Federal Department of Labour has moved to eliminate government inspection of federal health- and safety standards and instead rely on employer selfinspection. This move has been strongly critisized by the Canadian Labour Congress (Rabinovitch, 1979, as quoted by Willox, 1980).

Even when the situation is less characterised by conflict over the general status of work environment considerations, rules are to a certain degree necessary. This notwithstanding, there are also arguments against a rule-based strategy. In the following pages these arguments will be developed, as they are of particular relevance to an understanding of the Norwegian work environment reform.

What has been attempted in this reform is not a complete abandonment of traditional rules, such as threshold limit values, but rather the development of a new kind of balance between the use of rules and the use of other approaches. In the following sections we will summarize some of the main arguments against an exclusive reliance on rules.

Limitations of efforts

General, unequivocal and positively founded rules can be developed within some areas of the work environment, such as concerns many of the issues falling under the heading of technical threats agains safety, and within those fields of occupational medicine where threshold limit values are possible. There are, however, important areas where such rules simply cannot be developed and where any normative effort cannot proceed beyond the level of generalities and fairly open standards. This holds, for example, for ergonomics, or physiological loads and problems, an issue of broad importance in a work environment context (in most societies these constitute the single most frequent work environment problem). Another example could be psychological and social loads («stress»).

As long as rules are the sole parameter brought to bear on the problems, little or nothing will be done within those fields where rules cannot be developed.

Proof requirements

A second consequence relates to an issue which can be called *burden of proof*. Departing from the point of view that general rules are the main action parameters, while reasons for new rules are insisted upon, a situation is created where the consequences of uncertainty must generally be carried by the employees. Activities and processes are allowed *unless* there are rules prohibiting them. Such rules must, however, not be issued before positive reasons are present. In many instances, however, doubt and uncertainty prevail in relation to work environment issues and problems. This is in fact rather common because of such factors as rapid technological development which continuously creates new situations with uncertain consequences. «Work environment research» is far from able to keep up with all the developments taking place in working life. This research does, in terms of resources, make up only a tiny fragment of the resources used in support of technological development. In such situations, when negative effects might be suspected, but necessary documentation is lacking, the activity will be allowed. To this it must be added that even under conventional legislation a number of countries, Norway included, had started to make modifications in relation to this point of departure. As an overriding principle, this allocation of the «burden of proof» was, however, still prevailing in the early seventies.

One example of a discussion where opinions are influenced by what proof requirements one uses, is the well known debate on the relative frequency of occupationally induced cancer, relative to all incidences of cancer. Widely different estimates, ranging from practically zero to about 30 percent are given (see, e.g. Bridbord et al, 1978). The issue of burden of proof emerges on at least two points in this debate: Firstly, within the scientific community itself, where differences may emerge between on the one hand researchers who demand proof positive of relatively simple chains of causality between condition and effect, and on the other researchers who depart from the point that much is unknown about cancer and that the problem is to distribute possible conditioning factors in a situation of uncertainty where estimates and probabilities are core elements in the decision-making process. However, even if the scientific community can agree internally, a new problem emerges in the transition from science to practical use. Even if one believes that science offers objective and efficient models for describing the development of cancer (as, e.g. Saffiotti (1977) does), lawyers, administrators, industry and labour inspections might not necessarily accept the viewpoint of the scientists. Legal-administrative decisions in society often emerge from other rules about evidence than those of scientific estimates and recommendations. When the problem of occupationally induced cancer is mentioned as an example of an issue where doubt and uncertainty makes itself felt we have, furthermore, chosen a topic where there is after all quite a lot of research and at least some possibilities for the unbiased to suggest a reasonable point of view on the basis of available knownedge. But what about all the other possible dangers and hazards in the work environment such as, for example, stress? What do we know about them?

The problem of interaction

A further point inherent in the traditional system is lack of systematic recognition of interaction or interdependence between problems or loads. The emphasis on general rules which are to be unequivocal makes it necessary to proceed item by item, because consideration of interaction between loads makes the situation so complex that rules are no longer able to cope with it. One of the most important recognitions to emerge from work research of later years has been precisely the need to see the work environment *as a whole* (i.e. Arbejdsmiljøgruppen af 1972). This need to apply a total perspective also contributes to the problems attached to the traditional location of the burden of proof or evidence. If we accept, as it seems that we have to, that many problems in the work environment, and society in general for that matter, are not caused by single factors through simple chains of events, but through a multiplicity of conditions often implying long sequences of events, uncertainty and doubt about «what leads to what» will be the rule rather than the exception. Every now and then an issue might be «clarified» through research, but new problems will continually emerge.

Concerning interaction between work environment loads, or the effects of a total work environment on employees, it may be worth while to give the following example.

Some time ago the Norwegian Central Bureau of Statistics compiled data on the relationship between mortality and occupational background (Central Bureau of Statistics, 1976). To the surprise of many, the hotel- and restaurant workers emerged as one of the groups with the shortest average life span. In an effort to discover the reasons for this unexpected result, the Hotel- and Restaurant Workers Union requested the Work Research Institute to undertake a study of this occupational group. (Karlsen & Næss, 1978).

The study was done as a survey of a representative sample of the members of the union. The main picture to emerge from the survey data is given in Figure 6.

The main point is that a number of factors in the work environment *unite* in producing complex and many-sided effects on health. The effects include cardiovascular diseases, cancer due to stress control through smoking, and a slow but steady deterioration of function-

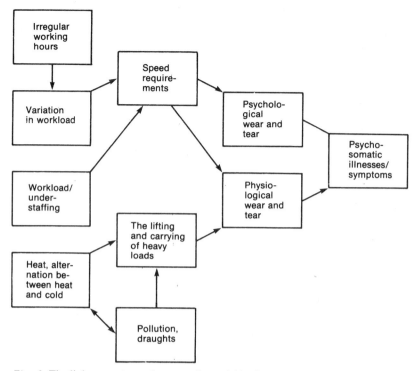

Fig. 6. The linkage structure between the variables in a study of hotel- and resturant workers (N = 989).
Source: Karlsen & Næss (1978)

al abilities due to physiological problems of various kinds such as pains in the neck, back and shoulders. There is no single factor in the environment which can be singled out as *the* cause. Looked at in isolation, each of the contributing factors can appear harmless enough, but the total impact is nevertheless a major threat to health.

A further point of major importance is that feedback effects also occur. When negative effects on health and welfare start to make themselves felt, the workloads will often be experienced as heavier, the speed requirements as tougher, the shift system as more inconvenient, with reinforcement of the negative effects on health as a consequence. In actual practice we confront a highly complex network of circular processes where «causes» and «effects» are intermingled.

A problem situation of this type can to some extent be dealt with through the use of general rules of the threshold limit type. The difficulties, however, will be major. The rules about each and every factor will have to be very conditional, because the function of each factor as a load depends very much on the total situation. It is, furthermore,

122

necessary to issue rules about conditions which have traditionally not been the object of rule making, such as staffing, workload and work organisation. Some of the factors emerging in this study have traditionally been the object of some degree of regulation, for example, heat and cold, but it is worth noting that the temperature variations these employees confront do not generally fall outside acceptable limits, if these variations were the only problems they encountered.

Demand for experts and pressure on public resources

A fourth point is that work environment issues at the level of the individual organization are turned to a large extent into problems of measurement and interpretations of measurement results. Work environment issues become issues requiring experts, often external experts, as many of the types of expertise called for are rarely to be found within such organizations as industrial companies. The possibilities for engagement and activity on the part of the employees who experience the problem becomes severely limited. They usually have to stand back and await the judgement of the experts, if there are any experts to call upon in the first place. One should not forget that work environment problems are, after all, the problems of the employees – often rather pressing problems that are personally experienced.

To the extent that work environment problems can not be dealt with on the local level, they constitute a pressure on public resources. The government or the municipalities will have to employ the necessary resources of experts, inspectors and so on. Such public resources have been present in most industrialized countries for quite a long period of time; most «factory inspections» date back to the previous century. It is quite clear that a certain amount of public resources are necessary. The problem does not lie here, but in the *balance* between what tasks are handled locally and what tasks need the intervention or support of external resources. It seems beyond the practically possible to assign all responsibility for work environment improvement and control to public institutions. We are, after all, not even able to control the traffic in a modern society, which constitutes a relatively simple problem of control compared to the complexity of working life. At the same time the number of policemen on the roads far exceeds the number of work inspectors in the factories. One possible solution to problems of this type is of course to develop the public resources further. It seems, however, as if even though most societies, including Norway, should use more public resources in support of developments in working life, one must at the same time face the fact that the public resources can not be expanded to a magnitude which would enable them to solve all the problems. In fact, when considering public resources it seems necessary to start from the thesis that the *main* responsibility for control and improvement of the work environment must be allocated *locally*. The use of public resources should be the exception rather than the rule.

«Frozen standards»

A further consequence of the conventional, rule-based approach, is that work environment conditions and standards tend to be «frozen» for long periods of time. When work environment issues are turned into a set of minimum requirements, that are not changed until the need to do so is «documented», the general situation in working life tends to become frozen. Little happens from one year to the next, the rules of yesterday are the rules of today and will be the rules of tomorrow. It sometimes happens that particular work environment problems surface in public debates. In the middle 1970's, for example, a public debate took place on the problems relating to vinylchloride and asbestos. This resulted in renewed efforts to clarify the effects and led to the eventual revision of applicable rules. The fact that such incidents are occasionally reported by the mass media must, however, not overshadow the point that with the great majority of work environment issues there is little change and improvement.

Lack of long term development

From the fact that unequivocal rules by necessity must convert work environment standards into minimum requirements, a further consequence also follows: improvement of the work environment is generally *not* defined as long term developmental work, but instead as short term adaptations to given rules. Minimum requirements must be *met*, at least when somebody points out that something is wrong, and this must be done *soon*. A long term approach will imply that a situation of «illegality» will prevail for a longer period.

This immediate adaptation to the requirements seems, at first glance, to be an advantage to those exposed to the problem. It is of course better that something is done immediately rather than having to wait until a long term change programme has eventually reached its goal. This line of reasoning would be valid if the question of what was allowed and what not allowed was defined independently of the strategic decision relating to the choice of approach needed to deal with a given problem. Such is manifestly not the case. Instead, what

124

actually happens is that steps are generally not taken at all within those areas where one or two step solutions can not be specified and where one would have to rely on a long term development. Hence, the conventional strategy does not function in support of defining improvement of the work environment as *developmental* work. The losers are the employees, who are compelled to continue their work in the face of work environment problems which can not be easily solved through application of the traditional rules approach.

Administrative practices

Given the rule based approach to work environment problems, the administrative practice to be developed by the labour inspection will acquire certain characteristics. For an issue to be defined as a work' environment problem, the following requirements must, as a point of departure, be fulfilled.

- It must be sufficiently *visible* to be seen during a relatively short visit to the workplace.
- There must be a rule defining the issue as *relevant* within a work environment context.
- The rule must define the existing situation as *illegal.*
- The rule, or supplementary material, must *specify what is to be done* to remedy the situation.

This is a point of departure. It is not argued that all labour inspectors in all situations have acted according to these requirements. There have been exceptions and deviations, for example when inspectors have reached broader evaluations based on an integrated view and have then taken responsibility for their decisions. These criteria must be seen not as absolute guidelines but as something around which actual behaviour tends to cluster and which, in spite of exceptions, still constitute the main generating premises for the work done by public authorities.

We have already touched on the point that the complexity of problems, frequently generated by a number of elements in interaction with each other, and with composite and longterm effects, are not easily taken up and dealt with by a system departing from this type of administrative practice. One might as well change the point of departure and say that the majority of work environment problems can not be dealt with through such a strategy. The traditional approach is relevant first and foremost within certain fields, particularly as concerns technical threats against safety and some related areas, and even within these areas the fruitfulness of the approach is dependent upon the possibilities of finding solutions to the problems without having to engage in a long term developmental process requiring step by step improvements combined with a learning process. Such a developmental process will often be necessary even within areas where the problem is relatively easily defined, such as for instance noise. A problem easily defined is not necessarily a problem easily solved.

The traditional approach and the role of research

Given such a legal superstructure and a corresponding administrative praxis, what is the role of research?

Research can play various roles also under this type of overall strategy. Emphasis, however, is particularly heavily placed on the following three functions (Gustavsen, 1980a):

- Discover what factors in the work environment constitute relevant loads.
- Find out how much people can tolerate of the various negative factors.
- Contribute to the visibility of problems in particular instances.

The first two tasks relate to production of general norms, the third to the use of research in particular workplace settings to clarify problems that are found to be difficult to handle by the labour inspection or the enterprise itself. There is an interdependence between this last type of research and the first two – e.g. in many instances the dangers attached to the use of chemical substances have first emerged through investigations on the enterprise level.

Given such main tasks as these, the bulk of work environment research has traditionally been medical, or cross-disciplinary with medicine in interaction with other sciences, such as chemistry. The role of social research has been much more modest. In the brief remarks to be made on the role of research, we will depart from social research as this is the type of research which has had most problems in fulfilling a relevant role under the conventional strategy.

Social research has played a role under the conventional approach in that it has contributed to the definition of factors of relevance in the work environment, particularly in the direction of a broad definition. Social research has, naturally enough, pointed at factors that can generate stress, psycho-social loads, dissatisfaction, alienation, etc. Such factors can to some extent differ from those commonly emphasized in medical research. Furthermore, social research has contributed to the visibility of work environment problems that in a sense «belong» to other disciplines, by bringing to light conditions detrimental to the health of workers. The established apparatus of society was, at least until recently, not particularly apt at identifying some of the major threats against health in working life, and the use social research has made of self-reported problems – problems and conditions as seen and experienced by those who confront them – made it possible to help bring new issues to light.

To some degree problems uncovered by social research have been taken over by others. Pointing out health risks can, for example, activate medical research and medical remedies. The task of social research has, in other words, been limited. However, there are important areas in working life where the relevance of social research is of more fundamental importance. In these areas, social research must not only identify the problem, it will also have to follow through until the level of specific action is reached and solutions begin to emerge. It is also here that problems begin to emerge. Relatively few factors or conditions in the work environment constitute a problem immediately upon presence. It is often a question of degree or amount, and research then confronts the demand of defining how much people can tolerate. If we believe that short work cycles are a problem, it is demanded that we specify how short in seconds or minutes. Unless the question of «how much» can be answered, the last link towards administrative operationality is lacking. Even if it is a question only of either-or, the traditional strategy demands that research must at least be able to say exactly under what conditions such and such factors generate negative effects. It is within this area that social research seems to fall short.

Partly, one is not able to specify how much, and even where this is not called for, the «contingency theories» that generally emerge when social science tries to state that something functions in this way or that way become so complex that it is hardly practical to use them as a basis for a system of conventional rules.

The result is a lack of cumulative mutual dependence between reform efforts and social research. Research does not lock into publicly initiated reform efforts and is left with the choice of criticizing these efforts from the sideline.

This lack of administratively operational knowledge is not necessarily for lack of trying. Even though terms like positivism and naturalism are ambiguous and difficult to use, it is still perhaps possible to say that a quest for knowledge which can be converted into unequivocal, general rules, demands a «natural science» oriented social research: social research should produce results of the same type as are produced, for intance, by medical research. And there has clearly been a strong tendency in this direction in social research. When a fruitful relationship is still lacking, it is because coincident expectations are not enough, the task to emerge from this coincidence must be viable. And this seems to be the core of the problem. Social and human phenomena cannot be treated «as nature» and social research will consequently not be able to produce threshold limit values, generalizable contingency theories, or whatever might be called for to penetrate a conventional legal-administrative grid (Gustavsen, 1980a).

There exists a tension between the conventional, rule-based strategy on the one hand, and social research on the other. Worth noting is that this tension, quite som time ago, started to make itself felt in other branches of work environment research, for example in medidal research, when some Scandinavian researchers began to take up the limitations of «tolerance research» with its emphasis on defining and establishing threshold limit values. To determine the limits of exposure of a given substance on employees is of course important, and such research must continue. The problem, however, is the context. It is commonly accepted today that threshold limit values are rarely based on absolutely certain knowledge. Most societies and public authorities will, furthermore, be reluctant to issue rules and regulations which, for technological or economic reasons, cannot be implemented. An additional problem exists in that the knowledge upon which such values are built is generally evaluated on the basis of the burden of proof rule described previously in this chapter, according to which positive and rather strong evidence is needed to prohibit, for example, a chemical substance. A substance will hence only be prohibited when it is positively proven that it has harmful effects. Conversely, as long as one is in doubt about the effects, the substance will continue to be used.

Given such problems and difficulties attached to most efforts at establishing unequivocal rules, some medical researchers have questioned the advisability of putting all eggs into this basket. Why not instead develop a mixed strategy, where threshold limit values are used as rough guidelines, but where the essential point is to get a successive lowering of exposure until one is down at levels where no damage can possibly occur? The pursuance of such a policy requires that each enterprise and workplace develop a programme for step-by-step improvement. Such a view is now taken by some of the leading medical researchers in Scandinavia, for example by the head of the Norwegian Institute for Occupational Health, Tor Norseth. In this way, the situation of medical research to some extent starts to resemble that confronted by social research. How to cope with these problems, is a question we will return to in Chapter VIII.

Concluding summary

The use of general, unequivocal and positively founded rules has been the basis for publicly initiated work environment improvement in the industrialized world. Under certain circumstances, such rules fill positive functions. However, there are also limitations and problems inherent in an exclusive reliance on rules:

- Efforts become limited to areas where it is technically possible to generate rules.
- Rules are generally defined as encroachments upon the freedom of people and enterprises, and the tendency is to demand positive proof or documentation of the need before a rule is issued. In situations of uncertainty rules are not issued. Hence, the rule-based approach implies a particular distribution of risk, generally at the expense of the workers.
- The problem of interaction between work environment loads largely falls outside the frame of reference of the traditional approach.
- Public initiation, supervision and follow-up are of critical importance, with a resulting strong pressure on public resources.
- Work environment issues become issues demanding experts and the workers who experience the problems end up in a passive position with few possibilities of influencing their own situation.
- There is little dynamism and development as concerns standards.

Decisions on work environment problems tends to be «ad hoc» decisions, hurriedly taken in the wake of a visit by a labour inspector and in the hope that it will be some time till the next visit.

The administrative practices of such bodies as the Labour Inspection can of course vary even under a rule-based system, but the preference will generally be in the direction of tackling problems that are visible and covered by existing rules. This makes it difficult to develop long-term strategies with respect to more complex problems. Under these conditions, research has a tendency to be limited to «tolerance research», that is to efforts in determining how much employees can safely tolerate of a given substance or process. In the light of these factors, the need to consider basic strategy in relation to improvements in the work environment, emerges as a high priority.

VII. The merger between work environment and participatory democracy

Introduction

In the search for a new strategy to cope with the limitations inherent in the traditional approach to workers' safety and health, a link came to be forged between work environment and industrial democracy. The Work Environment Act can, in principle, be viewed as legislation for participatory democracy within the field of work environment.

The key factor in this merging of ideas about industrial democracy with ideas about improvement of the work environment is the way work is organized. The relevance of work organization for industrial democracy is outlined in Chapter II. The relevance of work organisation for the issue of health will be touched upon below and also in Chapter IX. However, the chief point in this merger is not so much to introduce organization of work as the cause of «another illness» (e.g. stress) as to emphasize its importance as a *key to participation* while participation is at the same time the key to a new approach to work environment development within all fields. In this Chapter some of the main steps of this merger will be spelled out.

Freedom, competence and worker control: ability to cope with work environment loads

Historically, work environment and industrial democracy have given rise to different research traditions. Work environment research has mostly departed from the concept of health, and consequently had medical research as its core element, with chemistry and biology as important supportive disciplines. The factors of possible threat to health have largely been defined as various physical conditions in the workplace, such as noise, draught, or toxic substances. Industrial democracy, on the other hand, has been the domain of social scientists with limited interest in issues of health. The focus has instead been on such issues as, for example, participation in decision-making in the light of variations in technology and organization. To some extent, however, organization of work has been approached from a health perspective, be it physical or mental health, e.g. Baker et al (1969), Langner and Michael (1963), HEW (1973). Of particular importance in the Scandinavian setting have been studies that link poor mental health, psychosomatic disorders, sick leaves, cardiovascular diseases and other characteristics of negative health development to the dimensions of freedom and competence in work, e.g. Bronner and Levi (1969), Bolinder and Ohlstrøm (1971), Sundbom (1971), Ager et al (1975), Frankenhäuser and Gardell (1976), Gardell (1976; 1977; 1980). Of particular importance to practical efforts, has been the research of Gardell and colleagues:

In intensive studies of relatively small samples, methods from social psychology and from physiology have been integrated in efforts at identifying adverse factors in work processes. The concept of stress was the point of departure, as this concept has one foot in the field of medical research and another in the field of psychological and social research (Gardell, 1976; 1977; 1980, Frankenhäuser & Gardell, 1976). It is shown that machine-paced work, characterized by short work cycles and lack of control over the work by the operators, leads to problems of health in both its physiological and social/psychological dimensions. Biological stress reactions and psychological reactions do, in other words, roughly follow each other as well as interact with each other. Through these studies the concept of stress became linked to such work conditions as machine-pacing and monotony; job characteristics that had previously been linked more exclusively to dimensions like alienation and dissatisfaction.

It also became clear that a crucial factor in counteracting the negative effects of problematic work conditions is the *degree of control* the operator can excert over his or her work situation. Under equal conditions with respect to loads and problems, the worker who can to some degree control the work situation in terms of work rhythm, sequences of operations and choice of methods, is less subject to adverse effects than a worker who has to follow fully pre-structured sequences, cycles and methods.

This research demonstrates two interdependent points:

- Firstly, that lack of control over one's own work situation is in itself a work environment problem which can constitute a threat to health.
- Secondly, that the ability of the workers to counteract pressures and generally «live» with difficulties in the work environment without adverse effects, is generally better if they can exercise a reasonable degree of control over their work situation.

When degree of control, of the freedom and competence inherent in the work role, emerge as a critical factor in a work environment context it means that a direct link is made to issues of central importance within an industrial democracy context (Chapter II).

A re-analysis of data from a broad survey in Sweden, (Levnadsnivåundersøkningen) (Johansson, 1971, Karasek, 1978; 1980) has illustrated the same general relationship and further documented the critical importance of the degree of control exercised by workers.

Karasek departs from a framework of which a simplified version is given in Figure 7:

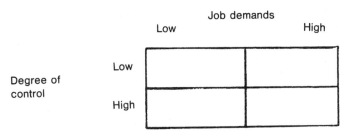

Fig. 7. Job demands and degree of control.

Source: Karasek, 1978; 1980

Jobs falling in the upper left hand quadrant are called passive; jobs in the upper right quadrant are heavy, those in the lower left quadrant are leisurely, and those in the lower right quadrant are active.

In terms of possible negative consequences of work environment conditions, the jobs in the upper right hand quadrant are the most critical ones. Such effects as, for example, depression and exhaustion occur at higher frequencies here than in any of the other quadrants. Individuals in active jobs may confront difficulties but the possibilities of coping without negative consequences are much better. This may be part of the explanation of why people who are commonly believed to be under much stress, like managers and professionals, still tend to come out as groups with (relatively) good health and long life expectancies (Chapter IX).

Job characteristics, work environment and safety work

The studies of Gardell and colleagues bring together the problem of health and the problem of work organization, the focal point being the degree of control exercised by the operator. In a study done at the Work Research Institutes in the middle seventies, the focus was on

133

safety- and health work on enterprise level (Karlsen et al, 1975).

The main purpose of this study was to determine the optimum organizational model for health and safety work at the enterprise level. With the re-organization of safety and health work at the enterprise level as an important part of the emerging work environment reform, this issue was given high priority. The project was designed as a comparative study of enterprises. The selection was undertaken in collaboration with two of the district offices of the Labour Inspection. About one half of the total of 44 enterprises had a reasonably good work environment, as defined by the Labour Inspection, while the other half represented the opposite. The immediate purpose of the study was to determine which factors were decisive in creating good and/or bad work environments.

A number of seemingly obvious questions can be raised about the organization of health- and safety work, and those that lent themselves to testing in this study were taken up. Did, for example, enterprises with a fairly well developed formal safety- and health organization produce better work environments? The study showed that the formal health- and safety apparatus was of limited importance. In line with this, the existence of a safety manager was also of limited importance, the same was the case for the formal allocation of this role, for example in terms of «closeness» to top management. The material was tested for other possible correlations. For example, it would be reasonable to believe that enterprises with a high level of work environment problems would also exhibit increased activity in health and safety work. This study, however, did not support this hypothesis.

The most important conditioning factors, on the basis of this investigation, seemed to be the *resources of the workers.* Worker's resources are made up of two components, one relating to skills or competence and one to organization. A force of skilled workers is in this respect richer in resources than a force of unskilled workers. The organizational component relates to those factors that determine the possibilities for joint action by the workers, the better these possibilities, the greater are the resources of the workers.

The link between workers' resources and results within the field of safety and healt work was established via *workers' activity* with work environment problems. Workers with more resources were found to be more active with work environment issues than workers with fewer resources.

The relevance of workers' activity, is to be found along two dimensions:

– Firstly, a number of problems can only be understood and adequately attacked by those who have a direct experience of the problems and the problem-generating situation.

- Secondly, activity on the part of the workers, will generally bring them to raise work environment issues with management, and thus management resources are also brought to bear on these problems. This does not imply that workers' activity is a necessary condition for management activity. Management can act also on its own, and there were instances where this occurred. Generally, however, management engagement seemed best ensured by an initiative on the part of the workers.

Management committment was of crucial importance with respect to two dimensions:

Firstly, work environment improvements often need investments. There is, in other words, a need for committment of economic resources. This need can vary, and is sometimes overestimated in the debate about work environment problems and the cost of their solutions. Nevertheless, economic support for this work is necessary, and here management control over the economic resources enters the picture.

There is, however, another factor of importance: the committment of human resources, or experts. As it is often overshadowed by economic considerations, it is relevant to underline its importance. A constructive approach to work environment problems requires the integration of these improvements with general developmental work in relation to technology, rationalization and organizational changes. Unless work environment improvements are fully integrated in this way, they will generally fall short of their full potential. It is difficult to achieve meaningful and long-term improvements in «bursts» following infrequent demands for change made by labour inspectors (Gustavsen, 1979c). If work environment considerations are to be taken seriously, the continuous participation of managers and experts as well as workers is essential.

The study also illustrated a further point of importance relative to work environment considerations on the local level and that relates to the degree of control exercised by an individual enterprise or workplace over its own development. If work environment considerations are to play a meningful part in the development of an enterprise, full, or at least partial, control over this development must rest at the enterprise level. This, in turn, depends on two conditions:

- Firstly, that there are options on the level of the enterprise.
- Secondly, that the enterprise has the resources necessary to utilize these options.

135

An enterprise or a workplace without options, or with very few options, is an enterprise which «imports» its production system from outside without exerting any influence on the design of this system. The study indicated, for example, that production units belonging to bigger groups or concerns, that had placed technological development in units far away from the places where the technology was to be used, had a tendency to end up on the more negative side as far as work environment improvements were concerned. Another variant of the same problem exists when there are technological options, but the enterprise is unable to use them because it lacks the necessary internal expertise. This situation is found most typically in certain parts of working life where the technology in use has been considered relatively «non-demanding» from a traditional operational point of view, while it is much more problematic from a work environment perspective. Traditional sawmills and many fish processing plants are of this type; they have very little technical expertise within their own production systems, because the technology has traditionally been considered relatively simple to operate and consequently in little need of engineering competence.

Workers resources are, as mentioned above, the crucial elements for successful health- and safety work at the local level. It has already been mentioned that these resources are based on competence and organizational capacity. As concerns the last factor, it is clear that the extent to which the workers are unionized is of considerable importance. Other conditions being equal, the level of workers resources in non-unionized enterprises will be lower than in unionized ones. Of considerable importance is also to what extent development of workers resources is supported by the surrounding community. Studies (e.g. Sørensen, 1979) show that local communities can differ considerably in their ability to give support to the development of workers resources. This ability can, in turn, depend upon a number of dimensions, such as degree of stability in the population, degree of stratification, and so on. These are dimensions that can only be hinted at; considerable further research is necessary to clarify them.

The study showed, futhermore, that the characteristics of jobs were of crucial importance: A high degree of freedom and competence in work was positively related to workers resources and through this to a better work environment. Hence, freedom and competence in work is of critical importance not only to what the worker can do within his or her specific work role, but also to what relationship each worker can have to such broader issues as work with health- and safety questions on enterprise level.

136

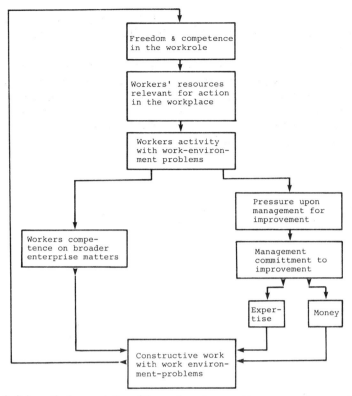

Fig. 8. Schematical presentation of the work environment improvement process (in the version of the positive dependence cycle).

Concluding remarks

The studies mentioned here were not the only ones of importance in this particular process of the merger between ideas derived from the concept of industrial democracy and ideas derived from the concept of work environment. Others could be quoted, and we could trace the threads back to the history of social and to some extent also medical research but such an effort would take us too far afield in this particular connection.

These and other studies did not make it possible to hammer out a «complete» theory and full specifications of action parameters. For that, they were too fragmentary. The fragments made it, however, possible to define certain new action parameters (Chapter VIII).

These studies indicate structures and processes of a relatively high degree of complexity. To simplify them into elementary «models» is an exercise to be performed with the greatest of care and with a number of reservations. Nevertheless, at the end of this chapter it may be useful to summarize some of the major points in a simplified figure (Figure 8).

The figure highlight some elements and links in a picture which is in reality much more complex. It is seen that the picture has important characteristics in common with a general model for industrial democracy where overall enterprise structure and worker influence depend upon workers' activity, which in turn depends upon freedom and competence in work (Chapter II).

VIII. The Work Environment Act of 1977
– Legislation in support of local activity

Introduction

Given the premises sketched in the previous chapters, we have seen that support of local activity emerged as a main strategic goal in the formulation of work environment legislation. No one believed that local activity could be generated by legislation alone. But the legislative framework does constitute one of the conditions hindering or furthering such work. Besides, legislation provides the basis for the operation of various public bodies such as the Labour Inspection. Through its influence on such bodies legislation can also support a particular strategy.

Legislation in support of local activity is not common in modern industrial societies; this is certainly the case for legislation that not only aims at rather simple measures but tries to generate long-term, complex processes. We have mainly come to rely on élites, experts and central solutions to social and technological problems. Experience in designing an alternative type of legislation is therefore limited and, when looked at in retrospect, the Norwegian Work Environment Act falls short of providing a complete answer. However, it contains a number of the principles that are of paramount importance if the goal is to activate local resources.

That the local resources must be activated, is a point of departure which in many ways seems trivial. It is obvious that public resources will never be sufficient to make work environment development a purely public responsibility. Consequently, all reforms in working life stress the responsibility of the parties involved. What is new in the work environment reform is the recognition that it is not *sufficient* to declare local responsibility and activity as the ideal in some general sections of an act, and then proceed to lay the foundations for publicly defined rules and control mechanisms. If local activity is really to be encouraged, there is a need for additional supportive mechanisms. It will not be possible, for example, to get people in the workplace to engage themselves in relation to reforms and changes if their own opinion concerning problems and solutions is not a legitimate basis for change. If, for example, management or external experts maintain an unconditional right to review and change decisions made by the people in the workplace, it is a certainty that the employees will soon discover that it is not worth their while engaging themselves in work environment reform. Consequently, activating local resources implies a more thorough revision of the *balance* between the different parties involved: public authorities, management and the workers. This is one example of a point which needs to be considered, there are others. They all rotate, however, around the need to support local activity, and include the following:

- Priority for work environment issues.
- Selection of relevant standards.
- Emphasis on issues requiring local experience for their settlement.
- A demand for a total evaluation of the work environment.
- Improved legitimacy to the evaluations of those who experience the problems.
- Changes in the requirements of proof or evidence.
- A concept of causality consistent with the needs for practical work.
- New ways of working with work environment problems.
- Work environment improvement as a developmental process.
- The need to consider the content of work.

Below, a brief comment will be made on each of these points. The ideas and principles will be presented in a pure form; we can only briefly go into the question of how these principles are actually expressed in the Act as this would take us too far into issues of legal interpretation. However, it must be mentioned that the legal expression of the various principles is not on all points as clear and unequivocal as, in the light of hindsight, one would have wished. Being one of the persons who took part in the design of this legislation, one of the authors of this book, Bjørn Gustavsen, must to some extent share the blame for a lack of a clear and lucid legal expression of all major principles. The excuse is that the Act was developed under heavy time pressure and that it to some extent pioneered new patterns of legislation in Norway. In this first effort at developing something which in important respects breaks with until then prevailing practices, one would perhaps have had to be more than lucky to emerge with a full-blown expression of new principles. Some additional problems were created by the pressure for a more conventional rule-based approach making itself felt in the legislative process. However, in spite of its shortcomings, it is no doubt that the Act as it stands, together with some of the supplementary guidelines issued afterwards (particularly the guidelines to sect. 14 about the duties of the employer, Order No 326 from the Labour Inspection; not available in English) provides a sufficient legal basis for the development of local activity with work environment problems. In the development of legal principles the issuing of an act is, furthermore, in itself not so much of a definite step as is often presumed. An act must be interpreted, and this interpretation is an ongoing process which lasts as long as the act exists. In later interpretations (e.g. Gustavsen, 1978b, see also Gustavsen, 1977a; 1978a; 1979a; 1980a; 1980b) the emphasis has been on developing and underlining the principles pertaining to local work with work environment issues.

Priority on the work environment considerations

It is fairly obvious that the relative importance attached to work environment issues must be enhanced. Unless these issues are given reasonable priority, no local activity will be possible. The political act of promulgating a new law, plus various of the rules to be found in the Act and in the related regulations, is in itself enough to get work environment issues «on the agenda» in enterprises. It is also quite evident that work environment issues are generally taken seriously in Norway today, even though there are still many exceptions. Safety delegates, shop stewards, safety directors and others need no longer fear a long uphill struggle to have work environment issues seriously discussed in the enterprise.

Minimum standards and the demand for improvement

The Act provides for minimum standards as well as for the improvement of all work environments irrespective of the point of departure. The rule-based approach turns all work environment issues into questions of minimum standards, at least as long as unequivocal rules are insisted upon. To be sure, the conventional approach can be modified by allowing for more open, flexible standards. But this is to move at least some of the way towards an alternative strategy. The new Act lays down minimum requirements, but it is also based on the idea that any work environment should be improved, irrespective of its initial level. Let us imagine that all work environments can be measured against a scale ranging from the best to the worst as in figure 9.

In this extremely simplified illustration the minimum standards define a cut-off point below which conditions may not fall. The demand for improvement does not stop once conditions have attained this

141

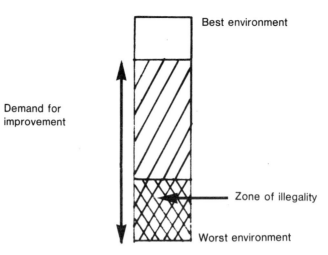

Best environment

Demand for
improvement

Zone of illegality

Worst environment

Fig. 9. Schematical presentation of work environment demands.

level; it still applies to conditions better than the minimum even though they do not constitute an infringement of established limits. The reasons for this provision are as follows:

First, the idea is to make it easier to raise issues and present demands without starting an argument about the «legality» of the existing situation. Such discussions tend to result in employees and management digging in their heels instead of developing efforts to make improvements. It is now possible to demand improvements without having to argue that the existing situation falls short of statutory requirements.

Secondly, and this is perhaps the most important point, between the best and the worst on the scale we have in between situations where it is very difficult to reach a clear opinion on the positive and negative aspects of the environment. Take, for example, a typical office landscape with some noise, the same air and temperature for everybody, a certain level of social pressure, and so on: is this a «good» or a «not so good» environment? It is often difficult to determine, and it is much better to try to improve it than to try to reach a final judgement which will have the agreement of everyone concerned. It is much easier in practice to reach agreement on what would constitute an improvement in a situation than attempt to reach agreement on a precise definition of the «quality» of work environment in a specific instance.

In the above figure it will be seen that the demand for improvement stops some way short of the top. This is because, as we proceed upwards, we eventually come to those jobs or workplaces where there can be little doubt that they are positive in most important respects

142

and where improvements would add very little beyond a waste of society's resources.

The general demand for development is given its most general expression in the concept of «*fullt forsvarlig arbeidsmiljø*» which translated is something like «fully satisfactory work environment (in all respects)». That this is a goal to strive for through developmental work rather than an unconditional requirement valid from the first of July 1977 when the Act went into force, did, however, not emerge clearly from the Act. It was of course impossible to expect that deficient work environments could be made fully satisfactory on July first 1977. In a society where legislation is traditionally expected to lay down requirements and not premises for development, such a mistake is, however, easily made.

Emphasis on issues demanding local experience for their settlement

A basic weakness of the rule-based approach is its lack of ability to come to grips with problems that for their definition and solution require local experience and insight. Hence, conventional workers protection legislation generally gives low priority to issues that need this particular input, in favour of stressing topics that lend themselves to regulation through rules and external experts. If one wants to develop legislation in support of local activity, it would be an advantage to reverse the priorities and *stress* topics where local insights are absolutely necessary and where external solutions can not be developed at all.

To some extent this philosophy has gone into the Norwegian Act. It is seen particularly clearly in section 12 (below) but also in other sections, such as 7 (below) and in the general developmental standard mentioned above. However, the Act also has shortcomings from this point of view. It contains, for example, no section on the issue of physiology or ergonomics, an area of major importance in a work environment context, which is also at the same time dependent upon local acting for improvements. The Act contains, furthermore, parts where a heavy reliance on the rule-based approach emerges. Of particular importance in this respect is chapter X relating to work time, shift systems and overtime. Hence, there are enough conventional rules in the Act to give those in favour of working from such a basis enough to do. Such rules are also, of course, to some extent a necessity. The point is to strike the right balance, and even the Norwegian Act, with its emphasis on developmental norms and local work is perhaps still too heavily biased in the direction of conventional rules. However, the need to base improvements on local development also emerges in some areas where rules and expert-based solutions are possible, for example in a section on toxic substances (8,d) where local improvement programmes are placed in focus instead of an exclusive reliance on the development and sanctioning of general threshold limit values.

A holistic approach

Section 7 of the Act expresses the principle that any given work environment is not to be evaluated only factor by factor but also from a holistic perspective. Such a perspective implies looking for possible interaction between the factors in the work environment. At this point it is worth recalling the study of the hotel- and restaurant workers (Chapter VI). With a few exceptions such as noise, when exposed to the music of bands using electronic amplifiers, these workers did not confront conditions which were in themselves of a major negative character. However, factors that are relatively harmless when evaluated in isolation, can unite in the generation of an environment which puts fairly heavy loads upon the workers.

The need to apply a total or holistic perspective has emerged along with the increasing importance of ecological thinking. An ecological frame of reference stresses the interplay and interdependencies between the elements and the wholeness of the situation. Emerging in the environmental debate as a key to the understanding of the impact of pesticides on animal life (e.g. Carson, 1962) this frame of reference has become more common in relation to other issues, including the internal environment of the workplace. It was, for example, stressed in a series of reports issued by a Danish work group on work environment issues (Arbejdsmiljøgruppen af 1972).

The holistic approach to work environments is not easily applied under a conventional rule-based strategy and conventional approaches to the questions of evidence and legitimation. Hence, changes are called for also within these areas.

Improved legitimacy of the experiences and evaluations of those who «have» the problems

The right to define problems and decide on solutions can in principle rest with one or more of three instances: Those who «experience» the problems, generally the workers, with management or with external authorities such as the Labour Inspection or public research institutes. A strategy for work environment reform emphasising local work must hence distribute «the right to decide» between these instances in a way which is optimal from the point of view of generating local activity.

The point of departure must be that the right to decide rests with those who experience the problems. This must hold not only in relation to management but also in relation to external authorities. However, it is also necessary to consider such points as the need to integrate development of the work environment with the general technological and organizational development of the enterprise, issues that generally rest with management, albeit with some modifications due to a certain degree of employee participation having been introduced. Hence, the issue of the right to decide can not be settled by drawing up a simple demarcation line between management and the workers, giving management the right to decide on issues pertaining to, for example, technological development as following from the ordinary economic goals of the enterprise, while the workers decide on the same issues from a work environment perspective. The considerations must instead be brought together in one decision making process. As concerns the relationship to external bodies, such as the Labour Inspection, it must be remembered that public interference might be necessary if the rights of the workers are to be protected with sufficient strength. One can, furthermore, not always presume that the workers will automatically pursue health- and safety interests when, for example, confronted with the need to make as much money as possible out of a piece-rate wage system. In this fairly complex situation a legal system must be developed that considers all these and other aspects without departing from the principle that the right to decide must as far as possible rest with those who experience the problem situation by living and working in it.

What solutions are developed to this problem in the Norwegian Act and its supplementary material, will emerge from later sections in this chapter. In principle, the main vehicle is *the work environment improvement programme* on the enterprise level. Each enterprise is under the obligation to generate a programme for systematic improvement over a reasonable time. The basis for this programme is to be a mapping of problems with the employees taking an active part in the process. As a corollary to this right to define problems, the employees must, however, share the responsibility for assigning priorities, and for developing a programme for step-by-step improvements. Such programmes can be demanded by the Labour Inspection if the enterprise does not develop a programme by itself. Programmes are reviewed by the Labour Inspection, thereby ensuring that public considerations enter the picture, if this is found to be necessary.

Shifting the burden of proof

Section 8 (d) of the new Act provides that « . . . pollution in the form of dust, smoke, gas, vapours, unpleasant odours and radiation is to be avoided, unless it is known that the pollution cannot have any adverse effects upon the employees». This is just one of a number of provisions that aim at shifting the burden of proof. Traditionally, in order to ban the use of a particular chemical in the workplace, it had to be proven that the chemical in fact *had* negative consequences. As long as no such proof was available, the use of the substance was generally allowed. Given the great complexity of many workplace situations and the rapid rate of change in production processes, it is, however, very difficult to carry out the investigations necessary to clarify each new issue as it arises. This is one of the reasons why it was deemed necessary to change the requirements regarding the burden of proof, so as to allow more developmental activity on work environment problems and quicker adaptation to new conditions. A further reason for the change was that even though research might have been done on a particular issue, its results might not be easily accessible and might be difficult to interpret. Work environment activity at the enterprise level should not be made too dependent upon the ability to find one's way about the scientific journals.

The point is, however, not primarily to introduce a new burden of proof rule to be applied unconditionally in all instances. This can in fact be done within the framework of a conventional rule based approach through issuing a general rule prohibiting everything unless it is proven that negative effects can not occur. The problem here is that such a rule would lead to a large number of plant closures and workers would consequently exchange work environment problems for unemployment problems. Any *general* burden of proof rule, in whatever direction it may go, will be associated with major negative consequences. The critical issue is really who is to make the decisions. It seems reasonable to put the workers themselves in focus here, letting them excert influence over the choice between work environment considerations and security of employment, to the extent that such choices have to be made. Hence, what is needed is burden of proof rules that make it possible and legitimate to make these decisions on the basis of information available to the workers, their choice should not be what expert to believe in.

Many supporters of workers' rights will say that workers should never be forced to chose between health and employment, the right to a hazard free work environment should be unconditional. In this these authors wholeheartedly agree. However, there is no society

146

known to these authors that has gone to the point of introducing a *general* rule giving the workers the unconditional right to refuse any work to which the worker himself find that any hazard whatsoever may be attached while the right to employment is maintained. Even the societies that claim to have gone farthest in the protection of the workers have dissolved the issue of worker protection into a number of specific rules, countless technicalities and measurement demands. Such a general rule would not have been politically possible in Norway in the middle seventies, nor, for that matter, today. It should, however, be possible to let the workers excert influence over these choices as long as the workers are generally well organized, have the right to decide on the basis of evidence directly accessible to them, are backed by a full employment policy from the government, and by the possibilities of special loans and other forms of publicly financed supports to work environment improvements which will go far towards pushing the real choice between employment and environment into the realm of relatively marginal situations not too often encountered. These conditions are generally present in Norway. Section 8 d can be seen to have its main function in underlining the necessity of developing a local strategy for the step-by-step reduction of exposures until one eventually reaches a level where safety is complete and unconditional. It must also be added that the rights of the Labour Inspection to demand, for example, plant closures are broader than before, as the Labour Inspection can also utilize the new burden of proof rules and hence need not establish the same documentation for such decisions as they previously had to do.

New concepts of causality

Scientists use various concepts of causality. In the field of work environment problems, however, the traditional one dating from John Stuart Mill has been of great importance. This concept says that for x to be defined as a cause of y, it must be demonstrated that y would not have happened if x had not occurred. But in highly complex situations, where long-term composite effects of a number of possible conditions are the rule rather than the exception, it is clear that such a criterion of causality often leads to endless discussions and to demands for «more research». By contrast, in order to get anything practical done about a work environment problem, *all* the factors that could *possibly* contribute to it as relevant causes have to be considered whatever future research may subsequently show to be the actual cause or causes. If all the factors cannot be tackled simultaneously, the workers must have an important say in deciding which to tackle first and which to leave until later.

To find an adequate legal expression of this idea is another example of a task not easily solved. The Norwegian Act is not absolutely clear on this point, and its expression in the Act depends upon some degree of interpretation (Gustavsen, 1978b).

New ways of tackling work environment problems

According to the «classical» rule based model, work environment improvements will come about as a result of «something wrong» being discovered, for example, by the Labour Inspection. As a labour inspection bound by a rule-based approach will often deal only with defects which are so apparent that they can be seen during a relatively short visit, and be referred to general rules and made the object of specific remedies, it is obvious that the classical model does not offer an adequate basis for bringing about broader and more thoroughgoing changes. In contrast, the new Norwegian Act and the regulations issued under it require the process to start with an over-all evaluation of the total situation by those working in the enterprise, who have to ask themselves: What problems do we appear to have, and in what order should we try to solve them? The aim is to develop a consensus within the enterprise and to make plans accordingly. If consensus can not be reached, conflicts can be settled by voting in the work environment committee (below) or by submitting the issue to the Labour Inspection. A plan must be flexible and subject to change in the light of experience gathered in the course of its execution, for example if it is found that some problems that were believed to be important are not so important, while other issues emerge as more urgent. It is essential that the workers take part in making these evaluations and formulating these plans.

These points are expressed in guidelines to sect. 14 of the Act, developed jointly by the Ministry of Labour, the Labour Inspection and the Work Research Institutes (Order No 326 from the Directorate of Labour Inspection, available only in Norwegian).

A learning process

Work environment improvement is a step-by-step developmental process, based on feedback and learning. The classical improvement model is a simple two-step one: a shortcoming is «discovered» and related to an existing rule, and corrective measures are specified and put into force. This approach is feasible only in the case of relatively sim-

148

ple issues concerning technical details. More comprehensive improvement of the total work environment can only be achieved, like any other complex goal, in a step-by-step fashion involving systematic evaluations, feedback and learning. This point is expressed primarily in the guidelines to sect. 14.

Rules on the organization of work

The part of the Norwegian Work Environment Act which has perhaps attracted most attention and discussion is section 12 which deals with the way work is organized. To the best of our knowledge, the Norwegian Act is the first of its kind to contain such rules. The major part of the section reads as follows:

§12
Planning the work

1. General requirements
Technology, organization of the work, working hours and wage systems shall be set up so that the employees are not exposed to undesirable physical or mental strain and so that their possibilities of displaying caution and observing safety measures are not impaired.

Conditions shall be arranged so that employees are afforded reasonable opportunity for professional and personal development through their work.

2. Arrangement of work
The individual employee's opportunity for self-determination and professional responsibility shall be taken into consideration when planning and arranging the work.

Effort shall be made to avoid undiversified, repetitive work and work that is governed by machine or assembly line in such a manner that the employees themselves are prevented from varying the speed of the work.

Otherwise efforts shall be made to arrange the work so as to provide possibilities for variation and for contact with others, for connection between individual job assignments, and for employees to keep themselves informed about production requirements and results.

3. Control and planning systems.
The employees and their elected union representatives shall be kept informed about the systems employed for planning and effecting the work, and about planned changes in such systems. They shall be given the training necessary to enable them to learn these systems, and they shall take part in planning them.

4. Work involving safety hazards.
a) Performance premium wage systems shall not be employed for work where this may materially affect safety.
b) . . .
(The rest of the section deals with issues not directly related to the organization of work.)

This section is treated extensively in publications from the Work Research Institutes (e.g. Gustavsen & Seierstad, 1977; Gustavsen 1978b; for English language publications the reader can be referred to Gustavsen, 1977a; 1978a; 1979a; 1980b).

The chief reason *why* this section came into the Act, has already been presented and discussed: To cope with all work environment problems, physical ones included, those concerned − the workers themselves − must have an active relationship to the problems and the situation they confront. Such an active relationship emerged as the key factor in constructive work with work environment problems (Chapter VII). It emerged, furthermore, that the possibilities for such an active relationship were dependent upon the degree of freedom and competence in work. Hence, a section on organization of work emerged as critical in the Work Environment Act, because this topic is the key to a successful approach also to other issues (Gustavsen, 1980b).

The section also fulfills other functions. From descriptive studies (e.g. Gardell, 1976; Frankenhäuser & Gardell, 1976) we know that there is a positive relationship between degree of control over the work situation and possibilities for withstanding work environment loads. Under equal conditions, people with more freedom and competence in their work are better able to withstand loads than people whose work behaviour is largely structured by outside forces. As we also know that, for example, stress has negative consequences on health and welfare (Bolinder & Ohlstrøm, 1971; Bronner & Levi, 1969; Ager et al., 1975; Frankenhäuser & Gardell, 1976), the degree of control becomes directly related to the concept of health.

In this way section 12 also plays a role as part of the system of rules that establishes substantive protection against illness and reduction in welfare due to loads and problems in the workplace. This second function overlaps in practice with the first function of section 12. The reason why jobs with freedom and competence function as a bulwark against loads and problems is precisely because they allow the operator to have an active relationship to his or her problems.

The third consideration relates to accidents, and emerges from much the same arguments as the other two. It is commonly believed today that «human mistakes» account for the great majority of accidents occuring in industry and related fields (e.g. in atomic power plants, to take an example of topical interest). This may be true from a certain point of view. The question is, however, what lies behind these «human mistakes». An increasing number of studies (e.g. Powell et al., 1971; Gardell, 1976; Frankenhäuser & Gardell, 1976) show that the possibilities for correct behaviour are to a large extent dependent upon the organization of work, supervision, and other conditions pertinent to the work situation. The ability to develop and maintain the necessary alertness is, for example, dependent upon the avoidance of overstimulation as well as understimulation (Frankenhäuser & Gardell, 1976) and this, again, is dependent upon the job providing for a reasonable degree of variation, possibilities for making judgements, taking initiatives, and so on. The link between accidents, alertness and organization of work is a further reason for section 12.

The last specific consideration was the need to be able to approach work environment problems through the use of an assortment of means or parameters in integration with each other. To take an example: the reduction of long term negative effects of one-sided work postures is a major goal in the improvement of work environment, as this is perhaps the most widespread single work environment problem (Central Bureau of Statistics, 1977). One way of attacking this problem is to change, for example, workbenches, chairs and so on, in the direction of making the equipment more flexible and easily adjustable and to allow the operators the chance of changing work posture throughout the workday, as no single posture is perfect in itself. However, if such changes are made, their effect will depend upon what support they get with respect to the wage system, supervisory practices, the possibilities for rotating jobs etc. Consequently, to really be able to do something to reduce physiological problems, one might have to attack a whole battery of aspects. To do this, one needs a reasonable array of means. Studies made at the Work Research Institutes (e.g. Ødegaard, 1979) indicate that work organization interferes with a number of other work environment problems. In a shipbuilding yard, such things as exposure to cold and noise depend on how long people have to stay in exposed areas, and this is often a function of production planning and work organization. An operator might be sitting on the top of a superstructure for an unnecessary length of time on a midwinter day waiting for parts that do not arrive, and so on. To deal with these contributory factors there is a need for a special section on work organization which legitimizes the use of means taken from this field as well as giving some degree of direction to these means.

To sum up, section 12 of the Work Environment Act is founded on the following considerations:
- The need to generate employee activity in relation to all work environment issues.
- Achievement of protection against certain types of work environment loads.
- Improvement of safety in the workplace through improvement of the conditions pertinent to alertness.
- The need to be able to use planning and organization of work as a systematic parameter when different types of work environment problems are to be solved.

The formal work environment organization on enterprise level

Improvement of the work environment is a task for the whole organization. A main point of the new legislation is to stress this and get away from work environment issues as something to be dealt with solely by spesialists, such as the safety manager (if such a role exist at all – it is generally not compulsory in Norway) and the safety delegates. There is however, a need for some special roles and bodies within the work environment field and such bodies are established by the Act. It also allocates responsibilities with some of the ordinary organizational units. In this section we will take a brief look at the structure of roles and bodies that are the bearers of special responsibilities. The more detailed rules pertaining to them are given in Appendix.

In brief, the formal system can be expressed as in Figure 10.

To start with the *employer* the duties are primarily defined in sect. 14 * of the Act (Appendix). Briefly, the employer carries the main responsibility according to the Act. To ensure that this responsibility is lived up to, various more specific considerations must be taken, and these are stated in sect. 14 and in a special set of guidelines pertaining to this section. (Order No. 326 from the Labour Inspection, not available in English translation).

The responsibility of the employer is generally carried out by top management. There are certain legal questions emerging concerning the right to delegate tasks and duties, a topic we can not take up for closer analysis here. In principle, there are limitations on this right. These limitations are given to ensure that a split does not emerge between top management decisions on the one hand and work environment considerations on the other. To the extent that such a split occurs, it will weaken the work environment considerations, as these will not be an integral part of the ordinary development of the enter-

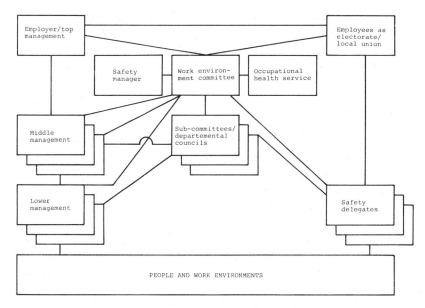

Fig. 10. Schematical presentation of the formal health- and safety organization on enterprise level. The actual legal relationships are much more complex than actually reflected in this figure. Some of the bodies, as for example the safety manager, can also have a varying position. Hence, this is an example rather than a complete presentation of possibilities.

prise. This does not, however, mean that top management itself has to give consideration to all the specifics and details of work environment issues.

Where the Act explicitly uses the term «employer», the interpretation of this term relates specifically to the relevant budget authority, that is: the right to decide on those investments or other general resource allocations which are called for in relation to a given issue. The concept of employer is hence to some extent relative, its definition must depend upon what issues are under discussion.

Safety manager is a role now found in a number of the middle sized and larger organizations in Norway. The legal status of this role is relatively weak, as it is barely mentioned in the Work Environment Act, as one of the roles under the heading of «safety and health personnel». Safety manager is a role in transition. Traditionally, the safety manager has been a part of the ordinary managerial structure, and generally held a staff position somewhere in the vicinity of top- or middle management. However, the rules found in the Act, now places the safety manager among the safety and health personnel, who, according to sect. 30, point 3 «shall have a free and independent position

153

as regards work environment matters». Hence, the safety manager is no longer a role which is completely instrumental in relation to top management, but a role which has some degree of independent professional responsibility. This aspect is underlined by the fact that the Labour Inspection has recently proposed a set of prescriptions concerning this role. Such prescriptions will underline the independent position of the safety manager and contribute to the professionalisation of this role. There is also in existence in Norway a safety managers' association, which at the moment has 250 members and is still growing. It encompasses safety managers from private as well as public organisations; the chairman at the time this is written is, by the way). As a collectivity the employees carry no specific legal obligations

The counterpart of top management is the *employees as a collectivity, or an electorate*, to some extent as represented by the *local union(s)*. As such a collectivity the employees represent «the other party». (Cf. Chapter I on the general patterns of labour relations in Norway.) As a collectivity the employees carry no specific legal obligations according to the Act, but they are the bearers of certain rights. The employees carry legal obligations as individuals, as parts of larger units of work organization, or as union members to the extent that there are relevant agreements.

One of the chief tasks of the employees as a collectivity is to elect people to fill certain roles, for example in the *work environment committee*. Such a committee is compulsory in any company employing at least fifty persons, it can be demanded by one of the parties if there are at least twenty persons employed, and the Labour Inspection can order the creation of such a committee in any organisation. (Sect. 23, see Appendix). The committee is to have an equal representation from management and the employees and a rotating chairmanship. As the chairman's vote is decisive in cases of fifty-fifty splits, the parties each hold the majority vote half of the time.

The main task of the work environment committee emerges more clearly from supplementary material issued after the Act, than it does in the Act itself. Its chief task is linked to the programmes for work environment improvement mentioned above, to which we will return in somewhat greater detail below. The work environment committee is designed to be the body where the threads and strands of local work with work environment issues and problems run together. It is designed not so much to curtail the rights of management, as to relieve management of some of those duties which top management may find difficult to handle. One of these duties is to assign priorities to work environment problems when developing a programme for improvement. As we have touched upon previously, the employees now have broad rights to take part in the definition of problems, and this can lead to a broad range of problems being brought to light as part of a work environment improvement programme (this point will be illustrated by the first case study to be presented below). As a corollary to this right to decide, the employees must, however, be prepared to share the responsibility for the settlement of priorities.

The work environment committee is located close to top management. The idea was to make it into a «high level» body working in close contact with the chief decision making bodies of the organization. In order not to create too much of a distance between the committee and the rank and file, the work environment committee can establish sub-committees. Another possibility, which will emerge from the Berger Langmoen case below, is to link the work environment apparatus to the system of joint committees developed in the Basic Agreement. Joint employee-management committees, or so-called production committees, were developed after the Second World War, a system which was revised and expanded in a revision of the Basic Agreement in the latter sixties. There is one general committee on company or organization level and in addition to this there are committees in the various departments. It is particularly the committees on departmental level that in many organizations have become actively involved with work environment problems.

The Act demands that top management is to participate in the work environment committee, or, to phrase the point differently, that at least one of the management representatives has top management authority. This demand is created by the need to avoid later revisions and changes of the decisions taken or agreed to by management representatives in the committee.

If an Occupational Health Service is present in the company, this service is to be represented in the work environment committee and take part in its meetings. The representative(s) of this service have, however, only consultative status without voting rights. The service is treated in the Act section 30, and to some extent also in sect. 22 (Appendix).

Safety delegates are treated in sections 25 – 27 (Appendix). In workplaces with five or more employees it is obligatory to elect a safety delegate.

If there is more than one safety delegate, one of them is to take care of coordination. In actual practice, this role is called head safety delegate.

According to a study done at the Work Research Institutes (Karlsen et al., 1975, see chapter VII) the safety delegate can, in principle, play three different types of roles:

- As a «neutral» expert.
- As part of management's health- and safety apparatus.
- As an employee representative.

All three versions could be found in Norwegian workplaces in the middle seventies. To some extent under the influence of the study of the WRI, which stressed the constructive importance of employee engagement in relation to work environment issues, it was decided to stress the «shop steward» aspect of the role of the safety delegate when the new Act was prepared. Sect. 26, point 1, first sentence (Appendix) says that «safety delegates shall safeguard the interests of the employees in matters relating to the work environment». However, as the safety delegates function within a particular context – the Work Environment Act – there will clearly be elements also of the two other roles present. The safety delegates are not only «pure bargainers», acting on behalf of employees, they also have to abide by the Act.

The head safety delegate is now generally a member of the local union board, as well as of the work environment committee. His or her membership in the local union board has become more common after the new Act came into force, reflecting the increased priority given to this section within union work.

Section 16 outlines the duties for employees in general, while subsection 2 deals with employees with «middle» or «low» level managerial responsibilities. Generally, middle and lower level management act on the basis of delegation from top management and not on the basis of rights and duties directly defined in the Act.

The development of a work environment improvement programme – the case of Berger Langmoen A/S

In describing the application of broad principles, as contained in the Work Environment Act, to actual situations at the enterprise and local level, we will now turn to case studies. The first study (based on Ryste, Seierstad & Ramberg, 1979) illustrates the development of a work environment programme, while the second study relates more specifically to the organization of work (section 12 of the Act).

Berger Langmoen A/S is a wood processing company, employing about 950 people. The product range is relatively broad, encompassing wall panelling, ready-made parquet floors, fibreboards, other prefabricated elements for the building industry, and ordinary boards, planks and other standard building materials. Generally, the production process starts with a common input – timber – and then branches off into a number of different processes. The factories are located in Brumunddal, on the shore of Norway's biggest lake, Mjøsa, approximately 150 kilometers north of Oslo.

The initiative

The way the project in Berger Langmoen came about, illustrates a project model which has become common in later years: initiative and central control from a national union, in combination with union-management collaboration on enterprise level. In this case the initiative emerged from the Building Workers Union, which wanted to gain experience in the application of the new Work Environment Act. In 1977, just before the Act went into force, the union approached the Work Research Institutes, and asked for professional assistance in a project. Contact was then established with Berger Langmoen, a company where the employees are organized in the Building Workers Union. On company level a union-management project group was established while centrally the project was based on collaboration between the Work Research Institutes and the national union. In actual practice one of the full-time officials of the union followed the project from start to finish. Such a project model is important since there is a need among unions to utilize research to further their aims and interests, while it is at the same time necessary to establish a relationship to management to be able to work with programmes of development in specific companies.

The chief purpose of the project

The main idea behind the project was to concretize the ideas of the Work Environment Act, particularly as it relates to work environment programmes. Hence, the case illustrates what can be called «the normal approach to work environment issues» under the new Act.

The main steps in the development of a work environment programme, are the following:

Organization: This element is described above. Let it be repeated that while the special bodies and roles such as the work environment committee, have special responsibilities in the context of work environment problems, the main organization for improvement of the work environment consists of all the elements of the ordinary enterprise organization. Special organizational units set up for the purpose of dealing with work environment issues must, furthermore, not be limited to those units specifically mentioned in the Act. The use of, for example, project groups to deal with specific issues will often have to be considered, together with a number of other organizational parameters (Gustavsen, Seierstad og Ebeltoft, 1978).

Education and training: This can take on various forms. Of major importance in Norway has been a basic forty hour course aimed at all persons who have any special role within the work environment area, such as work environment committee members and safety delegates. By the summer of 1980 about 150 000 people have gone through this course, which amounts to almost 10 percent of all employees.

Mapping: The next step is to find out what problems one confronts on the level of the individual organization and workplace. The guidelines stress the need to involve the employees actively in this process, and suggests various ways of doing this.

Organization of problems and settling of priorities: The mapping process can bring a number of problems to the surface. These problems need to be organized and priorities must be made concerning how to deal with them.

The development of a plan for improving the work environment.

Execution of the plan.

Feedback: Work with work environment problems is to be a continuous learning process, where definition of problems and plans for dealing with them are continuously revised in the light of practical experience.

Organization

The ordinary work environment roles and bodies were already present when the project in Berger Langmoen started. At the time of the start of the project, the managing director himself became a member of the work environment committee. The managing director is also one of the owners of the company.

The gap between a relatively high level work environment committee on the one hand, and the grass roots on the other, was filled by using the agreement-based departmental committees, and not by the establishment of work environment sub committees.

Berger Langmoen had a very limited occupational health service when the project started. It was decided to develop this service and the Work Research Institutes provided professional assistance for this purpose. A researcher with medical background made a study of con-

158

ditions and problems in the enterprise, and recommended specific steps for the development of the service which were subsequently acted upon.

Education and training

At the time the project began, the forty hour basic training course, mentioned above, was being implemented. Apart from this initial training, education in this project can be defined as learning through experience. By coming to terms with practical work and problems the employees were assisted by the researchers.

Mapping of problems

Mobilizing resources for improvement of the work environment, presupposes some ideas about what problems to attack. Hence, a mapping of the situation as it is, becomes necessary. Such a mapping has to be a compromise between different considerations. It should, of course, be as detailed and correct as possible. On the other hand, it is of major importance not to be stuck with a mapping process without end. This can easily happen, as many work environment problems are highly complex and difficult to describe and evaluate. The point is to arrive at a basis for practical work which is as solid as possible, but which is also open, in the realization that a number of issues can emerge in a new light as work proceeds and one starts to learn from experience.

Berger Langmoen has a number of work environment problems well known in the wood processing industry, such as noise, vibration, air pollution (e.g. sawdust) and temperature (relatively much of the work is done out of doors or in unheated production rooms). Such problems have a strong «physical gestalt» and are relatively easy to see. There are, however, other problems present, such as problems emerging from one-sided, repetitive work.

It was decided to let the departmental committees organize this mapping process. Using these committees ensured an anchoring in a reasonably general body that could perform overviews and see broader lines, without going so high up as to risk loosing contact with the rank and file.

The process of isolating and defining problems had various elements. The basic forty hours course to some extent includes an analysis of the workplace and mapping of problems. These data were used as a point of departure. Emphasis was put on establishing direct contact with all workers to elicit their points of view. These contacts

159

were, according to circumstances, taken by various people, ranging from management representatives to safety delegates and union representatives («shop stewards»). The general experience from this phase was that the safety delegates and shop stewards seemed to have the best possibilities for establishing open contacts to the workers, and hence to learn their real opinions.

Together with the mapping much discussion took place among the workers about work environment issues. This is a very important part of the total process, as insight into the problems presupposes a consciousness-generating process and such a process needs time and dialogue (these needs constitute, by the way, some of the chief arguments against the use of questionnaires in this type of process (Gustavsen, 1980c)).

The researchers largely played the role of stimulating the discussions. Generally, the researchers showed a very «low profile» in the sense that they did not want to play a leading role in the definition of problems. The mapping process resulted in a list of 350 to 400 different problems.

Structuring and priorities

Such a large number of problems initially constitute a disorganized mass. If the problems are attacked one by one in a haphazard sequence, the results will be limited and the improvement process unneccesarily lengthy. Hence, the problems need to be ordered and priorities assigned to them. The need to assign priorities emerge from various reasons: One of the chief ones is the need to bring order and method into the solution process and to receive the benefits from looking at issues in connection with each other. Another reason has to do with the participation of the employees. The employees have the right to influence the definition of problems. As a corollary to this they must, however, also share the responsibility for priorities and action programmes.

In Berger Langmoen the issues were grouped according to various criteria. One of these related to the extent to which issues could be:
- handled within each department without any need for additional investments,
- handled by the company's own service- and maintainance units with or without additional investments,
- handled by the company in collaboration with external help and requiring additional investements.

This way of grouping issues is of relevance for various reasons. Of particular imprtance is the need to get to work on some issues without delay. When people have contributed to a mapping of problems they should not be exposed to a long period of waiting while the issues are treated in various higher level line and staff bodies. This has a tendency to kiil the interest and engagement generated by the mapping process. Hence, it is necessary to sort out issues that can be dealt with immediately on the local level.

Programme

The programme for improvement of the work environment partly followed from the distinctions mentioned above. In relation to the third level issues in need of a more comprehensive analysis and long-term planning, the work environment committee played the central role. In the autumn of 1977 it was possible to launch a programme pertaining also to these issues, covering thirteen of the more important points which had emerged. Of these, eight had to do with noise, and two with air pollution.

The action programme also involved physiological as well as psycho-social problems emerging from machine-bound, one-sided work. In relation to these issues it was decided to start a development programme. Altogether, however, the problems following from noise and pollution were found to be the most pressing ones and hence in need of being dealt with quickly. There is, however, a link between such issues as noise on the one hand and psycho-social ones on the other. Noise can, for example, function in hindrance of contacts between people and generally contribute to stress and other negative experiences in the workplace. When priority was given to noise abatement, considerations of this type played a role.

Execution of the programme

When an improvement programme is to be converted into concrete efforts and practice, two points are particularly important:
- actively engaging the workers, those who experience the problems,
- maintaining openness and flexibility, making it possible to learn from what one does so as to be able to revise mappings and plans and over time develop a more and more adequate understanding of the work environment and of how to deal with it. Ultimately, such an understanding can only be developed through praxis.

In Berger Langmoen various mechanisms have been used to achieve these aims:

As mentioned above, a number of issues were immediately brought

161

back to the local level for action. Here the employees have taken part in the development, both directly on the shop floor as well as via representatives in the departmental committees.

The employees were participating in project groups set up for the purpose of developing new installations. It is generally of importance to see that the «organization for improvement of the work environment» also includes such units as project groups, and not only bodies like the work environment committee (Gustavsen, Seierstad & Ebeltoft, 1978).

Where direct employee participation is not possible, issues are dealt with in bodies where the employees are represented on a parity basis.

The local union is actively engaged in all work environment issues.

To support the possibilities for participation from the employees, a number of channels are used to keep people informed. Union officials and safety delegates are actively engaged in this process, in addition to the ordinary administrative channels. A factory newsletter carries all relevant information. In all departments, the results of the mapping are set up in the form of lists which are posted on a wall and information about what happens in relation to each and every problem is given on these lists, making it possible for everybody to keep track of developments throughout the enterprise.

By the autumn of 1978, one year after the programme had started, an inventory of achievements was made, showing that 76 percent of the smaller problems, 48 percent of the medium ones and 18 percent of the larger ones were either being dealt with or had already been corrected.

Part of the improvement programme pertained to the organization of work. The prime method applied here was job rotation. The reasons for increased use of job rotation are partly to be sought in the psycho-social field and partly in the physiological field. One-sided, monotonous work, of which there is quite a lot in this type of production process, produces effects in both of these categories. Job rotation had to some extent been introduced before the project started, but has now been expanded, to encompass the majority of workers in the main departments. It is necessary to stress that the system of job rotation was carried through with the active participation of the employees, and not as something forced on them from outside because «it is good for you». Rotation requires the active support of the workers involved, individually as well as collectively.

162

Using the work environment act sect. 12:
The letter department, Oslo Post-terminal

The initiative

In the early seventies, a new post-terminal was built in Oslo, to go into operation in 1975. The letter department handles and sorts all incoming and outgoing mail. While Oslo has about ten percent of Norway's population, about fifty percent of all mail goes in and out of Oslo, indicating that the volume of work is fairly large in the Oslo-terminal. The letter department employs about 1300 people distributed over three shifts. It occupies one floor of the terminal building and is structured as one single «landscape» of approximately 6000 square meters.

Among the people working in the postal services in the Oslo area the expectations towards the new terminal were great. The terminal was to provide for spacious and bright working conditions, and it would contain more advanced technological resources than what was previously available. However, when the new terminal was opened, many people seem to have experienced acute disappointment. This led to unrest among the employees. It was, however, not easy to pinpoint the problems experienced by the employees. The new Work Environment Act made it possible for the Labour Inspection to issue demands for clarification and analysis of work environments, and such a demand was issued concerning the new terminal. The Work Research Institutes were asked to provide professional assistance in this analysis. (The description to be given here is based on Gustavsen, 1980g).

When this project started the safety delegates at the new terminal had already gone through a forty hour basic course on work environment issues and had begun the process of registering emerging problems.

They had focussed mainly on physical problems like noise and temperature. In the first meeting between the Work Environment Committee and the researchers, the latter started probing for broader issues, like the degree of mechanisation that had taken place, and the extent to which employees experienced difficulties in meeting work loads. The employee representatives on the committee responded to this immediately and in a few minutes the discussion moved to the psychological and social aspects of work. While these dimensions had not surfaced earlier, it took very little initiative to bring them to the surface. At that point it was decided to continue the analysis in the context of the Work Environment Act, Section 12.

163

Sect. 12 and mapping of problems

Let us briefly repeat the legal framework:
- The Act makes the organization of work and related problems into legitimate work environment issues.
- The Act contains some standards and guidelines, but not an absolutely fixed set of prescriptions.
- In dealing with these issues on the local level it is necessary to seek the active participation of those who experience the problems from «inside», as external evaluations can not generate a complete set of premises for evaluations and decisions.

In designing a strategy on the basis of sect. 12 there are, however, options. One can stay fairly close to the text of the Act and try to develop and use criteria that follows rather directly from the legal text. In some instances this will be preferable. In other instances it is necessary to seek a point of departure less directly linked to the Act, and depending more on the concrete work experiences already present in the system. Staying within the broad frame of reference contained in sect. 12 this last course was decided on in the letter department. In this connection it must be remembered that for improvement to be done, it is not necessary to document that existing conditions are in conflict with general rules or standards. The extistence of problems and the identification of problem-generating factors is a sufficient reason for the change-process to be initiated.

As management and the employee representatives in the letter department agreed that the developmental standard was to apply to the terminal, an analysis based on existing experience in the system was used.

It was mentioned that the department employs about 1300 persons. The turnover is relatively high. It was, at the same time, felt that the fact that the analysis had come about because of a demand from the Labour Inspection meant that it had to be done within certain time limits. These points considered, it was decided to base the analysis on the safety delegates, of which there are about thirty in the department. This meant refraining from involving each individual employee directly. The safety delegates have, on the other hand, a legally defined responsibility for being informed about the working conditions of those they represent. They were, furthermore, asked to make contact with the constituency to the extent that they felt it necessary to complete the evaluation.

Departing from existing experience meant that one had to depart from criteria inherent in this experience. The process began in a meet-

ing with the safety delegates. At the first of these meeting, the following questions were raised:
- To what extent are there jobs in the letter department that are generally considered to be (relatively) good and to what extent are
  there jobs considered to be (relatively) bad?
- If there are such differences, what criteria do you use to distinguish between them?

The problems were discussed in two consecutive meetings. General
agreement was reached on a list of such criteria, which emerges from
Table 3.

From the table it will be seen that the criteria which emerged are
aspects of (work) situations, rather than characteristics of total work
roles. This change was, however, necessary.

On the basis of these criteria, a simple questionnaire was compiled,
which was to guide the safety delegates in the gathering of the data.
The safety delegates decided themselves to base the questionnaire on
simple either -or categories and to avoid graded responses.

Table 3. The safety delegates' evaluation of work in the letter department: negative characteristics of work ordered from highest to lowest
frequency.

Negative characteristics of work situation	Frequency
Enforced job rotation decided on an ad hoc basis by supervisors	17
Continuity of input	15
Workload	15
Turnover of personnel	13
Enforced job rotation according to lists	10
The human qualifications of supervisors	9
Unstable social environment due to job rotation and turnover	6
Low status	5
Do not know what tasks one will be assigned	3
The professional qualifications of supervisors	2
Maximum	23

23 areas or sub-departments were covered by the investigation. The table does not show the distribution of problems on the various areas. This would have made the table rather complex and it would in addition probably not have told people unfamiliar with post terminals very much. Briefly, this distribution turned out to be uneven, with a «heaping up» of problems in the various sub-departments performing bulk sorting. The sub-departments dealing with the more detailed sorting — for example on the various postal areas of Oslo — were in an in-between position, while some smaller, specialised units, together with code punching, showed the fewest problems. Code punching is, as the name indicates, the punching of code numbers, an extremely simple and routinized job. At the time when this analysis was done, however, there was still not much code punching performed in the letter department, making it possible to rotate on this function and limiting the period spent on such work to two hours for each individual. If further automation increases the relative importance of this function, its importance as a source of problems is sure to grow.

Problem structure

The next step in the analysis was to use these and other data to make a simple «process model» of the problems in the letter department. The list of problems was split in the middle — or rather beyond the sixth most frequent problem — and these six problems were taken as a point of departure.

Of these issues, two can be said to pertain to inputs into the system, three to the way the system reacts to characteristics of the inputs, and one to problems following from these patterns of reactions. They can be ordered as in Figure 11.

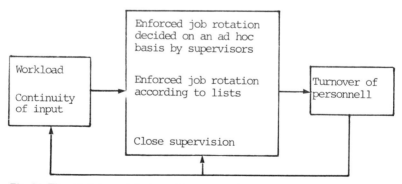

Fig. 11. The chief elements in the problem generation process in the letter department.

To meet a heavy workload in the form of a continuous stream of mail pouring into the system, various methods were used. Of these, job rotation, ad hoc as well as according to lists set up in advance, were experienced as problems, the same held for close and continuous supervision. These problems seemed, in their turn, to contribute to turnover, which in itself was seen as a problem. The existence of turnover of some magnitude increased the difficulties in meeting the workload, leading to more job rotation, and probably to more turnover. This can easily become a vicious circle.

Ad hoc job rotation, in particular, was viewed as a serious problem as it creates acute anxiety among the employees who can be rotated, without advance warning, to any position within the letter department. Frequently, such rotation occured at the beginning of a shift, which resulted in a spillover of anxiety from the workplace to the home.

When interpreting job rotation of both kinds as a source of problems, two factors must be considered:

Firstly, that this was not a self-determined rotation based on the needs of the individual for variation in work, for learning new skills, and such like. It was a system of imposed rotation, carried out by the first line supervisors to fill «holes» emerging in the system because of turnover, absences due to illness and variations in workload.

Secondly, due to the large size of the terminal and the large number of people involved, the rotation implied major shifting around in terms of physical and social space. Here we see clearly the negative effects of large units. The individual was continuously placed in environments with people he or she did not know.

If we proceed to the less frequent problems, we see that «unstable local environment» is a problem emerging with a lower frequency than the turnover problem, but it appears in all instances together with the turnover problem.

The holistic perspective

The Work Environment Act demands that work environment problems are to be considered not only one by one but also from a total or holistic point of view. The next step in the analysis was to bring together data from the analysis presented above, with data pertaining to other aspects of the work environment.

Noise. The letter department contains about 600 motors and hundreds of meters of transport lines.

167

The lifting of heavy loads. Trolleys, cassettes and bags are used in the transport process. The size of these, and their weight, was to a large extent determined by what is technologically optimal rather than by what was best from a human point of view.

Incorrect work postures were also a problem.

Climate and temperature. Again, the size is an important factor. In the letter department all kinds of work is performed, ranging from physically very light work to work which is very heavy. The temperature is, however, the same all over, with the result that those doing heavy work tend to sweat while those performing light work may freeze. In actual practice the temperature is set at a level which makes it reasonably comfortable for those who do ordinary office work, making it rather hot for those having physically more demanding work.

Illumination. Again, size and uniformity contributes to the problems. Different types of work demand different types of illumination, a demand not easily met when the «benefits of large scale» are to be reaped.

Dust in the air, produced in the handling of the mail bags, which are made of rough cloth. The size of the «landscape» makes it difficult to get rid of it in spite of an air exchange- and conditioning system.

The analysis of the relationships between the various problems, showed a complex pattern, which we will not discuss here, except to state that there was a tendency towards an accumulation of problems: employees in those areas with a heavy concentration of primary problems (rotation, close supervision etc.) also tended to experience a concentration of such problems as for example bad work positions.

Programme for improvement

This analysis led up to elements of a strategy for improvement, of which some points will be touched upon here:
   Two issues can be said to have emerged as particularly important.
   - First: the size of the department; a number of problems seemed directly or indirectly linked to this.
   - Second: the relationship between amount and continuity of input (mail) on the one hand and the mechanisms for coping with the workload on the other.
Starting with the second problem, one approach would be to reduce input. The position of both management and employees, was against taking up this issue. In the long run, the question of more terminal ca-

168

pacity can perhaps be taken up, but the point of departure for seeking solutions was that mail is to be handled within the framework of the given facilities at high speed and with few mistakes, criteria which the postal service of Norway clearly lives up to. Given that solutions had to be found without reduction in input, there were three areas emerging as important in the change programme:

- Even though the main physical outline of the terminal had to be taken as given, some of the social and psychological consequences of size could be changed by developing alternative patterns of work organization.
- The degree of control exerted by the operators over the speed and continuity of the flow of mail had to be looked into with a view to seeing to what extent this control could be improved on.
- Various physical problems, such as noise, would have to be attacked.

Starting with the first issue, various approaches suggested themselves. A breaking up of the department into organizational sub-departments was a first step. By sub-departments are meant units not as small as work groups, but something in between work groups and the total system. A sub-department is in most ways a framework for further organizational changes, such as the development of autonomous work groups. Such a breaking up into sub-departments can be supported by some physical signs, such as semi-walls.

A next step was to limit job rotation to each sub-department. Nobody will then be rotated outside his or her department and some of the problems following from the original rotation system, such as continuously having to move into new social environments, could be eliminated.

To the extent that compulsory job rotation would be necessary for some time ahead, for example until a new pattern of work organization has been developed and stabilized, one possibility was to let people rotate in pairs, sometimes even in bigger groups. the individual will then not «move alone» to a new place.

Relatively shielded autonomous work groups were already in existence in the department, particularly in those areas where few problems were recorded. This pattern of organization could be expanded in the letter department, provided that the turnover is reduced and a reasonable system of sub departments to provide a framework for group development, is established. Ideally, the sub-departments can in the future be imagined as consisting of a network of autonomous work groups. As most work to be done within each sub-department is of a rather similar nature, there are limited reasons in providing for job rotation beyond the framework of each group.

By the time this is written, parts of these improvements have been implemented. The breaking up of the terminal into sub-departments had already started before the project got under way. Such a sub-division had in fact been in existence ever since the terminal went into operation but one had not drawn sufficiently broad organizational consequences from this division. Instead, one tried to reap the benefits of the large scale, which was, of course, natural as it was just to allow for these (presumed) benefits that the terminal was built with such a large work area. The system of rotation in pairs has to some extent been introduced. A further expansion of the idea of autonomous work group has as yet not taken place.

It is possible to go some way towards a better work environment by changing the patterns of work organization as suggested above. However, there are limits to what can be gained through such an approach alone. The degree of control which the operators can exert over the flow of mail emerges as a critical issue in its own right as well as a condition of importance to further organizational changes. This control is largely a technological problem which requires two interdependent developments: more and better buffer areas and improved technological controls available to the workers. These issues are probably the key factors in a long term development in the letter department. Relatively little has as yet been done. Unless solutions for these problems are found, the possibilities for the operators to control the speed and rhythm of work will be limited.

As concerns the third area, an improvement programme has already been implemented. The key factor here is noise abatement. This programme was started by placing noice absorbers by the hundreds under the roof, in addition to changes in parts of the transport system and the better isolation of motors. These solutions did, however, not prove sufficient and a whole new roof is now being installed. This roof is below most of the motors and the transport system (these are as far as possible located under the roof to leave the floor space fre for work) and will hence encapsulate the most important sources of noise. A physiotherapist has been put to work on the issue of ergonomics with a view to developing proposals for change in equipment (e.g. chairs).

Some social perspectives

The postal services is one of the large-scale public services, which have recently experienced a process of automation and mechanization. It has, at the same time, experienced changes in the composition of the labour force: fewer and fewer men, who see the postal services

170

as a place for a total life career based on some degree of professionalization, are to be found in the letter department. Instead, an increasing number of women, and generally without the basic professional training provided for by the postal services' own training system, are moving in. There are particularly two categories of importance: young women around twenty years of age, generally unmarried, and middle aged married women. An increasing number work part time, particularly the married women.

The employees have traditionally been well organized, in the Postal Workers Union, which has various sub-branches for employees in different categories. Practically everybody in the postal services is organized, including management. The union belongs to the LO.

Traditionally, there has been a well developed pattern of management-employee collaboration, largely based on joint consultative committees. Before the terminal was built, the drawings and plans were dealt with in various such committees. In spite of such a set of «democratic» institutions, the end product had important deficiencies as a work environment. This illustrates some of the problems attached to democratization through a relatively high-level representative system, where issues are dealt with on a fairly broad and general basis and where the possibilities for bringing in specific work experience are limited, simply because committees are places where «the few» discuss issues pertaining to «the many» and the few can never transmit all the detailed, concrete work experience of a large number of people.

The type of employees found in the letter department, women of whom many have a short time perspective on their work in the terminal, and of whom many others are part time employees as well as housewives, belonges to those who are thought to be rather passive in relation to problems in their workplace. One of the most interesting aspects of the development in the letter department is, however, the slow but steady emergence of a will to improve conditions. The key person is the head safety delegate. This is linked to the point that the safety organization has gained in importance lately. The issues and topics under discussion, have gained in legitimacy due to the Work Environment Act. Even though this apparatus is integrated with the old union system, one can nevertheless see the emergence of a new pattern with greater emphasis on work environment issues, with women in leading roles and with emphasis on the day-to-day problems, which can not be solved unless those who have a direct experience of the problems take active part in their definition and in the working out of solutions. Hence, the letter department is an example of the development of womens resources in the workplace.

It must also be added that the relationship between employees and management is characterized by a mixed situation in terms of conflicts and collaboration. During the winter of 1980, a go-slow and over-time refusal campaign took place in the letter department, as a protest against some of the jobs of the department being rationalized away.

Concluding remarks – the current status of the reform

The work environment reform is still very much in its developmental phase. It is still too early to make any broad evaluation in terms of «success» or «failure» – to the extent that such broad evaluative terms are at all applicable to such a highly complex reality as the development and fate of such a reform. This is written in the early summer of 1980, three years after the Act went into force. This might sound like a long time perspective to some, but to those having experience in complex social change it will be clear that the period is actually short.

At the moment it looks like we are approaching the end of what can loosely be called «the first phase of hesitation and confusion» after the passing of the Act. This period of three years has seen the emergence of work environment programmes like those described above. Such programmes have been, however, more pioneering efforts than results of broadly recognised and established practices. Adaptation to such a reform as the Work Environment Act, which after all is a fairly complex reform, always take time. The initial phase will invariably be one of some confusion and hesitation, and such a phase clearly emerged in the wake of the Act. In this phase most enterprises stepped up their activity with work environment problems, but largely kept on along the older patterns of such work, giving priority to the well known and long recognized issues such as noise; the Labour Inspection inspected in more or less the same way as before; and the politicians generally considered the issue of work environment reform to have been adequately dealt with, through the passing of the Act. However, since the beginning of 1980 there are signs of a broader understanding of, and adaptation to, the new Act. More improvement programmes are developled, greater emphasis is being placed on such issues as the organisation of work and total evaluations of work situations. The Labour Inspection seems to be giving more priority to getting organizations to develop their own improvement programmes instead of performing the more conventional inspections. A parliamentary report on the status and future of the implementation of the Act is to be written, emerging from a realization that the Work Environment Act is the opening of a process of social change rather than the laying down of a particular social structure. The application of the Act, however, exists only in embryonic forms in Norwegian working life, and it is still not certain that the reform will mature into broad and systematic patterns of a new reform praxis encompassing all Norwegian workplaces. The fate of the work environment reform is bound up with the broader development of Norwegian society, issues that to some extent will be touched upon in the last chapter.

In the period between the writing up of the second last and the last version of the manuscript for this book – June 1980 – a new factor has entered the picture. As part of the parliamentary report on the Work Environment Act it has been decided to make a study pertaining to the status of work environment programmes on enterprise level. Contacts have been made with the Employers' Confederation, the Federation of Trade Unions and with bodies within the public sector. Agreement is emerging about a joint questionnaire study to be developed and administered by the Work Research Institutes. The aim will be to reach a reasonably broad sample of enterprises and other organizations with a view to finding out to what extent work environment programmes, such as described in the Berger Langmoen case, have been developed and what issues they include. Recent contacts with the employers in connection with this study indicate that the status of work environment development programmes on enterprise level may in fact be more positive than we thought when we wrote this book. Nobody argues that broad and ambitious work environment programmes, encompassing all issues, including organization of work, have been developed in the majority of private and public organizations in Norway. What is indicated, is that such programmes may already be frequent enough to give grounds for saying that a positive development is clearly under way. To what extent this is really the case, the investigation will hopefully uncover. The results will be published in English as soon as they are available.

IX. Concluding remarks on work reform and contemporary problems in Norwegian society

Introduction

The focus of this book has been on working life and its institutions. While we have attempted to sketch the surrounding societal framework we are aware of the fact that this has been inadequate for a full understanding of the historical roots of contemporary Norwegian working life. To some extent all developments in working life are culture bound, and without specifying the culture which gives rise to a particular development, the reader may be left with a number of unanswered questions. In spite of the fact that an overall presentation of Norwegian society has not been given here, we will in this last and concluding section of the book locate the work environment reform in a broader context of national development.

We have discussed various approaches to reform in working life and various frameworks or reasons for such reforms. We have, for example, seen that the issue of work organization can be related to productivity, satisfaction, industrial democracy and work environment and that each of these frameworks gives a different meaning to the issue of work organization. However, it can also be said that the industrial democracy context presented in chapter II and the work environment context presented in chapters V – VIII are both part of a larger context of participatory democracy on the societal level. Participatory democracy is here defined in line with Pateman (1970), as a model of society where development can be influenced by people through processes emerging from the grass roots. Its conceptual counterpart within modern political science theory is «elite democracy» (Cfr. Schumpeter, 1947; Dahl, 1960; Lipset, 1961).

From this point of departure a broad treatment of work reform within the framework of participatory democracy in Norway in general, is warranted. Such a treatment would, however, take us beyond the confines of this book. When a few remarks on the relationship between the work environment reform and broader issues in Norwegian society are nevertheless to be made, we will choose a more limited framework, in the form of two specific processes that make themselves relatively strongly felt in Norwegian society at the moment. One of these processes has to do with the issue of centralisation versus decentralisation, the other departs from macro-economic problems, such as counteracting inflation and maintaining full employment.

Centralization, decentralization and stragtegy

To understand these specifics, we need to go back to Chapter I and recall the relatively centralized structure on the employer, as well as on the employee side, and the resulting centralized mechanism for conflict resolution between the parties. This relatively centralized structure in working life is, however, not something which exists in a vacuum: it is to some extent a corollary to characteristics of centralization in society in general. The social democratic societies are sometimes thought to be somewhere «between» the relatively decentralized type of society found in, for example, the United States or Canada and the more centralist structure found in Eastern Europe. Even though these authors are a little reluctant to use this «in between model» to describe the Scandinavian societies, it is reasonably useful in this particular respect.

Norwegian society has a relatively strong and well developed public sector with the state in the center. How does this structure function?

There is a strong committment to such goals and values as full employment, equality in life opportunities, a good environment, and so on. While such values are to be found in many countries, it has been noted that the committment to such values is particularly strong in Norwegian society, or, to phrase the point differently, the values are taken relatively seriously. Hence, it is difficult to oppose proposals for new legislation or other public efforts that can be grounded in such values and they generally pass through the political apparatus with limited resistance. To some extent the political fate of the Work Environment Act can be seen in this light.

In order to operationalize these values and ideals Norwegian society has imposed certain duties and obligations on the private sector, both, on individuals and on enterprises. These obligations and duties are imposed for «the common good» of the whole population. The development of public organizations has been a chief parameter, not least because obligations on the population need to be administered and supervised by somebody. This public sector can function in various ways, and the points we make must be seen as broad generalizations, not necessarily applicable to all public organizations in Norway.

176

It seems as if the public sector in Norway, which has grown throughout the main part of this century, has more and more fallen victim to what can be called a *process of concretization*. By a «process of concretization» (Gustavsen, 1972a) is meant, for example, the type of development described by Selznick (1949) in his analysis of the Tennessee Valley Authority in the United States.

This organization was developed to realize a number of general goals and ideals of an economic as well as of a social character. In the process of turning these ideals into reality, a number of concrete steps had to be taken. Administrative practices had to be developed, ways of dealing and collaborating with a number of interest groups established, and so on. The TVA was, for example, originally entrusted with the task of developing recreation areas accessible to the broad public. Through its necessary collaboration with farmers and their organizations it did, however, slowly abolish this goal in favour of letting the farmers get the exclusive rights to use the land originally intended as public grounds.

Such a process of concretization must always take place and it will always to some extent affect the goals of the organization. Glittering generalities can remain so only as long as they are not to be implemented. However, even if this is true, it is also a question of what balance is struck and how the relationship is developed between goals and «tactics». And this brings us to a point of major importance − the problem of *mediation* between goals and specific efforts.

The description and analysis of the work anvironment reform done in this book give an illustration of such a mediation; on the one hand one has certain goals, such as improved health, and on the other the need to make a large number of specific decisions. It was pointed out that this relationship can be settled in different ways. One way is to develop as many general and unequivocal rules as possible and rely on a public apparatus to enforce these rules, the other approach is to generate conditions for local development in each and every workplace. Both ingredients are of course needed, but the approaches can still be balanced in various ways.

The way this particular balance is struck relates to the question of *strategy*.

The overall situation in Norwegian society today can perhaps be characterized by a *lack of strategic considerations*. There is strong committment to various general ideas and there are a number of public institutions that perform tens of thousands of specific acts each day. However, when strategy is lacking, these tens of thousands of specific acts become more and more «technical» and narrow in frame and conceptualization and − of most critical importance − they do not constitute consistent steps towards a general goal. Such overall goals as full employment and better environment will only rarely include specifications as to what acts should be preferred on the local level.It is only through the mediation of a strategy that such selections can be made in a way which is consistent with the final goal. Lack of strategy will often mean that specific acts go in all possible directions and that little overall progress is achieved.

Such a situation can easily develop into a vicious circle: the existence of a committment to general goals means that there is a continuous pressure for improvement and reform. More resources are spent on the development of public initiatives and public control, but the results do not necessarily constitute coherent steps towards real improvements. Hence, the pressure remains, followed by increased investment, controls and so forth. It has been pointed out (e.g. Holter, Gustavsen and Reigstad, 1974) that the development of a comprehensive public welfare system does not only often fail to realize the underlying aims but sometimes it shatters the natural mechanisms among people, such as social networks for mutal help and support. Such a development will further strengthen the pressure for «more reforms» as the problems grow, rather than disappear.

To the extent that this analysis is correct, it locates the work environment reform in a field of tension. It is an effort at breaking this vicious circle of development while it is at the same time located in a society where this type of development exists. Hence, the work environment reform can be of critical positive importance if it succeeds, because it can make a major contribution to the turning of the tide. To succeed it must overcome not only certain factors acting contrary to this reform within working life itself, it must also function contrary to what is perhaps the chief critical development in Norwegian society as a whole. There is a distinct danger that the work environment reform itself will be converted from the emphasis on participatory democracy to end up as another set of «technical specifications».

Economic instability

Like all industrial societies, Norway has been characterized by an increased economic instability throughout the seventies, particularly from 1974 onwards. Up until that point the system for control of the economy, largely following the patterns suggested by Keynes, but further developed by a Norwegian school of economists of whom the Nobel Prize winner Frisch is perhaps the best known, functioned quite well. Full employment was maintained together with a reasonable check on inflation and a contiuous growth in the buying

178

power for the population in general. After 1974 changes have occurred. While employment has continued to go up also after 1974, it is a fairly widepread belief that in the future there will be increasing difficulties in maintaining full employment. As concerns buying power, fairly borad groups, particularly in the middle income brackets without any fringe benefits attached to their jobs, complain about reductions in their standard of living. The key factor seems to be inflation. To stabilize the economy, economists generally argue that wage developments must be kept within limits.

These limits follow from the state and prospects of the total national economy. As these limits are not easy to see and define for everybody, and to ensure that they are really respected, it can be argued that wage settlements need to be under a high degree of central control and that this central control must be performed in a way which is integrated with the national economy. In the light of this, the validity of which we will not attempt to judge, the high degree of centralization existing between the parties in working life has been developed into more of a tripartite system with the government as the third party (Chapter I).

This picture can easily create the impression that wages in Norway are fairly well controlled from central quarters and that Norway is consequently in a better position − when seen from the particular point of view of keeping inflation in check through wage controls − than what is the case for the less well organized societies, such as the United States or Canada. However, the picture is more complex.

Even though most wages are settled through central mechanisms, it does not mean that the critical *social* mechanisms for pushing wages upwards are under central control. Here we confront the difference between an economic versus a sociological outlook on the issue of wage settlements. It is not necessarily so that the biggest groups in numbers are the most important as wage settlers. Relatively small groups can avoid the main mechanisms of central bargaining, for example, by remaining unorganized and bargaining directly with the employer on an individual or small group basis, as most middle and top managers in the private sector still do. Among mechanisms to increase one's wages is fringe benefits systems. «Multiple jobs» providing for more than one source of income is another possibility, pioneered in Norway by, for example, the medical profession. High mobility between companies, such as in advertising and computer systems, is frequently combined with higher wage settlements at each and every move. In addition, certain unions, such as the Iron and Metalworkers' Union, have the right to local wage bargaining in addition to the central settlements. Some unions, generally outside the LO or the other federations, resort to the frequent use of strikes in order to achieve a higher wage settlement. Various groups, such as airline personnel and employees in parts of the offshore oil industry, have developed a pattern of relatively frequent strikes for that purpose.

If wage increases can be «pioneered» by groups of limited size, the centralized system can in fact become a major mechanism for *diffusion*. In a society where equalization is a prominent value, the fact that somebody else has achieved a wage increase is a fairly potent argument for raising one's own. Hence, there is an inbuilt danger of a major wage drift upwards encompassing the whole economy. Such a situation has as yet not developed in Norway. The big organizations representing the major groups of employees have clearly considered the needs for economic restraint when the wage claims have been defined. However, the situation can easily change. Of particular importance in this respect is the increased instability in the world economy which may make it more difficult than before to raise everybody's standard of living. As an ever increasing number of wage earners may have their buying power reduced, the level of industrial conflict can increase, thus putting additional pressure on the system. Norway is accustomed to a low level of strikes (Chapter I). The ability of the economy to tolerate conflict is, however, also low. Norwegian planning and economic development, ranging from the national to the enterprise level is based on a relatively conflict-free situation in working life. A sharp increase in the level of conflicts will produce pressures for major changes in the entire system.

Given this background there is an emerging need, expressed particularly by economists in positions of responsibility for the national economy, to take «the heat» off the wage issues on the local level and get people to focus on something different. Development of work environment is an obvious factor here. In simple terms this point of view can be expressed like this: Wages must be defined centrally and work environment locally. Traditionally, it has more or less been the other way around, as the public approach to work environment improvements has been mediated through a system of centrally defined rules, while the centralized wage bargaining system has not prevented «wage pioneering» from being mostly locally initiated. Hence, a support for the work environment reform is at the moment emerging from people who have generally had a centralist preoccupation with macro-economic issues.

The work environment reform can give a significant contribution to the stabilization of the national economy. On the other hand, it has to withstand the pressure from some of the forces that generate the economic problems, such as «wage pioneering» among some groups, and a consequent risk of diffusion to the rest of working life with increasing instability in Norwegian economy as a possible result.

One reason for accepting central control over wage bargaining as a positive goal is that this may well be the only approach for a long term equalization of wages. As the economic problems of the industrialized world keep piling up, and there is little to indicate that they will not keep on doing so as the energy situation alone seem sufficient to bring this about, the question of wages will become more and more difficult to settle. There are no objective criteria for a just wage structure, and no way in which differentiated wages can be defined to everybody's satisfaction. Hence, the only way out of problems in many societies, may be to go for a policy of equal pay for everybody – some form of «society member's pay» as it is generally referred to. This may happen not for ideological, but for practical reasons if and when a society reaches a stage where the positive effects on effort, creativity and productivity, believed to follow from differentiated wages, will be more than made up by the losses following from a bitter struggle for slices of a shrinking economic pie. Because of the oil incomes, Norway will in all probability be one of the last nations in the Western world to reach this stage and will probably not come to pioneer the issue of equal pay. Some countries, such as for example Britain, may already have reached a stage where the introduction of equal pay would solve many more problems than it would create and hence make a major contribution to a positive economic development.

A note on work organization and health

Freedom and competence in work is a key factor in the work environment reform. Organization of work is in this reform located within a network of concepts where local activity, safety and health are imprtant ones. It is, however, mentioned (Chapter VII) that when organization of work and health are linked, it is not with a view to reinforcing a «stress» approach to workplace problems, according to which changes need to be legitimized through a medical diagnosis characterising the workers as «ill». Rather the opposite: after 40 years with the concept of stress in its medical and semi-medical content, so little has been done that this approach lacks attractiveness. When organization of work is placed in the center of the reform, it is because freedom and competence in work mediates between problems and *human action*. Here we will make a brief remark on an aspect of this mediation not mentioned previously:

As a point of departure we use data from a study made in the Oslo area about mortality among middle aged men, see Table 4.

The «inequality of death» (WHO, 1980, see also Romøren, 1974)

181

emerging from this table, where mortality rate for unskilled workers is about four times as high as for academics, is not peculiar to Norway (for US data, see House, 1976) Why do these differences occur? It must be remembered that the important reasons for death are coronary diseases and cancer. Such diseases are, in medical terminology, often referred to as «life style» diseases, as they have something to do with the acts and choices of people, e.g. the choice to smoke. Then, however, we enter the field of what factors *decide* «peoples' choices» in such respects. More and more evidence suggests that the type of work people have is important (see, for example, Meissner, 1971; Karasek, 1978; 1980). If the work enables people to take initiatives, perform judgments, raise support in their environment, participate in collective action, it seems as if they are better able to make constructive decisions pertaining to their health also outside the work situation. In Norwegian studies it has, for example, been shown that an anti- smoking campaign achieved much better results among academics than among unskilled workers (Statens Tobakkskaderåd, 1979). We will not expound on this point here. Considerably more research is needed to establish it more firmly. If this link stands up it means that organization of work becomes of the most extreme importance to the total health policy in society. It means, furthermore, that health will be strongly interwoven with a participative structure, in the same way as Emery & Thorsrud (1976) argued that productivity is (Chapter II).

Table 4. Mortality for men aged 40 – 49 years, in promillae (deaths per thousand).

	Academics	Function- aries	Skilled workers	Unskilled workers
Mortality, all causes	16,0	15,1	24,2	55,1

N   24.864 males in the Oslo-area.
Source: Holme et.al. (1980)

This does not mean that health should «take over» as the one and only factor in policies for the future, at the expense of the other concepts that have traditionally guided a development towards a more egalitarian society. What it means is rather that health is torn out of the realm of naturalistic research and expert decisons where it is largely located today, and brought back to the people. The Secretary for Environmental Issues in the Norwegian Federation of Trade Unions, Børre Pettersen, has argued that this has to be the platform on which the future welfare policy of the Federation must be erected.

Concluding remarks

The Industrial Democracy Programme can be said to pertain to the issue of reform in working life from a democratization perspective. The work environment reform also pertains to working life and includes a democratization perspective but it emerged originally from health and safety considerations. Both reforms link, in various ways, to issues and processes in society in general. The logical sequence to the reforms described in this book would be a reform where participatory democracy in working life *as well as* in other spheres of life was approached in an integrated way, where various means and categories are brought to bear on the problems and where all relevant reasons for the development of participatory democracy – ranging from health to democratic values – are brought together.

Such an idea for a process of democratization is, of course, not new. The problem does not lie here, but *in the hammering out of a multi-mean and multi-level strategy which can lead to practical results under the prevailing conditions in society.* Such an approach needs to consider such issues as treated in our description of the work environment as well as the industrial democracy reform. Solutions need to be developed at least on the same level of specificity as are done in the work environment reform. Legislation needs to be considered, so must rules and institutions for public administration, difficult issues of centralization and decentralization will have to be taken up, ways and means of enterprise development must be reconsidered, and so forth. Treating all these highly complex issues as questions of broad principles is of course very well. Such analyses on the level of principles are not lacking. To transform these principles, via a series of political, legal and administrative reforms, down to the level where all the nitty-gritty details can be attacked is, however, far more difficult. Given such a demand for practicality, we still lack a total approach to the problem of participatory democracy. The development of such a strategy is the major task for the future.

References

Abell, P. (1980): Hierarchy and Democratic Authority. In: Burns, T.R., Karlsson L.E. and Rus, V (eds.): *Work and Power: The liberation of work and the Control of Political Power.* Sage studies in International Sociology, Vol. 18, London

Ager, B., Aminoff, S., Baneryd, K., Englund, A., Nerell, G., Nilsson, C., Saarman, E. och Søderkvist, A. (1975): *Arbetsmiljøn i sågverk. En tvärvetenskaplig undersøkning.* Undersøkningsrapport AM 101/75. Arbetarskyddsstyrelsen, Stockholm.

Agersnap, F. (1973): *Samarbejdsforsøg i jernindustrien.* Foreningen af Verkstedfunktionærer i Danmark/Centralorganisationen af Metalarbejdere i Danmark/ Sammenslutningen af Arbejdsgivere indenfor Jern- og Metalindustrien i Danmark, København.

Agurén, S., Hansson, R. och Karlsson, K.G. (1976): *Volvo Kalmarverken.* Rationaliseringsrådet SAF-LO, Stockholm.

Agurén, S. och Edgren, J. (1979): *Annorlunda fabriker.* Svenska Arbetsgivareføreningen, Stockholm.

Anker-Ording, Aa. (1965): *Bedriftsdemokrati. Eiendomsretten og grunnloven.* Universitetsforlaget, Oslo.

Arbejdsmiljøgruppen af 1972: *Rapporter* 1 – 6. København.

Aspengren-Komitéen (1965): *Innstilling om demokrati i arbeidslivet.* Felleskomitéen LO – DNA, Oslo.

Attføringsutvalget ved Norsk Jernverk (1972): *Arbeids- og helseforhold.* Arbeidsdirektoratet/Norsk Produktivitetsinstitutt, Oslo.

Baker, F., McEwan, M.P.J.M. and Sheldon, A. (1969): *Industrial Organization and Health.* Travistock Publications, London.

Batstone, E. and Davies, P.L. (1976): *Industrial Democracy: European Experience.* H.M.S.O., London.

Berg, O. (1975): Health and the Quality of Life. *Acta Sociologica*, Vol. 18, No. 1.

Berg, P.O., Eskild, A. og Webster, R. (1975): *Reglene om bedriftsdemokratiet.* Tiden, Oslo.

Berglind, H. (1978): Pension or Work? A Growing Dilemma in the Nordic Welfare States. *Acta Sociologica*, Vol. 21, Special issue for the ISA World Congress in Uppsala.

Bernstein, P. (1976): *Workplace Democratization. Its Internal Dynamics.* Kent State University Press.

Biderman, A.D. and Drury, T.F. (1976). *Measuring Work Quality for Social Reporting.* Sage/Halstead, New York, London, Sidney, Toronto.

Bjørk, L., Hansson, R. och Hellberg, P. (1972): *Økat innflytande i jobbet.* Personaladministrativa Rådet/Utvecklingsrådet før Samarbetsfrågor, Stockholm.

Blauner, R. (1964): *Alienation and Freedom.* University of Chicago Press.

Blichfeldt, J.F. (1974): The Educational Autonomy Project: An Overview. *Work Research Institutes*, Oslo.

– « – (1975): Relations Between School and the Place of Work. *Acta Sociologica*, Vol. 18, No. 4.

Blumberg, P. (1968): *Industrial Democracy: The Sociology of Participation.* Constable, London.

Bolinder, E. och Ohlstrøm, B. (1971): *Stress på svenska arbetsplatser.* Prisma, Stockholm.

Bolweg, J.F. (1976): *Job Design and Industrial Democracy: the Case of Norway.* Nijhoff, Leiden.

Braverman, H. (1974): *Labor and Monopoly Capital.* Monthly Review Press, New York.

Bridbord, K. et al (1978): Estimates of the Fraction of Cancer in the United States Related to Occupational Factors. National Cancer Institute/National Institute of Environmental Health Sciences/National Institute for Occupational Safety and Health.

Bronner, K. och Levi, L. (1969): *Stress i arbetslivet.* Personaladministrativa Rådet, Stocholm.

Brown, W. and Jaques, E. (1965): *Glacier Project Papers.* Heinemann, London.

Bull, E. (1979): Norge i den rike verden. *Norges Historie,* Bind 14. Cappelen, Oslo.

Bullock Report (1977): *The Report of the Committee of Inquiry on Industrial Democracy.* H.M.S.O., London.

Burns, T. and Stalker, G.M. (1961): *The Management of Innovations.* Tavistock Publications, London.

Carson, R. (1962): *Silent Spring* Houghton Mifflin, New York.

Central Bureau of Statistics (1976): Yrke og dødelighet. *Statistiske Analyser,* nr. 21.

– « – (1977): *Helseundersøkelse 1975.* Oslo

– « – (1978b): *Historical Statistics.* Oslo.

– « – (1980): *Statistical Yearbook.* Oslo.

Clegg, H.A. (1960): *A New Approach to Industrial Democracy.* Oxford.

Cummings, T.G. and Molloy, E.S. (1977): *Improving Productivity and the Quality of Work Life.* Praeger, New York.

Dahl, R.A. (1961): *Who Governs? Democracy and Power in an American City.* Yale University Press, New Haven and London.

– « – (1963): *A Preface to Democratic Theory.* The University of Chicago Press. Chicago and London.

Dahlstrøm, E. (1978): The Role of Social Science in Working Life Policy: The Case of Postwar Sweden. In: Berglind, H., Hanisch, T. and Haavio-Mannila, E. (eds): *Sociology of Work in the Nordic Countries. Themes and Perspectives.* The Scandinavian Sociological Association, Copenhagen, Helsinki, Oslo, Stockholm.

– « – , Eriksson, K., Gardell, B., Hammarstrøm, O. och Hammarstrøm, R. (1971): *LKAB och demokratin.* Wahlstrøm og Widstrand, Stockholm.

Dorfman, H. (1957): *Labor Relations in Norway.* The Norwegian Joint Committee on International Social Policy, Oslo.

Eckhoff, E. (1964): Representantskapet i norsk aksjelov. *Lov og Rett,* nr. 3.

Eckhoff-Komiteen (1971): *Innstilling om demokrati i bedriftslivet.* Statsministerens kontor, Oslo.

Eckhoff, T. and Dahl Jacobsen, K. (1960): *Rationality and Responsibility in Administrative and Judicial Decision-Making.* Munksgaard, Copenhagen.

Eckstein, H. (1966): *Division and Cohesion in Democracy.* Princeton University Press.

Edwards, R. (1979): *Contested Terrain: The Transformation of the Workplace in the Twentieth Century.* Basic Books, New York.

Elden, M. (1975): Sharing the Research Work – Researcher's Role in Democratizing Organizational Change. *Work Research Institutes,* Oslo.

– « – (1977): Political Efficacy at Work: More Autonomous Forms of Workplace

186

Organization Link to more Participatory Politics. Paper presented to seminar on social change and organization development, Inter-University Center, Dubrovnik.
– « – (1979): Three Generations of Work-democracy Experiments in Norway: Beyond Classical Socio-Technical Systems Analysis. In: Cooper, C.L. and Mumford, E. (eds): *The Quality of Working Life in Western and Eastern Europe.* Associated Business Press, London.
Emery, F.E. (1959): Characteristics of Socio-Technical Systems Doc. No. 527, Tavistock, London.
– « – (1963): Second Progress Report on Conceptualisation. Doc. No. 125, Tavistock, London.
– « – (1967): The Next Thirty Years: Concepts, Methods and Anticipations. *Human Relations,* No. 3.
– « – (1969): *Systems thinking.* Penguin.
– « – (1978): *The Emergence of a New Paradigm of Work.* Center for Continuing Education, the Australian National University, Canberra.
– « – and Oeser, O.A. (1958): *Information, Decision and Action.* Cambrigde University Press, Melbourne.
– « – and Thorsrud, E. (1969): *Form and Content in Industrial Democracy.* Tavistock Publications, London.
– « – and Thorsrud, E. (1976): *Democracy at Work.* Nijhoff, Leiden.
– « – and Trist, E.L. (1969): The Causal Texture of Organizational Environments. In: Emery, F.E. (ed): *Systems Thinking.* Penguin.
Engelstad, P.H. (1970): *Teknologi og sosial forandring på arbeidsplassen.* Tanum, Oslo.
– « – (1973): Industrielle lønnssystemer – noen utviklingstendenser. *Bedriftsøkonomisk informasjon,* nr. 9.
– « – (1980): Developments in a National Strategy of Democratizing the Work Organization. In: Trebesch, K. (ed): *Organization Development in Europe. Vol 1: Concepts.* Paul Haupt Verlag, Bern.
– « – og Qvale, T.U. (1977): *Innsyn og innflytelse i styre og bedriftsforsamling.* Tiden, Oslo.
– « – and Ødegaard, L.A. (1979): Participative Redesign Projects in Norway, Summarizing the First Five Years of a Strategy to Democratize the Design Process in Work Organization. In: *Working With the Quality of Working Life.* Nijhoff, Leiden.
Frankenhäuser, M. and Gardell, B. (1976): Underload and overload in Working Life: Outline of a Multidisciplinary Approach. *Journal of Human Stress,* September issue.
French, J.R.P. and Caplan, R.D. (1972): Organizational Stress and Individual Strain. In: Marrow, A.J. (ed): *The Failure of Success,* Amacom, New York.
Gardell, B. (1971): *Produktionsteknik och arbetsglädje.* Personaladministrativa Rådet, Stockholm.
– « – (1976): *Arbetsinnehåll och livskvalitet.* Prisma-LO, Stockholm.
– « – (1977): Autonomy and Participation at Work. *Human Relations,* Vol. 30, No. 6.
– « – (1980): Psychosocial Aspects of Industrial Production Methods. In: Levi. L. (ed): *Society, Stress and Disease, Vol IV, Working Life.* Oxford University Press, London, New York, Toronto.
– « – and Gustavsen, B. (1980): Work Environment Research and Social Change – Current Developments in Scandinavia. *Journal of Occupational Behaviour,* Vol. 1, No. 1.

187

– « – and Svensson, L. (1980): Codetermination and Autonomy. A Trade Union Strategy for Democracy at the work Place. Dep. of Psychology, University of Stockholm (Draft)

Glud, T., Jensen, P. og Nielsen, N. (1971): *Malerrapporten*. Fagkritiske Tekster nr. 3, Studenterrådet, Århus Universitet.

Goldthorpe, J.H., Lockwood, D., Bechhoffer, F. and Platt, J. (1969): *The Affluent Worker in the Class Structure*. Cambridge University Press.

Gouldner, A.W. (1954): *The Patterns of Industrial Bureaucracy*. The Free Press, Glencoe.

Graham, F. (1970): *Since Silent Spring*. Fawcett Crest Books, New York.

Grøholt, K., Gustavsen, B., Lysgaard, S., Samuelsen, K., Terjesen, S.G. og Wiig, O. (1979): *Arbeidslivs- og arbeidsmiljøforskning, særlig på bakgrunn av den teknologiske utvikling*. Hovedkomitéen for norsk forskning, Oslo.

Gullvåg, H. (1953): Attitudes and Perceptions of Representatives in Industry. Institute for Social Research, Oslo.

Gulowsen, J. (1971): *Selvstyrte arbeidsgrupper*. Tanum, Oslo.

– « – (1974): Bedriftsdemokrati ved Norsk Hydro? Samarbeidsforsøket i Fullgjødselavdelingen 1967 – 72. *Arbeidsforskningsinstituttene*, Oslo.

– « – (1975): *Arbeidervilkår. Et tilbakeblikk på Samarbeidsprosjektet LO-NAF*. Tanum, Oslo.

Gunzburg, D. (1976): *Industrial Democracy in Sweden*. National Productivity Institute, Melbourne.

Gustavsen, B. (1972a): *Industristyret*. Tanum, Oslo.

– « – (1972b): Changing the Organization on the Service Stations: Basis and Elements of a Programme. *Work Research Institutes*, Oslo.

– « – (1973): Styrearbeid. *Bedriftsdemokrati*, hefte 2. Arbeidernes Opplysningsforbund, Oslo.

– « – (1975): Redefining the Role of the Board. *Journal of General Management*, Vol. 2, No. 3.

– « – (1976a): The Social Context of Investment decisions. *Acta Sociologica*, Vol. 19, No. 3.

– « – (1976b): Aktionsforskning. *Rapporter*, nr. 13. Psykologiska Institutionen, Stochholms Universitet.

– « – (1976c): The board of directors, company policy and industrial democracy. In: Bebin, R. (ed): *Handbook of work organization and society*. Rand McNally, Chicago.

– « – (1977a): A Legislative Approach to Job Reform in Norway. *International Labour Review*, Vol 115, No. 3.

– « – (1977b): Styret – noen kjennetegn og utviklingstrekk. I: Isachsen, K. (red.): *Aktivt styrearbeid*. Tanum, Oslo.

– « – (1978a): A Legislative Approach to Job Reform. In: McLean, A. et al (eds.): *Reducing Occupational Stress*. DHEW (NIOSH) Publication No. 78 – 140.

– « – (1978b): *Innføring i arbeidsmiljøloven*. Tiden-Arbeidernes Opplysningsforbund, Oslo.

– « – (1979a): A Strategy for Reform of Working Life. In: Levinson, C. (ed.): *Designing and Organizing the Workplace of the Future*. International Federation of Chemical, Energy and General Workers Unions, Geneva.

– « – (1979b): Liberation of Work and the Role of Social Research. In: Burns, T.R., Karlsson, L.E. and Rus, V. (eds.): *Work and Power. The Liberation of Work and the Control of Political Power*. Sage studies in International Sociology, Vol. 18, London.

188

– « – (1979c): Arbeidsmiljøloven og de dårlige tidene. *Bedriftsøkonomen*, nr. 6.

– « – (1980 a): Legal-Administrative Reforms and the Role of Social Research. *Acta Sociologica*, Vol. 23, No. 1.

– « – (1980b): Improvement of the Work Environment: A Choice of Strategy. *International Labour Review*, Vol. 119, No. 3.

– « – (1980c): From Satisfaction to Collective Action: Trends in the Development of Research and Reform in Working Life. *Economic and Industrial Democracy*, Vol. 1, No. 2.

– « – (1980d): Arbeidsmiljøreform og organisasjonsforskning. *Forskningsnytt*, nr. 3.

– « – (1980e): Research in Action: Reflections on the Relationship between Knowledge and Social Change. *Work Research Institutes*, Oslo. (Draft)

– « – (1980f): Work Reform and Social Research. In: Gardell, B. and Johansson, G. (eds.): *Man and Working Life* (in preparation) Wiley, London.

– « – (1980g): Kartlegging av arbeidsmiljøet på Brevavdelingen, Oslo Postterminal. *Arbeidsforskningsinstituttene*, Oslo.

– « – og Skaarud, T. (1971): Servicestasjonen. *Arbeidsforskningsinstituttene*, Oslo.

– « – og Seierstad, S. (1977): *Arbeid og menneskelige hensyn. Arbeidsmiljølovens krav og praktisk vernearbeid.* Tanum, Oslo.

– « – , Seierstad, S. og Ebeltoft, A. (1978): *Hvordan skal vi gjennomføre arbeidsmiljøloven?* Tiden-Arbeidernes Opplysningsforbund, Oslo.

– « – and Ryste, Ø. (1978): Democratization Efforts and Organizational Structure: A Case Study. In: Negandi, A.R. and Wilpert, B. (eds.): *Work Organization Research: American and European Perspectives.* Kent State University Press.

Hanoa, R. (1971): *Rapport fra Borregaard.* Pax, Oslo.

Hellstrøm, B. (1977): Bedre vern mot helseskader i arbeidslivet. Foredrag på konferanse om arbeidsmiljøloven arrangert av Kommunal- og Arbeidsdepartementet og Statens Arbeidstilsyn, januar 1977.

Herbst, P.G. (1962): *Autonomous Group Functioning. Explorations in Behaviour Theory and Measurements.* Tavistock Publications, London.

– « – (1974). *Socio-thechnical Design. Strategies in Multi-Disciplinary Research.* Tavistock Publications, London.

– « – (1975): *Alternatives to Hierarchies.* Nijhoff, Leiden.

HEW (1973): US Department of Health, Education and Welfare: *Work in America.* MIT Press, Cambrigde.

Hill, P. (1971): *Towards a New Philosophy of Management.* Grower Press, London.

Holme, I., Helgeland, A., Hjermann, I., Leren, P. og Lund-Larsen, P.G. (1980): Oslo undersøkelsen. Fire års dødelighet, koronare risikofaktorer og sosioøkonomiske indikatorer. *Tidsskrift for den norske legeforening*, nr. 22.

Holter, H. (1965): Attitudes Towards Employee Participation in Company Decision Making Process. *Human Relations*, Vol. 18, No. 4.

– « – Gustaven, B. og Reigstad, A. (1975): *Sosiale problemer, helse og arbeidsliv.* Hovedkomitéen for norsk forskning, Oslo.

House, J.D. (1976): Using Health Criteria in a System of Indicators of the Quality of Employment. In: Biderman, A.D. and Drury, T.F. (eds.): *Measuring Work-Quality for Social reporting.* Halstead, New York.

Jaques, E. (1951): *The Changing Culture of a Factory.* Tavistock Publications, London.

Johansen, R. (1979): Democratizing Work and Social Life on Ships. A Report from the Experiment on board M.S. Balao. In: *Working With the Quality of Working Life.* Nijhoff, Leiden.

Johansson, S. (1971): *Om levnadsnivåundersökningen. Låginkomstutredningen.* Almänna Førlaget, Stockholm

Jensen, P.L. (1977): *Job Design*. AMT-publikation D.I. 77 103-A, Danmarks Tekniske Højskole.

Karasek, R. (1978): Job Socialisation: A Longitudinal Study of Work, Political and Leisure Activity in Sweden. Paper presented in the Research Committee on Sociology of Work under the IX World Congress of Sociology, Uppsala.

– « – (1980): Job Socialisation and Job Strain. The Implications of Two Related Psychosocial Mechanisms for Job Design. In: Gardell, B. and Johansson, G. (eds.): *Man and Working Life. A Social Science Contribution to Work Reform*. Wiley, London (in preparation).

Karlsen, J.E. (1978): *Arbeidsmiljø og helseskader*. Tiden-Arbeidernes Opplysningsforbund, Oslo.

Karlsen, J.I. (1976): *Samarbeidsprosjektet ved Hotel Caledonien*. Samarbeidsrådet LO-NAF, Oslo.

– « – , Qvale, T.U. og Lange, K. (1971): Tariffstridige aksjoner. *Arbeidsforskningsinstituttene*, Oslo.

– « – , Næss, R., Ryste, Ø., Seierstad, S. og Sørensen, B. AA. (1975): *Arbeidsmiljø og vernearbeid*. Tanum, Oslo.

– « – , og Næss, R. (1978): *Arbeidsmiljø i hotell- og restaurantnæringen*. Arbeidsforskningsinstituttene, Oslo.

Karlsson, L.E. (1971). *Uddevallarapporten*. Føretagsdemokratidelegationen/Utvecklingsgruppen før Uddevallavarvet AB, Stockholm.

– « – (1975): Experiences in Employee Participation in Sweden. *Economic Analysis*, Vol, IX, Nos. 3 – 4.

Kelly, J.E. (1978): A Reappraisal of Sociotechnical Systems Theory. *Human Relations*, Vol. 31, No. 12.

Kollberg, J.E. (1974): *Trygde-Norge*. Gyldendal, Oslo.

Kornhauser, A. (1965): *Mental Health of the Industrial Worker*. Wiley, New York.

Korsnes, O. (1979): Duality in the Role of Unions and Unionists: the Case of Norway. *British Journal of Industrial Relations*, Vol. XVII, No. 3.

Kronlund, J. (1975): *Praktik och teori*. Økonomiska Institutionen, Linkøpings Høgskola.

Langner, T.S. and Michael, S.T. (1963): *Life Stress and Mental Health*. Free Press, New York.

Lawrence, P.R. and Lorsch, J.W. (1967): *Organization and Environment*. Harvard University Press, Boston.

Lewin, K. (1951): *Field Theory in Social Science*, Tavistock Publications, London.

Lindqvist, S. (1978): *Grav där du står*. Bonniers, Stockholm.

Lipset, S.M. (1963): *Political Man*. Mercury Books, London.

LO-DNA (1973): Program for bedre arbeidsmiljø. Oslo.

LRN (1975): The Norwegian Joint Council on Industrial Social Policy: *Labour Relations in Norway*. Oslo.

Lysgaard, S. (1960): *Arbeiderkollektivet*. Universitetsforlaget, Oslo.

Mayo, E. (1945): *The Social Problems of an Industrial Civilization*. Harvard University Press, Boston.

McLean, A. (ed.) (1970): *Mental Health and Work Organization*. Rand McNally, New York.

Meidner, R. (1978): *Employee Investment Funds: An Approach to Collective Capital Formation*. Allen and Unwin, London, Boston, Sydney.

Meidner, R. Hedborg, A. and Ford, G. (1977): Employee Investment Funds. *Economic Analysis*, Vol. XI, Nos. 3 – 4.

190

Meissner, M. (1971): The Long Arm of the Job: A Study of Work and Leisure. *Industrial Relations*, Vol 10, No. 3.

Merton, R.K. (1940): Bureaucratic Structure and Personality. *Social Forces*, Vol. 18.

Nichols, T. (1976): Management Ideology and Practice. *People at Work*. The Open University Press.

Norges Industri (1975): Staten eier 40 – 50 % av norske industriaksjer. Nr. 22.

Norsk Arbeidsgiverforening (1975): Taushetsplikten for medlemmer av styre og bedriftsforsamling. *Arbeidsgiveren* nr. 17.

– « – (1980): Lønnsstatistikk. *Arbeidsgiveren*, nr. 1.

NOU (1976): *Attføringsarbeidet. Om målsettinger og virkemidler.* Norges Offentlige Utredninger, nr. 3. Universitetsforlaget, Oslo.

Nygaard, K. og Bergo, O. (1974): *Planlegging, styring og databehandling I – II*, Tiden, Oslo.

OECD (1979): *Wage Policies and Collective Bargaining Developments in Finland, Ireland and Norway*. Paris.

– « – (1980): *Norway*. OECD Economic Surveys, Paris.

OT:PROP. Nr. 3 1975/76: *Om lov om arbeidervern og arbeidsmiljø m.v.* Kommunal- og Arbeidsdepartementet, Oslo.

Pateman, C. (1970): *Participation and Democratic Theory*. Cambridge University Press.

Powell, P., Hale, M., Martin, J. and Simon, M. (1971): *2000 Accidents: A Shop Floor Study of their Causes*. National Institute of Industrial Psychology, London.

Pugh, D.S. (1966): Modern Organisation Theory: A Psychological and Sociological Study. *Psychological Bulletin*, No. 4.

Quinn, R.P., Camman, C.C., Gupta, N. and Beehr, T.A. (1973): Effectiveness in Work Roles. Final Report to the Manpower Administration. *US Department of Labor*.

Qvale, T.U. (1976): A Norwegian Strategy for Democratization of Industry. *Human Relations*, Vol 29, No. 5.

Rabinovitch, V. (1979): Federal Inaction on Health and Safety. *Canadian Labour*. Vo. 24, No. 4.

Rhenman, E. (1964): *Føretagsdemokrati och føretagsorganisation*. Svenska Arbetsgivareføreningen/Føretagsekonomiska Forskningsinstitutet, Stockholm.

Roethlisberger, F.J. and Dickson, W.J. (1950): *Management and the Worker*. Harvard University Press, Cambrigde, Mass.

Roggema, J. og Thorsrud, E. (1974): *Et skip i utvikling*. Tanum, Oslo.

Romøren, T.I. (1974): Helsetilstanden 1950 – 1970; noen flere data. *Hovedkomiteen for norsk forskning*, Oslo.

Roustang, G. (1977): Why Study Working Conditions via Job Satisfaction? A Plea for a Direct Analysis. *International Labour Review*, Vol 115, No. 3.

Ryste, Ø., Seierstad, S. og Ramberg, I.G. (1979): *Praktisk miljøarbeid. Erfaringer fra Berger Langmoen A/S*. Arbeidsforskningsinstituttene, Oslo.

SAF (1975): Job Reform in Sweden. Conclusions from 500 Shop Floor Projects. *Svenska Arbetsgivareføreningen*, Stockholm.

Safiotti, U. (1977): Scientific Bases of Environmental Carciogenesis and Cancer Prevention: Developing an Interdisciplinary Science and Facing its Ethical Implications. *Journal of Toxicology and Environmental Health*, Vol. 2.

Samarbeidsrådet (1975): En undersøkelse av virksomheten i Bedriftsutvalg 1973 – 74. *Samarbeidsrådet LO-NAF*, Oslo.

Sandberg, T. (1978): No one is a Prophet in his own Country. On the Norwegian Work Organization Experiments. Work Paper, Uppsala.

Sandberg, Å. (1979): *Computers Dividing Man and Work*. Center for Work Life Studies, Stockholm.

Schumpeter, J.A. (1947): *Capitalism, Socialism and Democracy*. Harper, New York.

Seierstad, S. (1974): The Norwegian Economy. In: Ramsøy, N.R. (ed.): *Norwegian Society*. Oslo University Press/C. Hurst & Co., London/Humanities Press, New York.

Selznick, P. (1949): *TVA and the Grass Roots*. University of California Press, Berkeley.

– « – (1957): *Leadership in Administration*. Harper & Row, New York.

Silverman, D. (1970): *The Theory of Organisations*. Heinemann, London.

SIND (1975): Statens Industriverk: *Styrelsesrepresentation før anställda. Erfarenheter från førsøksperioden*. Liber Førlag, Stockholm.

Srivastva, S., Salipante, P. Jr., Cummings, T.G., Notz, W.W., Bigelow, J.D. and Waters, J.A. (1975): *Job Satisfaction and Productivity*. Case Western Reserve University, Cleveland.

Statens Tobakkskaderåd (1979): *Ikke mitt bord*. Oslo.

Studenterrapporten (1973): *Murerrapporten. Århus*.

Sundbom, L. (1971): *De førvärsarbetandes arbetsplatsførhållanden*. Allmänna Førlaget, Stockholm.

Sørensen, B. Aa. (1979): Industrien som levevei. *Arbeidsforskningsinstituttene*, Oslo.

Taylor, J.C. (1977): Job Satisfaction and Quality of Working Life; A Reassessment. *Journal of Occupational Psychology*, Vol. 50.

Thorsrud, E. (1970): A Strategy for Research and Social Change in Industry. *Social Science Information*, Vol, 9, No. 5.

– « – (1976): Democratization of Work as a Process of Change Towards Non-Bureaucratic Types of Organization. In: Hofstede, G. and Kassem, M.S. (eds.): *European Contributions to Organization Theory*. Van Gorcum, Assen.

Thurmann, J.E. (1977): Job Satisfaction: An International Overview. *International Labour Review*, Vol. 115, No. 3.

Torgersen, U. (1974): Political Institutions. In: Ramsøy, N.R. (ed.): *Norwegian Society*. Universitetsforlaget, Oslo/C. Hurst & Co, London/Humanities Press, New York.

Trist, E.L. and Bamforth, K.W. (1951): Some Social and Psychological Consequences of the Longwall Method of Coalgetting. *Human Relations*, No. 4.

– « – Higgin, G.W., Murray, H. and Pollock, A.B. (1963): *Organisational Choice: Capabilities at the Coal Face under Changing Technologies – the Loss, Rediscovery and Transformation of a Work Tradition*. Tavistock Publications, London.

Walker, C.R. and Guest, R.H. (1952): *The Man on the Assembly Line*. Harvard University Press, Cambrigde, Mass.

Walker, K.F. and Bellecombe, de, L.G. (1974): *Workers' Participation in Management Problems*. International Institute for Labour Studies, Bulletin No. 12. Geneva.

Westenholz, A. (1976): Lønmotagerræpresentation i Aktieselskabsbestyrelser. *Nyt fra samfundsvidenskaberne*, Handelshøjskolen, København.

WHO (1980): The Inequality of Death. Assessing Socioeconomic Influences on Mortality. WHO Chronicle, Vol. 34, No. 1.

Willox, P. (1980): The Capital Crisis and Labour: Perspectives in the Dynamics of Working-class Consciousness in Canada. Doctoral dissertation, Uppsala University.

Ødegaard, L. (1979): *Fra tegning til produkt*. Arbeidsforskningsinstituttene, Oslo.

Appendix: Selected parts of the Act relating to Worker Protection and Working Environment

Chapter I. Objectives and scope of the Act.

§ 1
Objectives.

The objectives of this Act are:

1. to secure a working environment which affords the employees full safety against harmful physical and mental influences and which has safety, occupational health and welfare standards that correspond to the level of technological and social development of the society at large at any time,

2. to secure sound contract conditions and meaningful occupation for the individual employee,

3. to provide a basis whereby the enterprises themselves can solve their working environment problems in co-operation with the organizations of employers and employees and under the supervision and guidance of the public authorities.

§ 2
Scope of the Act.

1. Provided that it does not expressly state otherwise, this Act applies to all enterprises that engage employees.

2. The following are exempt from the Act:
   a) shipping, hunting and fishing, including processing of the catch on board ship,
   b) aviation,
   c) agriculture and other enterprises covered by the Act relating to working conditions for agricultural workers.

3. The King may direct that enterprises associated with exploration for and exploitation of petroleum resources in the seabed or its substrata, Norwegian inland waters, Norwegian sea territory and that part of the continental shelf which is subject to Norwegian sovereignty, except for areas subject to private property rights, shall wholly or in part be exempt from this Act.

   The King may direct that parts of the public administration shall be exempt from this Act or from parts of it, when the nature of the enterprise is such that to adapt it to the provisions of the Act would be impracticable. The King shall decide which enterprises conducted by the public shall be deemed "administration".

4. The King shall decide whether and to what extent this Act shall be

applicable to work performed in the employee's home.

5. The King may direct that technical apparatus and equipment shall be subject to supervision pursuant to this Act though not used in enterprises covered by the Act. The same applies in respect of work not covered by this Act when such work takes place under conditions that may involve a hazard to life . or health.

§ 3
Employee.

1. For the purpose of this Act "employee" shall mean any person who performs work in the service of another.

If an enterprise is conducted by two or more persons jointly for their own account, only one of these persons shall be deemed an employer under this Act, the others being regarded as employees. The name of the person to be regarded as the employer shall be reported to the Labour Inspection without delay.

2. The King shall decide to what extent
   a) students at educational or research institutions,
   b) national servicemen,
   c) persons on non-military service in lieu of national service,
   d) inmates in Prison Authority institutions,
   e) patients in health institutions, rehabilitation institutions etc.,
   f) persons who for training or rehabilitation purposes are placed in enterprises without being employees,

shall be regarded as employees when performing work in an enterprise covered by this Act. Provisions relating to the employer shall apply correspondingly.

§ 4
Employer.

For the purpose of this Act "employer" shall mean any person who has engaged employee(s) to perform work in his service.

The provisions of this Act relating to the employer, shall apply correspondingly to the person conducting the enterprise in the employer's stead.

§ 5
Mandatory provisions.

The provisions of this Act cannot be set aside by agreement unless this is expressly provided.

§ 6
Compulsory registration.

Every enterprise covered by this Act shall register in writing with the Labour Inspection, unless it has registered with the Inspection earlier pursuant to Section 3 of the Protection of Workers Act of 7 December 1956. The Inspection shall also be notified when an enterprise intends to start using a new permanent workplace, whether in connection with removal or otherwise, and when a temporary workplace is taken into use for a period of more than six weeks. Registration shall take place as early as possible and not later than one week before the enterprise commences operation or starts to use. the workplace.

Further rules concerning the information to be given for registration shall be issued by the Directorate of Labour

Inspection. The Directorate may grant exemption from the rule relating to registration of a temporary workplace when such registration will involve excessive inconvenience for the enterprise and registration is not considered necessary for supervision under the Act.

Chapter II. Requirements concerning the working environment.

§ 7
General requirements.

1. The working environment in the enterprise shall be fully satisfactory when the factors in the working environment that may influence the mental and physical health and welfare of the workers are judged separately and collectively.

2. The King may issue rules restricting permission to employ certain groups of employees who may be exceptionally vulnerable to accidents or health hazards. In so doing the King may issue rules concerning the relocation of such groups.

§ 8
The workplace.

1. The workplace shall be arranged so that the working environment is fully satisfactory as regards the safety, health and welfare of the employees.

   In particular it shall be ensured that:
   a) workrooms, passageways, stairways etc. are suitably dimensioned and equipped for the activities being conducted,
   b) good lighting is provided, if possible with daylight and a view,
   c) climatic conditions are fully satisfactory as regards volume of air, ventilation, humidity, draughts, temperature etc.,
   d) pollution in the form of dust, smoke, gas, vapours, unpleasant odours and radiation is avoided, unless it is known that the pollution cannot lead to undersirable effects upon employees,
   e) noise and vibration is avoided or reduced to prevent undersirable effects upon employees,
   f) the necessary precautions are taken to prevent injury to employees from falls and falling or sliding objects or masses,
   g) precautions are taken to prevent fire and explosions, and to provide adequate means of escape in the event of fire, explosion or other emergencies,
   h) sanitary installations and welfare rooms are satisfactory in size and design,
   i) workrooms, sanitary and welfare rooms etc. are kept in good repair, clean and tidy,
   j) first-aid equipment is readily accessible.

2. The workplace shall be arranged so that employees of both sexes can be employed.

3. Living quarters made available to employees by the employer shall be properly constructed, fitted out and kept in repair. Any house rules shall be drawn up in consultation with employee representatives. The Directorate of Labour Inspection may issue regulations prohibiting house rules that have unreasonable effects upon employees.

4. The Directorate of Labour Inspection shall issue further rules concerning the requirements imposed under this Section for permanent,

temporary, ambulatory and outdoor workplaces. These rules may also be made applicable to the lessors of premises etc.

§ 9
Technical apparatus and equipment.
1. Technical apparatus and equipment in the enterprise shall be designed and provided with safety devices so as to protect employees from injury and disease.

   When technical apparatus is being installed and used, care shall be taken to ensure that the the employees are not exposed to undesirable effects from noise, vibrations, uncomfortable working positions etc.

   Technical apparatus and equipment should be designed and installed so that it can be operated by or be adapted for use by employees of varying physique.

   Technical apparatus and equipment shall always be maintained and attended.

2. The Directorate of Labour Inspection shall issue further rules concerning the requirement imposed under this Section, including:
   a) design, construction, installation etc.,
   b) approval,
   c) tests of materials, or the examination or inspection of technical apparatus and equipment by experts.
   d) use, maintenance and inspections.

§ 10
Boilers, tanks and pipes under pressure.
1. Boilers, tanks and pipes in the enterprise that are under steam pressure, shall be properly manufactured, equipped, installed and maintained.

Use of these shall not commence until permission has been obtained from the Labour Inspection.

2. The King shall issue further rules concerning the requirements to be imposed regarding boilers, tanks and pipes under steam pressure, concerning registration, inspection and maintenance, and concerning the assistanse to be provided by employers at inspections.

   The King may direct that the operator of the boilers or the person responsible for its operation shall possess certain qualifications.

   The King may direct that other tanks and pipes under pressure shall be subject to inspection under this Act.

   Provisions stipulated in or pursuant to this Section may be made applicable to owners or users of boilers, tanks and pipes, although the persons concerned are not employers or employees within the meaning of this Act.

§ 11
Toxic and other noxious substances.
1. In enterprises where toxic or other noxious substances are manifactured, packed, used or stored in a manner that may involve a health hazard, the working processes and other work shall be fully satisfactory so that employees are protected against accidents, injury to health and excessive discomfort. Containers and packaging for the substances shall be clearly marked giving the name of the substance and a warning in Norwegian.

   The enterprise shall keep a record of such substances showing the

196

name of the substance, its composition, physical and chemical properties, as well as information concerning possible poisonous effects (toxicological data), elements of risk, preventive measures and first-aid treatment. The enterprise shall have the necessary equipment to prevent or counteract injury to health due to such substances. Such dangerous substances shall not be used if they can be replaced by substances less hazardous to the employees.

2. In enterprises that manufacture, pack, use or store toxic or noxious substances in a manner that may involve a health hazard, the working environment and the health of the employees shall be kept under continuous control.

   The Directorate of Labour Inspection shall issue further rules concerning test methods, the extent and frequency of tests, and reports on results. Moreover, the Directorate may require the employer to carry out special studies or submit specimens for study.

   The cost of studies required under this Section shall be borne by the party under obligation to carry out the study or submit the specimen.

3. The Directorate of Labour Inspection may direct that a record shall be kept of all employees who are exposed to specified noxious substances in enterprises covered by this Act.

4. The Directorate of Labour Inspection may forbid the manufacture, packaging, use or storage of noxious substances in enterprises covered by this Act. Moreover, the Directorate may impose further conditions for the use or production of any substance.

5. The Directorate of Labour Inspection shall issue further rules concerning the manufacture, packaging, use and storage of toxic and other noxious substances in enterprises covered by this Act.

6. The Directorate of Labour Inspection may grant enterprises that use toxic or other noxious substances in connection with research and analysis work etc., full or partial exemption from the rules of this Section.

§ 12
Planning the work.
1. *General requirements.*

Technology, organization of the work, working hours and wage systems shall be set up so that the employees are not exposed to undesirable physical or mental strain and so that their possibilities of displaying caution and observing safety measures are not impaired.

Conditions shall be arranged so that employees are afforded reasonable opportunity for professional and personal development through their work.

2. *Arrangement of work.*

The individual employee's opportunity for self-determination and professional responsibility shall be taken into consideration when planning and arranging the work.

Efforts shall be made to avoid undiversified, repetitive work and work that is governed by machine or conveyor belt in such a manner that the employees themselves are prevented from varying the speed of the work. Otherwise efforts shall be made to arrange the work so as to provide possibilities for variation and for contact with others, for connection between individual job assignments, and for employees to keep themselves informed about production requirements and results.

3. *Control and planning systems.*

The employees and their elected union representatives shall be kept informed about the systems employed for planning and effecting the work, and about planned changes in such systems. They shall be given the training necessary to enable them to learn these systems, and they shall take part in planning them.

4. *Work involving safety hazards.*

a) Performance premium wage systems shall not be employed for work where this may materially affect safety.

b) If work is to be carried out in the enterprise that may involve particular hazard to life and health, a special directive shall be issued prescribing how the work is to be done and the safety precautions to be observed, including any particular instruction and supervision.

c) When the work is of such a nature that it involves danger of a disaster or disastrous accident, plans shall be drawn up for first-aid, escape routes and rescue measures, registration of employees present at the workplace and so on.

d) Employees shall be informed of the regulations and safety rules etc. relating to the area concerned and of the plans and measures mentioned under c).

e) When satisfactory precautions to protect life and health cannot be achieved by other means, employees shall be provided with suitable personal protective equipment. Employees shall be trained in the use of such equipment and if necessary shall be ordered to use it.

5. The Directorate of Labour Inspection shall issue further rules concerning the requirements to be imposed upon the enterprises under this Section. Moreover, the Directorate shall issue further rules concerning the design and use of personal protective equipment and concerning the approval of such equipment by public authorities.

§ 13
Occupationally handicapped employees.

1. Passageways, sanitary facilities, technical apparatus and equipment etc. shall, to the extent possible and reasonable, be designed and arranged so that the enterprise can employ occupationally handicapped persons.

2. If an employee has become handicapped in his occupation as the result of accident, disease, overstrain or the like, the employer shall, to the extent possible, effect the necessary measures so as to enable the employee to be given or to retain suitable work. Preferably the employee shall be afforded opportunity to continue his normal work, possibly after special adaptation of the work, alteration of technical apparatus, rehabilitation or the like.

3. In the event that, in accordance with the rules of subsection 2 above, there is question of transferring an employee to other work, the employee and the elected union representative concerned shall be consulted before any decision is made.

4. Further rules concerning implementation of the provisions of this Section shall be issued by the Ministry.[1])

Chapter III. Duties of employer and employees.

§ 14
Duties of employer.

The employer shall ensure that the enterprise is arranged and maintained, and that the work is planned, organized and performed in accordance with the provisions stipulated in or by virtue of this Act, cf. in particular Sections 7—13.

To ensure that the safety, health and welfare of the employees is taken into consideration at all levels throughout the enterprise, the employer shall:

a) when planning new workplaces, alteration of workplaces or production methods, procurement of technical apparatus and equipment etc., study and evaluate whether the working environment will be in compliance with the requirements of this Act and effect the measures necessary;

b) arrange continuous charting of the existing working environment in the enterprise as regards risks, health hazards and welfare, and effect the measures necessary;

c) arrange continuous checks of the working environment and the health of employees when there may be a risk of health injuries caused by long term effects from influences in the working environment;

d) arrange for expert assistance and for testing and measuring equipment

---

[1]) Ministry of Local Government and Labour.

when this is necessary in order to comply with the requirements of the Act;

e) organize and arrange the work giving due consideration to the age, proficiency, working ability and other capabilities of the individual employees;

f) arrange for systematic promotion of safety within the enterprise, and ensure that qualified persons with an understanding of safety matters are appointed to ascertain that the work is performed in a proper manner as regards safety and health;

g) ensure compliance with the provisions of the Act relating to systematic promotion of safety, cf. Chapter VII;

h) ensure that employees are informed of any accident risks and health hazards that may be connected with the work and that they receive the necessary training, practice and instruction.

The Directorate of Labour Inspection shall issue further rules concerning the employer's duties pursuant to the preceding paragraph.

§ 15
Two or more employers at one workplace.

1. When two or more employers are conducting activities simultaneously at one and the same workplace:

a) each employer shall ensure that his own activities and his employees' work are arranged and carried out so that the other employers' employees are also protected in accordance with the rules of this Act;

b) each employer shall co-operate to provide a fully satisfactory

working environment for all employees at the workplace;
c) the principal enterprise shall be responsible for co-ordinating the safety and environmental work of each enterprise.

2. At workplaces where more than 10 employees are employed at the same time, and no one of the enterprises can be regarded as the main establishment, the employers shall decide by written agreement which of them shall be responsible for co-ordination. In the event that no such agreement is reached, the Labour Inspection shall be notified and shall decide which employer shall be responsible for the co-ordination.

§ 16
Duties of employees.

1. Employees shall take part in the creation of a sound, safe working environment by carrying out the prescribed measures and participating in the organized safety and environmental work of the enterprise.

Employees shall perform their work in conformity with orders and instructions from superiors or from the Labour Inspection. They shall use the prescribed protective equipment, display caution and otherwise co-operate to prevent accidents and injury to health.

If employees become aware of faults or defects that may involve a hazard to life or health and they themselves are unable to remedy the fault or defect, they shall immediately notify the employer or his authorized representative, the safety delegate and, to the necessary extent, the other ômployees.

An employee who finds that the work cannot continue without danger to life or health, shall cease his work. Employees who suffer injury at work or who contract diseases which they consider result from the work or conditions at the workplace, shall report this to the employer or his representative.

2. Employees whose duty it is to lead or supervise other employees, shall ensure that safety and health are taken into consideration when work that comes under their areas of responsibility is being planned and carried out.

Chapter IV. Responsibility of manufacturers, suppliers etc.

§ 17
Manufacturers and suppliers of technical apparatus and equipment.

1. Any person who manufactures, sells, leases or lends technical apparatus or equipment that will or may foreseeably be used by enterprises covered by this Act, shall, before delivering same for use, or displaying them for sale or advertising purposes, ensure that they are designed and provided with safety devices in accordance with the requirements of this Art.

Care shall be taken when designing such technical appartus and equipment as mentioned in the preceding paragraph, to ensure that they can be used for their intended purposes without involving excessive inconvenience or discomfort.

They shall be accompanied by the necessary, easily understandable written in structions in Norwegian concerning transportation, installation, operation and maintenance.

2. Any person who undertakes independently to install such technical apparatus or equipment as mentioned in subsection 1 of this Section, shall ensure that it is assembled and installed in accordance with the requirements of this Act.

3. Before such technical apparatus or equipment as mentioned in subsection 1 of this Section is delivered or displayed, it shall be marked with the name and address of the manufacturer or, in the case of imported goods, of the importer, or otherwise be marked so that the manufacturer or importer can easily be identified.

4. The King shall issue further provisions concerning:
   a) design, construction, installation etc.,
   b) approval,
   c) materials testing, or the inspection or survey of technical apparatus and equipment by specialists.

5. The costs of inspection or survey required under this Section, shall be borne by the party under obligation to carry out the inspection or survey.

§ 18
Manufacturers and importers of toxic and other noxious substances.
1. Any person who manufactures or imports toxic or other noxious substances that will or may foreseeably be used by enterprises covered by this Act, shall:
   a) procure information concerning the composition and properties of the substance,

   b) effect the necessary measures to prevent accidents and injury to health or excessive discomfort or inconvenience for the employees,
   c) report to the agency named by the King the name of the substance and its composition, physical and chemical properties, and supply such additional information as may be required to determine how hazardous the substance is,
   d) ensure proper packaging so as to prevent accidents and injury to health,
   e) mark the packaging with the name of the substance, the name of the manufacturer or importer, and a clear warning in Norwegian. The marking label shall be submitted with the report required under litra c).

2. The King may require that the manufacturer or importer shall carry out tests or submit specimens for testing to determine how hazardous the substance is.

   The King may prohibit the sale of any substance if the manufacturer or importer fails to observe his duty to report or mark the substance, or fails to provide additional information required pursuant to litra c) subsection 1 of this Section.

3. The King shall issue further provisions concerning the duties of manufacturers and importers under this Section.

   The King may determine that all or part of the provisions of this Section shall apply to dealers.

   The costs of tests required under this Section shall be borne by the party under obligation to carry out the test or submit the test specimen.

4. Medicines, substances covered by Act No. 9 of 5 April 1963 relating to Insecticides etc., and foods covered by Act No. 3 of 19 May 1933 relating to Control of Foods etc., are exempt from the provisions of this Section regarding reports and marking.

Chapter V. Permits from the Labour Inspection to erect and alter buildings, reorganize production processes, etc.

§ 19

Any person wishing to erect a building or perform building work that must be reported under the existing Building Act and that will or may foreseeably be used by an enterprise covered by this Act, shall obtain prior consent from the Labour Inspection.

The same shall apply if an existing enterprise wishes to effect such alteration of the premises, production processes, machinery etc. as will result in a substantial change of the working environment.

The Ministry shall issue further rules concerning the extent of the duty to obtain prior consent from the Labour Inspection under this Section, the information that may be required by the Inspection, and the conditions that may be imposed for such consent.

Chapter VI. Reporting and recording occupational accidents and occupational diseases.

§ 20
Records of injuries and diseases.
The employer shall ensure that all injuries suffered by persons in the enterprise are recorded. The same applies to diseases believed to have been caused by the work or by conditions at the workplace.

The records must not contain medical information of a personal nature without the consent of the person to whom the information applies. The records shall be accessible to the Labour Inspection, safety delegates, working environment committees, and safety and health personnel. Otherwise the employer shall maintain silence regarding information in the records concerning personal matters.

§ 21
Employer's duty to report injuries and diseases.

If, as the result of an occupational accident, an employee loses his life or is seriously injured, the employer shall report the matter in the quickest possible way to the Labour Inspection and to the nearest police authority. The employer shall confirm his report in writing. The safety delegate shall receive a copy of the report.

If the enterprise is not subject to the duty to report pursuant to Section 18-2 of the National Insurance Act, less serious accidents that result in an employee being unfit for work for at least three days shall also be reported in writing to the Labour Inspection as soon as possible and not later than within three days.

Any employer who realizes or should realize that a disease is caused by the work or by conditions at the workplace, shall report this to the Labour Inspection.

In addition to the cases mentioned in the preceding paragraphs, any near accidents (serious accidents or acute poisonings that are averted) shall be reported to the Labour Inspection by the employer as soon as possible and not later than within 3 days.

Further rules concerning the accidents and occupational diseases to be reported under this Section shall be issued by the Directorate of Labour Inspection.

§ 22
Medical practitioners' duty to submit reports.

Any medical practitioner who attends an employee suffering from an occupational disease that is the equivalent of an occupational injury under Section 11-4 of the National Insurance Act, or any other disease which the medical practitioner believes is due to the employee's work, shall report this in writing to the Labour Inspection.
This duty to report applies also to company medical officers who, in the course of their work, learn of such diseases as mentioned in the preceding paragraph.

Subject to the consent of the employee concerned, the employer shall also be notified of the disease.

The Directorate shall issue further rules concerning the duty to submit reports, including the duty to report specified diseases that may presumably be caused by the nature of the work or by conditions at the workplace.

Chapter VII. Safety delegates, working environment committees, safety and health personnel.

§ 23
Working environment committees.
1. Enterprises which regularly employ at least 50 employees, shall have a working environment committee on which the employer, the employees and the safety and health personel are represented.

Working environment committees shall also be formed in enterprises having between 20 and 50 employees when so required by any of the parties at the enterprise.

Where working conditions so dictate, the Labour Inspection may direct that enterprises having less than 50 employees shall establish a working environment committee.

Working environment committees may appoint sub-committees.

2. When a working environment committee is established, this shall be reported to the local Labour Inspection office. Notices shall be posted at the workplace giving the names of the persons who are members of the committee at any time.

3. The employer and the employees shall have an equal number of representatives on the committee. Representatives of the employer and of the employees shall be elected alternately as chairman of the committee. Safety and health representatives on the committee have no vote. When votes are equally divided, the chairman has the casting vote.

4. The King shall issue further rules concerning working environment committees, including their composition, election and terms of offise.
Rules providing that on specified conditions other co-operative bodies in the enterprise may act as the

working environment committee, may be issued by the King.

§ 24
Duties of working environment committees.

1. The working environment committee shall work to establish a fully satisfactory working environment in the enterprise. The committee shall participate in planning safety and environmental work and shall follow up developments closely in questions relating to the safety, health and welfare of the employees.

2. The working environment committee shall consider:
   a) questions relating to the company health service and the company safety service,
   b) questions relating to training, instruction and information activities in the enterprise that are of significance for the working environment,
   c) plans that require the consent of the Labour Inspection pursuant to Section 19,
   d) other plans that may be of material significance for the working environment, such as plans for building work, purchases of materials, rationalization, work processes, working time systems and preventive safety measures.

Questions relating to work for occupationally handicapped employees may also be considered by the committee, cf. Section 13.

3. The committee shall study all reports relating to occupational diseases, occupational accidents and near accidents, seek to find the cause of the accident or disease, and ensure that the employer takes steps to prevent recurrence. As a general rule the committee shall have access to Labour Inspection or police inquiry documents. When the committee considers it necessary, the committee may decide that inquiries shall be conducted by specialists or by a commission of inquiry appointed by the committee. Without undue delay the employer may submit such decisions to the Labour Inspection for decision.

The committee shall study all reports relating to occupational health inspections and test results.

Before such reports as mentioned in the first and second paragraphs above are considered by the committee, medical information of a personal nature shall be removed from the reports, unless the person to whom the information applies consents to it being submitted to the committee.

4. If the working environment committee considers it necessary in order to protect the life or health of employees, it may decide that the employer shall effect concrete measures to improve the working environment, within the framework of the provisions stipulated in or by virtue of this Act. To determine whether a health hazard exists, the committee may decide that the employer shall have the working environment examined or tested. A time limit for effectuation of the decision shall be imposed by the committee. If the employer finds that he is unable to effectuate the decision, the matter shall be summitted without undue delay to the Labour Inspection for decision.

5. Each year the working environment committee shall submit a report on

its activities to the administrative bodies of the enterprise, to employee organisations and to the Labour Inspection.

Further rules concerning the contents and composition of the annual report shall be issued by the Directorate of Labour Inspection.

6. Further rules concerning the activities of the committee, including rules concerning procedure and concerning a duty of secrecy for members of the committee, shall be issued by the King.

§ 25
Safety delegates.

1. Safety delegates shall be elected at all enterprises covered by this Act. At enterprises having less than five employees, the parties may agree upon a different system or agree that the enterprise shall not have a safety delegate. At enterprises having more than 10 employees, more than one safety delegate may be elected.

2. The number of safety delegates shall be determined according to the size of the enterprise, the nature of the work and working conditions in general. Enterprises that consist of several separate departments or where employees work shifts, shall as a general rule have at least one safety delegate for each department or each shift team.
Safety areas shall be clearly marked and shall not be larger than that the safety delegate can have full control and attend to his duties in a proper manner.

3. Enterprises having more than one safety delegate shall have at least one senior safety delegate who shall be responsible for co-ordinating safety delegate activities.

The senior safety delegate shall be elected from among the safety delegates or other persons who hold or have held offices in the enterprise.

4. The employer shall notify the local Labour Inspection office when safety delegates are elected. Notices giving the names of those acting as safety delegates at any time shall be posted at the workplace.

5. The King shall issue further rules concerning the number of safety delegates, concerning elections including conditions governing the right to vote and eligibility, concerning the right of the local trade union to appoint safety delegates, and concerning the safety delegates' term of office.

§ 26
Duties of safety delegates.

1. Safety delegates shall safeguard the interests of employees in matters relating to the working environment. Safety delegates shall ensure that the enterprise is arranged and maintained and that work is carried out in such a manner that the safety, health and welfare of the employees is safeguarded in accordance with the provisions of this Act.

2. In particular safety delegates shall ensure that
   a) employees are not exposed to hazards from machinery, technical apparatus, chemical substances or work processes,
   b) adequate safety devices and personal protective equipment are provided in adequate numbers,

that they are readily accessible and in proper conddition,

c) employees receive the necessary instruction, drills and training,

d) work otherwise is arranged so as to ensure the safety and health of the employees,

e) the reports relating to occupational accidents etc. required under Section 21, are submitted.

3. Immediately a safety delegate learns of circumstances that may lead to an accident or present a health hazard, the safety delegate shall notify the employees at the place, and if he is unable to avert the danger himself, the safety delegate shall bring the matter to the attention of the employer or his representative. When so notified the employer shall give the safety delegate a reply. If no action has been taken within a reasonable space of time, the safety delegate shall notify the Labour Inspection or the working environment committee.

4. The safety delegate shall be consulted during the planning and effectuation of measures of significance for the working environment within the delegate's safety area.
The safety delegate shall be informed of all occupational diseases, occupational accidents and near accidents within his area, of occupational hygiene reports and tests, and of any faults or defects discovered.

5. The safety delegate shall become familiar with existing safety rules, directives, orders and recommendation issued by the Labour Inspection or the employer.

6. The safety delegate shall participate in the inspection visits of the enterprise undertaken by the Labour Inspection.

7. Further rules concerning the activities of safety delegates and their duty of secrecy shall be issued by the King. Such rules may stipulate that the safety delegate shall perform tasks allotted to the working environment committee under Section 24 when the enterprise has no such committee. Authority to make decisions in accordance with Section 24, subsection 3, first paragraph, first sentence, and subsection 4, may not be vested in the safety delegate.

§ 27
Safety delegates' right to halt dangerous work.

If a safety delegate considers that the life or health of employees is in immediate danger and such danger cannot be averted by other means, work may be halted until the Labour Inspection has decided whether work may be continued. Work may be halted only to the extent the safety delegate considers necessary in order to avert danger.

The halting of work and the reason for this shall be reported without delay to the employer or his representative.

The safety delegate is not liable for any loss suffered by the enterprise as a result of work being halted under the provisions of the first paragraph above.

§ 28
Spesial local or regional safety delegates and working environment committees.

In building and construction enterprises, for stevedoring work, and otherwise when special cirpumstances so necessitate, the King may decide that special local working environment committees or safety delegates shall be appointed. The tasks, rights and duties of these working environment committees and safety delegates may be such as mentioned in Sections 24, 26 and 27 above, in relation to all employees at the workplace.

Moreover, the King may direct that there shall be systems of working environment committees or safety delegates covering several enterprises within one geographical area.

Rules issued pursuant to this Section shall contain special provisions concerning how committees or delegates are to be appointed, their duties, and concerning distribution of the costs of their activities.

§ 29
Other provisions.

1. Costs associated with the activities of safety delegates and working environment committees shall be borne by the employer.

2. The employer shall ensure that safety delegates and working environment committee members receive the training necessary to enable them to perform their duties in a proper manner.

   Safety delegates and members of working environment committees are entitled to receive the necessary instruction at courses arranged by employee organizations. Costs associated with such training shall be borne by the employer. Further rules concerning the requirements for such training shall be issued by the Ministry.

3. Safety delegates and members of working environment committees shall be allowed the time necessary to perform their duties according to Sections 24 and 26 in a proper manner. As a general rule these duties shall be performed within normal working hours. Should it be necessary for one of them to be absent from his workplace, he shall notify his immediate superior in advance, or as soon as possible.

4. The employer shall ensure that holding office as safety delegate or as a working environment committee member does not result in any loss of income for the employee and does not in any other way impair his employment and contract conditions.

§ 30
Safety and health personnel.

1. When special supervision of the working environment or of the health of employees is necessary, the enterprise shall have safety and health personnel, such as a company medical officer, company nurse, safety manager etc.

2. Safety and health personnel shall assist the employer, the employees, the working environment committee and the safety delegates in their efforts to create safe and sound working conditions.

   Safety and health personnel shall cooperate with and assist the Labour Inspection.

3. Safety and health personnel shall have a free and independent position as regards working environment matters.

4. The King may issue further rules concerning when and to what extent enterprises shall have safety and health personnel, the professional qualifications of such personnel, and the duties they are to perform.

Back cover + is model for reform elsewhere
+ page 13

P.16 and proposal for withdrawal state cos

- BG+ evaluation

Mushroom argument page 69   also c 7 5 9

Good and evil discussion, P 73 doubtful

Action idea, p 74, individuals consulted in   P 75 - action idea false
                        document?

                75 a supporting the weak

78. explore alternative! (8 m.) p̃ → l)
                        as per P.O.
Mill & leadership. Eckstein? technical + politic dimensions
        and views l. important in this. (elsewhere?)

One lesson not fully developed (participation in research/progs)
                in legal programme.
                B G not discuss process issue   maybe msur by
                learning & the problem of imposing   right to remain for
                a procedural formula (WEC's)   out + H+S.
                → emergence of certain issues
                → avoid failure of others.

                New a formula to encourage
                both redist power &, in //?,
                new style problem solve?

A.R. traa devel⁰.   ⌉
        role of research & action⌋

Experience with WEC's and the British exp. also?
The 'political' context of WRI & sit. in Norway not hinted at.

And Questions connect on QWL